Fire in the Blood

—The New Spain—

Fire in the Blood

— *The New Spain* —

Ian Gibson

faber and faber
LONDON · BOSTON

BBC BOOKS

Published by Faber and Faber Limited
3 Queen Square
London WC1N 3AU

and

BBC Books
a division of BBC Enterprises Limited,
Woodlands, 80 Wood Lane, London W12 0TT

First published 1992
© Ian Gibson 1992

ISBN 0 563 36194 8

Designed by Graham Dudley Associates
Maps by Eugene Fleury
Picture Research by Lesley Davy

Set in 11.5/13 pt Garamond by Goodfellow & Egan Ltd., Cambridge
Printed and bound in Great Britain by Richard Clay Ltd., St Ives PLC
Colour separations by Dot Gradations Ltd., Chelmsford.
Jacket printed by Lawrence Allen Ltd., Weston-super-Mare

For Lulu

Contents

List of Illustrations

List of Maps

Acknowledgements

The publishers gratefully acknowledge permission to reprint the following copyright material:

The Spanish Temper by V. S. Pritchett, Chatto & Windus, 1954, by permission of Peters, Fraser and Dunlop; *Castilian Ilexes* by Charles Tomlinson and Henry Douglas, OUP, 1963, by permission of Oxford University Press; *The Quest for El Cid* by Richard Fletcher, Hutchinson, 1989, by permission of Hutchinson Ltd.

For details of photo copyrights, please see the List of Illustrations on p. ix.

Introduction

Recently a friend of my mother-in-law spent a holiday in Torremolinos. Asked if she had enjoyed herself, 'Spain?' she replied firmly. 'You can have Spain!' She had not been impressed, and, assuming that the rest of the country is similar to that unlovely tangle of jerry-built high-rise blocks, estate agencies and fish-and-chip shops, had decided to avoid Spain in the future.

I wonder how many other people have been put off by a package-tour sojourn in the famous Málaga resort or some analogous enclave straddling a once beautiful coastline now largely disfigured by specu-lation.

Happily Spain is more, very much more, than Torremolinos, with a fascinating hinterland undreamt of by the tourist who arrives with one goal in mind: a sun-drenched beach.

It is also a country that, since the death of General Franco in 1975, has carried through a quite remarkable transition from dictatorship to stable democracy, an achievement that has earned it international admiration and full membership of the European Community.

This book, intended to complement the BBC2 series of the same name, attempts to provide an idea of what Spain, behind the tourist scenes, is like on the eve of the 1992 Seville World Fair, popularly known as Expo 92 (9 million foreign visitors expected), the Barcelona

Olympics and Madrid's whirl as European Cultural Capital. On the eve, that is, of what Spain hopes will be its Great Year.

I have felt it imperative, after giving some account of the physical characteristics and variety of the country, to furnish one or two historical flashbacks. Above all I stress the uniqueness of medieval Spain, with its mixed population of Muslims, Jews and Christians and astonishingly rich cultural amalgam, and underline the cruel, and permanent, damage done to the Spanish spirit by the collapse of that unique world in 1492. It seems to me that no book on the country should fail to highlight the medieval period, nor to point out how today, at last, Spain is recovering what can be considered its true tradition of tolerance.

1492 was also the year, as everyone knows, in which Columbus happened upon America and opened up a New World which regaled Spain, for a time, with a seemingly inexhaustible supply of gold and silver. Expo 92 will be celebrating the 500th anniversary of what Spaniards call, simply, 'The Discovery', and one can confidently predict that many new books, as well as films and TV programmes, will soon appear about the enigmatic Columbus and Spain's colonial role in America. I do not examine that role, however, because it falls outside the framework I have set myself; nor, for the same reason, do I review the country's complex European involvement from the sixteenth century onwards, first under the Habsburgs and then, from 1700, the Bourbons. The story of Portugal is not told here either: lost to Spain in 1641, it gradually sank out of the consciousness of Spaniards, like another Atlantis, and is only now beginning to creep back in.

I look fairly closely at the 1930s, evoking the deeply traumatic experience of the Second Republic (1931–6) and the agonizingly long dictatorship that followed the Civil War (1936–9). Without some awareness of these decades no one could hope to grasp how the peaceful transition to democracy was possible once Franco died.

The book's pretensions, then, are modest. It is not intended for the specialist but, rather, for those who feel an incipient interest in modern Spain and might be considering a visit. In writing it I have tried to be true to my personal view of the country that has been my home since 1978. If I had produced too glowing an account of the New Spain (and the New Spaniards) I would have been criticized by those

Spanish friends who feel that the Socialists should have done far more to change the country for the better during the ten years they have been in power. If, on the other hand, I had quibbled too much, I know I would have received nothing but abuse from those who, all too ready themselves to run down their own country, hate anything approaching a rebuke from a foreigner, albeit a foreigner with Spanish nationality. I hope that these friends will concede at least that I have tried to be honest.

Finally, I would like to say how much I owe to the BBC teams with whom I was privileged to work on the TV series and, particularly, to Jenny Rivarola and Cristina Lago. Unfailingly they all came up with questions I couldn't answer, sending me scurrying to the library, or the telephone. Not only did I learn a great deal in their company as we travelled around Spain, but it was fun too.

Madrid, 24 July 1991

-1-

Landscapes of Spain

Spain is a large country by European standards. Only marginally smaller than France, its 190,115 square miles make it almost twice the size of England, Scotland and Wales taken together. In the south, the eight provinces of Andalusia, 34,089 square miles in area, are 2,000 square miles bigger than Ireland, well over double the extent of Holland and almost three times that of Belgium. Despite this Spain can boast considerably fewer inhabitants than Britain (in round figures 39 million), a result of the inhospitable nature of much of its terrain.

Neighbouring Portugal has a population of approximately 10 million and an area of 34,254 square miles. Which means that the Iberian Peninsula, all of 224,369 square miles in area, supports no more than 50 million people.

Visitors are often surprised to discover that Madrid, situated at the geographical centre of the peninsula, is the highest capital city in Europe. A bronze plaque affixed to the façade of the handsome Regional Assembly building in the Puerta del Sol, Madrid's Piccadilly Circus, indicates that the most famous square in Spain stands at 650.7 metres (2,134 feet) above sea-level. Only Berne, at 1,800 feet, can begin to match this.

Spain is Europe's most mountainous country after Switzerland,

1

with an average height of over 2,000 feet and many peaks that rise to more than 11,000 in Andalusia's Sierra Nevada range and in the Pyrenees. By way of comparison, Ben Nevis, Britain's highest mountain, attains only 4,408 feet above sea-level.

Salvador de Madariaga, that most European of Spaniards, wrote that 'the essential thing about Spain is its inaccessibility. Spain is a castle.' He went on to point out that the country has tall mountains along almost all the length of its seaboard, leaving in general only thin strips of coastal plain. The main exception to the rule is the Atlantic shoreline of Andalusia, which runs from the Portuguese border to south of Cadiz.

The Greek geographer Strabo, writing at about the time of Christ, compared the shape of the Iberian Peninsula to that of the stretched hide of an ox (with the shoulders facing towards Italy). The comparison caught on, and two thousand years later you will often find journalists using the 'bull's hide' cliché when they need a synonym for Spain. Perhaps they feel that the taurine equivalence is all the more apt because of the vital role of the bull in Spanish culture.

At the core of the peninsula stands an immense tableland, the Meseta, which Madariaga terms the 'inner citadel' of the Spanish fortress. Divided into Old and New Castile (from the Latin *castella*, 'castles') by the mighty transversal range of the Guadarrama and Gredos mountains, the Meseta extends from Burgos in the north to the Sierra Morena in the south, from the Portuguese border in the west to the edge of the east coast. Its slightly westward tilt explains why four of the country's five great rivers (the Duero, the Tagus, the Guadiana and the Guadalquivir) flow into the Atlantic, not the Mediterranean.

In colour predominantly burnt sienna, the Meseta is calcined in summer by a sun of tropical intensity; north of the Guadarrama, it is often bitterly cold in winter. Spring, all too briefly, decks its hedgerows and ditches in gorgeous flowers and freshens the fields with the green of young wheat. The Meseta's awesome, sierra-ribbed wastes and solitudes, conducive to mysticism, have inspired many painters and writers, among them Cervantes and Saint John of the Cross.

British visitors to Castile have always been struck by what Laurie Lee, in *As I Went Out One Midsummer Morning*, has termed 'those east–west ramparts that go ranging across Spain and divide its people into separate races'. Ninety years earlier George Borrow had evoked in *The Bible in Spain* (1843) 'those singular mountains which rise in naked horridness like the ribs of some mighty carcase from which the flesh had been torn'. Borrow's is the vision of a man who has walked or ridden across central Spain in the full heat of day. At sundown, however, the sierras become less forbidding as their barren features are transformed by the ebbing light into a symphony of mauves, indigos and purples.

The Romans only needed three words to define the predominant character of the Spanish interior: 'Dura tellus Iberiae', 'Harsh land of Iberia'.

Harsh it certainly is. Who could ever forget the first sight of the barren plains of Old Castile, just north of Burgos, after dropping down through the thickly forested mountains and lush pastures of the Basque Country, with their picturesque, Swiss-like homesteads nestling among the long grass? The Meseta stretches into the distance as far as the eye can see. One might be in Africa. What desolation! 'Ancha es Castilla', 'Wide is Castile', runs a Spanish saying. People use it to remind themselves and others that in the world there is, or ought to be, ample room for everyone's point of view and personal idiosyncrasies.

Of the travellers who have described the brusque transition from the Basque hills to the Meseta, I think Victor Pritchett comes closest to catching the peculiar excitement of the moment. The passage is taken from his splendid book *The Spanish Temper* (1954):

> The train enters the Pancorbo Pass, a place of horror like all the Spanish passes, for the rock crowds in, comes down in precipitous, yellow shafts, and at the top has been tortured into frightening animal shapes by the climate. Nine months of winter, three of hell, is the proverbial description of Castilian weather, the weather of half of Spain: a dry climate of fine air under a brassy sun, where the cold wind is wicked and penetrating, a continual snake-fang flicker against the nostrils. Castile is a steppe. Its landscape is the pocked and cratered surface of the moon.

3

South of Madrid, south of Don Quixote's La Mancha, after the seemingly endless vineyards that produce the light wines of Valdepeñas, the foothills of the Sierra Morena lead to another equally impressive defile marking, this time, the end of New Castile. It is called Despeñaperros, literally 'Place for Throwing the Dogs off the Cliffs', the 'dogs' being the infidel, not canine, variety. Despeñaperros, the gateway to Andalusia, was infested by bandits, like Pancorbo, in the nineteenth century. The English guidebooks of the period warned travellers to go well armed when traversing it, and to keep their eyes open. Today a new motorway speeds the traffic through the pass towards Seville, and much of the romance has fled. But it requires little imagination to conjure up what it must have been like coming through here on horseback a hundred years ago, particularly at night, or the relief felt by travellers on arriving at this portal to the fertile valley of the Guadalquivir after their long journey across the cruel plains.

Castile, with its cluster of fascinating historic cities (Burgos, Toledo, Avila, Segovia . . .), is rich in the remains of the fortresses from which its name derives. These often majestic ruins evoke *The Poem of the Cid*, Spain's great medieval epic, and speak of Castile's shifting frontiers and constant strife between Christians and Moors.

Other characteristic aspects of the Meseta are the huge crumbling churches that dominate the villages (you will often see them from the train or car window), and the occasional lines of poplars threading the flat countryside like intruders. One can be sure that the trees mark a stream or river. In early summer their greenery affords a striking contrast against the gold of the wheat, and when the wind rustles their leaves Castilians are reminded of the all-too-distant sea.

Central Spain was not always as bare as it is today. In medieval times dense woods clothed most of the land, and it is said that a squirrel could travel from Gibraltar to the Pyrenees without touching the ground. The uncontrolled destruction of the forests for centuries led to appalling denudation. This, in turn, has meant less rainfall. In the mountains just north of Madrid the vestiges of some ancient beech woods (the most southerly in Europe) give an idea of what Castile may have looked like in the past.

No poet has captured the sadness and severe beauty of Spain's heartland more poignantly than Antonio Machado (1875–1939), a

Sevillian who spent several years as a teacher in the high city of Soria, 140 miles north-east of Madrid. Machado's Castilian verse has a sobriety reflecting that of the terrain itself. In his poem 'The Ilexes' (*Quercus ilex* is the indigenous oak of Castile) he conveys the power of these stark uplands where icy blasts whip the face in winter, and spring comes late:

> *Woods*
>
> > *of Castilian ilexes*
> >
> > > *on slope*
>
> *and eminence*
>
> > *hillsides*
> >
> > > *and sudden fastnesses*
>
> *woods, that*
>
> > *dense with a brown and brambled dark*
> >
> > > *are where*
>
> *in the ilex tree*
>
> > *strength and humility agree...*

Castilian Ilexes[1]

Castile can with justice be considered the cradle of the Spanish nation, and deserves to be far better known to tourists. But of course there is much more to Spain than its vast central tableland. At the end of the nineteenth century the British naturalists Chapman and Buck were staggered by its variety. 'Among European countries,' they began their book Wild Spain (1893):

> Spain stands unique in regard to the range of her natural and physical features. In no other land can there be found, within a similar area, such extremes of scene and climate as characterize the 400 by 400 miles of the

[1] Versions from Antonio Machado, by Charles Tomlinson and Henry Gifford (London, Oxford University Press, 1963)

Iberian Peninsula. Switzerland has alpine regions loftier and more imposing, Russia vaster steppes, and Norway more arctic scenery: but nowhere else in Europe do arctic and tropic so nearly meet as in Spain.

It is easy to share Chapman and Buck's enthusiasm. Spain has over 3,000 miles of coastline, Atlantic as well as Mediterranean, and an even wider diversity of landscapes than suggested in the quotation. I have tried already to give some idea of what Castile looks like. But then there are the snowfields, high valleys, lakes and oak forests of the Pyrenees, the deep Atlantic *rías*, or inlets, of Galicia (which remind one of the west of Ireland or Scotland), the scorching beaches of the south, the orchards, market gardens and citrus groves of Murcia and Valencia, the Mediterranean coves of the Costa Brava, the hill villages of Málaga and Cadiz (with their whitewashed houses that make one think of Morocco, just across the Strait of Gibraltar), the tobacco plantations of Granada's fertile plain, the rolling steppes of Extremadura, where Wellington routed Napoleon, the towering volcanic pinnacle of the Teide, Spain's highest mountain, in the Canary Islands. . . and this is merely a selection.

Broadly, Spain can be divided into a temperate and a dry zone. From Galicia eastwards in a broad swathe across the north of León and Castile to the Mediterranean the weather is generally mild and humid (summer holidays on the north coast can be delightfully sunny but also disastrously wet, and there is a persistent drizzle, known as the *sirimiri*, in the Basque Country). This temperate zone accounts for about one third of Spain's surface. The rest of the territory has a Mediterranean climate and is semi-arid. On balance Spain enjoys the finest weather in Europe, with a national average approaching 2,800 hours of annual sunlight.

One of Spain's greatest headaches is water, scarce in most of the country and unevenly distributed. Over the last few years this situation appears to have been made worse by the 'greenhouse effect'. Thus, in November 1989, while the reservoirs of the north reached an all-time low after a year's drought (something unheard of there) and people were bathing as if it were high summer, Andalusia found itself subjected to torrential rains, the heaviest in fifty years. A friend commented to me: 'See what I mean? In Spain everything is black or white. You can wait years for rain – and when it comes the dams over-flow, the crops are destroyed and the water is lost in the sea!'

Linked to the water shortage is the problem of erosion. Each year many million tons of topsoil are blown away, and the experts agree that a quarter of Spain's surface is undergoing desertification. A particular sufferer is the south-eastern province of Almería, some 75 per cent of which is affected. There are villages there where it never rains, where you can travel for dozens of miles without seeing a tree. Parts of the province are indistinguishable from the Sahara, which explains why some of the scenes in *Lawrence of Arabia* were filmed in the region.

Erosion is aggravated by the fires, often started deliberately by vandals, that ravage the woods each summer, particularly in Galicia. The Franco regime's extensive reafforestation with pines and eucalyptus has proved a disaster, not least because these trees ignite much more quickly than the country's native species such as the ilex. A more intelligent replanting policy is now being implemented (Spain is becoming more environmentally alert), but it is a painfully slow process. Meanwhile every summer the fires continue to decimate the dwindling masses of trees. In 1989, the worst year for the last three decades, almost 988,000 acres of forest were destroyed in 19,000 conflagrations.

Someone has referred to 'the delirious geography of Spain, which creates half a million problems in half a million square kilometres'. One of the main problems has been travel between the regions, particularly complicated from north to south thanks to the country's east–west mountain divides mentioned by Laurie Lee. Such bars to communication have played a major role in shaping Spain's history and culture, inducing, among other things, a permanent tendency to separatism. A glance at the physical map of Spain (see Illustration 1) will show why road-building has always been laborious and expensive here, and why it took so long to connect the main cities by train. More than any other single factor it was the railway system, completed towards the end of the nineteenth century, that forged Spanish unity.

Earlier in the century, before the arrival of the railways (the first of which was opened between Barcelona and Mataró, eighteen miles up the coast, in 1848), Spain attracted a handful of adventurous travellers searching for scenes more Romantic, exacting and, they hoped, spiced with risk than could be expected along the well-tried and comfortable routes of the Grand Tour. Among these hardies, who always took good care to carry with them a copy of *Don Quixote*, Richard Ford (1796–1858) was outstanding.

Ford's *Handbook for Travellers in Spain and Readers at Home*, published by John Murray in two volumes in 1845, is arguably the greatest book ever written on Spain by a foreigner. A highly educated man of intensely inquiring mind, Ford rode the length and breadth of Spain between 1830 and 1833, sampling whatever was going, jotting down his impressions, sketching, botanizing and conversing with the high and the low. After that came ten years' study back home in Exeter, working at Murray's commission. Ford arrived at the conclusion that one of the fundamental characteristics of the Spanish people was what he termed their 'unamalgamating' tendency, their refusal to join forces for a common purpose – a result in large measure of the geographical isolation of the country's different regions.

Spaniards, Ford found, were loyal above all to their local community (town or village), and after that to their district; the concept of Spain as a nation had little meaning for them. How could it have been otherwise, he mused, given the enormous difficulty of travel? He recalled that from antiquity those visiting Spain had been struck by the fierce localism of its indigenous stock. Had not Strabo said that the Iberians were incapable of pooling their energies for the common good? Nothing much had changed since then. 'Spain is today as it always has been,' Ford wrote, 'a bundle of small bodies tied together by a rope of sand, and, being without union, is also without strength.'

Galicians, Asturians, Cantabrians, Basques, Navarrese, Aragonese, Catalans, Castilians, Murcians, Andalusians, Extremadurans, Valencians, each with their own customs, installed in widely varying landscapes and in some cases speaking their own languages. . . who, asked Ford, would ever be able to make them see eye to eye, to bind them into anything more than a temporary unity?

A scholar of our own day and age, Richard Fletcher, muses on the same subject in his book *The Quest for El Cid*. 'Spain', he writes, 'has always been a country of markedly fissile tendency, where a single political authority has had the greatest difficulty in imposing its will upon the provinces. This is not owing to any stubborn streak of

Spain today is a semi-federal state divided into seventeen regions, each with its own parliament.

cussedness or pride in the Spanish character. It arises simply from the size and physical conformation of the Peninsula.' That puts it well – although one might question the adverb 'simply'. The streak of cussedness and pride mentioned by the author, perhaps itself partly a consequence of geography, has surely helped to shape the destinies of a country peculiarly difficult to hold together.

The 1978 Constitution, promulgated three years after the death of General Franco, reflected the conviction that, unless Spain's 'historically differentiated regions' (the Basque Country, Catalonia and Galicia, each of which has its own language) were afforded a considerable measure of self-government, the new democracy would fail to take definitive root. The three communities immediately went ahead and applied for a degree of devolution, which was granted. After all, who better than they to run their own affairs – affairs never fully understood in Madrid? The Franco regime had despised and repressed their languages and culture. Now they desired to right the balance.

What happened next was that the other regions of Spain, not wanting to be left behind, also asserted their constitutional right to form themselves into autonomous communities. Finally, after an enormous amount of haggling, the country acquired its current configuration. Today Spain is a quasi-federal nation divided into no less than seventeen *comunidades autónomas*, each with its own local parliament (see map on p. 9).

The system appears to be working, although to many people it seems ludicrous that such small regions as, say, La Rioja, or Cantabria, should have, or need, self-government on a par with Catalonia, Galicia and the Basque Country. The languages of the latter communities are now being taught alongside Spanish in their schools, something utterly unthinkable while Franco was alive; and self-government has meant a considerable reduction of separatist tension. The radical Basque nationalists are not satisfied by the autonomy provided under the Constitution, however, and continue to dream of an independent Basque State, while their terrorist wing, ETA, is still assassinating army officers and members of the police, using techniques that vie for brutal efficiency with those of the IRA. Later on we shall be looking more closely at the Basque Country and its problems.

Salvador Dalí liked to maintain that the word *España* is etymologically related to *espina*, thorn. To the painter it seemed fitting that the

very name of Spain, a country in his view obsessed by death and suffering, should relate to laceration. But in fact the Latin *Hispania*,
which gives *España*, appears to derive from an ancient Iberian word
meaning 'abounding in rabbits', an altogether more gentle connota-
tion. Seventeen years after the death of the dictator, the only thorn in
the flesh of Spain is ETA. The rest of the body politic has never been
sounder, as I hope this book will make clear.

−2−

Jews, Muslims and Christians: The Three Cultures

In 218 BC a Roman army under the Scipios landed at the Mediterranean port of Ampurias, founded by the Greeks on what is today known as the Costa Brava. Their objective: to destroy the power of the Carthaginians, who had been in Spain since about 500 BC, and incorporate the Iberian Peninsula into their fast-expanding empire. The ensuing struggle, known to historians as the Second Punic War, continued until 206 BC, when the Romans took Gades (the modern Cadiz), the last Carthaginian stronghold in Spain.

Firmly implanted in the fertile and unwarlike south and along the Mediterranean coast and lower reaches of the River Ebro, the Romans now turned their attention to subduing the more recalcitrant western, central and northern areas of the peninsula.

In the former, the Lusitanians (predecessors of the Portuguese) put up a tremendous resistance before succumbing in 139 BC. The vast tableland of central Spain was inhabited by a mixture of Celts and Iberians. These Celt-Iberians fought tenaciously to defend their capital, Numancia (near the later city of Soria), and were eventually starved out in 133 BC. In the mountain fastnesses of the north, the wild Basques, who had been living there for thousands of years before the arrival of the Romans, held out until 19 BC – and were never fully subdued.

12

It had taken the Romans two hundred years to complete their conquest. Almost another five hundred were to pass before the western Roman Empire collapsed under the impetus of the so-called 'barbarian invasions'. Spain fell to the Visigoths, the last of a series of Germanic tribes who had been filtering into the peninsula since the third century AD.

Behind them the Romans left splendid roads and irrigation systems, Christianity and outstanding works of architecture and engineering. Many of the latter are still standing today (such as Segovia's stupendous aqueduct, the amphitheatre at Mérida, the great bridge over the Tagus at Alcántara, the ruins of Itálica outside Seville and the various monuments that attest to the former greatness of Tarragona).

The Romans also bequeathed their language. Spanish today, thanks to the South and Central American connection, is the most widely spoken of all the languages deriving from Latin and the mother-tongue of some 300 million people. Portuguese, spoken by about 150 million, comes second.

When the Visigoths pressed into Spain in the fifth century AD, shouldered out of Gaul by the Franks, they were already considerably Romanized, and knew Latin. It is believed that there cannot have been many more than 100,000 of them. Like the Hispano-Romans they were Christians but, unlike them, followers of the 'heretical' Arius of Alexandria, who held that Christ was less than God, though more than human. For almost a hundred years the Visigoths remained aloof from the local inhabitants. Then, in AD 589, the monarchy, which had made the old Roman city of Toledo its capital (after first settling on Seville), was converted to Catholicism. From this moment onwards the fusion of the Visigoths with the Hispano-Roman population accelerated. The Latin culture of Visigothic Spain was the most flourishing in Western Europe at the time.

Visigothic German left little mark on the colloquial Latin spoken by the inhabitants of the Peninsula. Traces remain, however, in hundreds of place-names, some warlike terms and a handful of Spanish Christian names alluding to heroism, chivalry and related attributes. For example, Alfonso means 'all-prepared', Rodrigo is a compound of 'fame' and 'powerful', Fernando combines notions of 'peace' and 'daring', and Gonzalo derives from a word for 'strife'.

The Visigoths introduced an architectural novelty usually ascribed to the Muslims, who adopted and developed it when they invaded the peninsula: the horseshoe arch. Another innovation was the abolition of the old Roman system of provincial government and the elaboration of a great legal code, the *Forum iudicum*, that envisaged Spain as an independent national unit.

One stain on the record of the Visigoths is that for reasons not fully understood they unleashed a fierce campaign of persecution against the Jewish communities which had been living peacefully in Spain since Roman times. Some scholars believe that, in self-defence, the Jews may have encouraged the Muslim invasion which destroyed the Visigothic State in AD 711 and inaugurated a new era in the history of the Iberian Peninsula.

The town of Tarifa stands at the southernmost tip of Andalusia, and hence of Europe. Here the Mediterranean and Atlantic meet in an often rough embrace that attracts windsurfers from all over the world. On the slopes behind the town graze herds of red cows, descendants of the cattle that Hercules stole from Geryon, King of Tartessos, in accomplishment of one of his twelve labours.

On clear days the view across the Strait of Gibraltar is stupendous. Tarifa is separated from the nearest point in Africa, Punta de Ceres, by a mere eight miles, and with binoculars one can see the smoke rising from fires on the foothills of the Atlas Mountains, and ships entering Tangiers.

It was at Tarifa that, in AD 710, an expeditionary force under the Berber leader Tarif, from whom the place was to take its name, landed to sound out the Visigothic defences. Hardy folk from the Atlas, the Berbers had recently been converted to Islam, and Tarif was persuaded by Musa, the Umayyad Caliph's commander in western North Africa, to reconnoitre Spain. He and his men met little or no opposition, and the following year an invading army commanded by another Berber chief, Tarik, landed to take possession of the country. Somewhere near the estuary of the River Guadalquivir they routed the forces of the last Visigothic king, Roderic.

It was the beginning of a period that was to run for almost a millennium – until the fall of the Moorish kingdom of Granada in 1492 and, beyond that, to 1609, when the converted Moors living under the Christians were expelled from Spain.

After the defeat and death of Roderic, the Muslims, reinforced by successive waves of warriors from Africa, quickly overran most of the peninsula, taking Toledo, the Visigothic capital, without difficulty. Only in the high mountains of the north was the Christian resistance successful. The battle of Covadonga in Asturias (c. AD 722), at which a warlike Visigothic chieftain called Pelayo, who appears to have been one of Roderic's courtiers, defeated a Muslim force (the strength of which was almost certainly exaggerated by subsequent chroniclers), has traditionally been considered by Spaniards as the beginning of the 'Reconquest'.

I place 'Reconquest' between inverted commas because the concept is the invention of Spanish Roman Catholic historiography. 'I do not know how you can apply the word reconquest to something lasting for eight centuries,' commented the philosopher José Ortega y Gasset in 1921. 'The Reconquest is a fallacy and a great historical lie!', the famous Andalusian playwright Antonio Gala has exclaimed more recently.

The Muslims made an incursion into France shortly after invading the peninsula. There Charles Martel did justice to his surname, 'hammering' the Moors so decisively in AD 732 at the Battle of Tours (the French call it the Battle of Poitiers) that they retreated back into Spain and never returned.

Over the following centuries, as the Christians of northern Spain gradually pushed south against the Muslims, there came into operation an idealized race memory of pre-Islamic times, and the Visigoths, certainly no angels, were increasingly mythified. By the late Middle Ages, according to historian Brian Tate, Spaniards believed them to have been 'frank, sober, masculine conquerors of the decadent, power-hungry Romans'. Part of the blame was due to Isidore of Seville (c. 560–636), the scholar bishop who had lauded the Germanic invaders in his celebrated *Book of the Goths*.

In the forefront of the Christian advance south were the fighting men of Castile, a small county that arose in the mountains of Cantabria fringing the north coast between Asturias to the west and the Basque Country to the east. The name Castile is recorded as early as AD 801. At its inception the county was subject to the neighbouring kingdom of León, heir to the Visigothic monarchy, but it was not long before the Castilians began to press for independence. This they

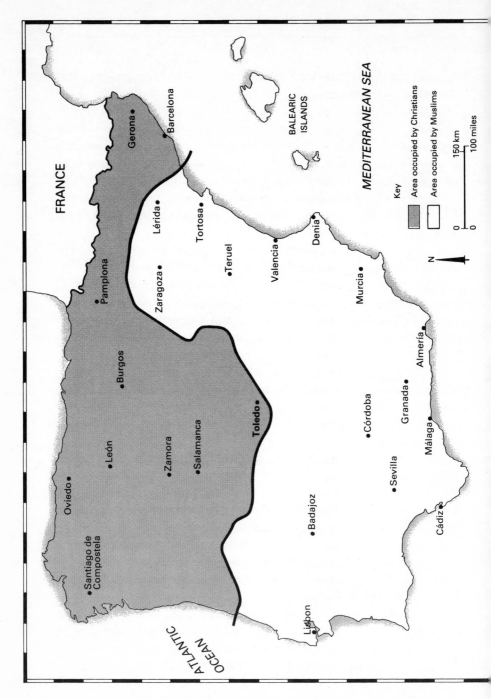

The approximate dividing line between Muslims and Christians after Toledo fell to the latter in AD *1085.*

achieved in the tenth century. The Romance spoken by the Castilians was destined eventually to become the 'official' tongue of Spain.

After three and a half centuries of ebb and flow, the boundary between the Christians and Moors was approximately that shown in the map on p. 16. An event of great symbolic and strategic importance had been the fall of Muslim Toledo in 1085 to King Alfonso VI of Castile and León: symbolic because it meant the recovery of the old Visigothic capital of Spain, strategic because Toledo, at the very heart of the peninsula, was ideally placed as a springboard for further operations to the south. Built on a steep rock almost completely surrounded by the River Tagus, the city posed few defence problems. With a mixed population of Christians, Jews and Muslims, Toledo later developed into one of the most flourishing centres of culture in the peninsula, and, indeed, in Europe.

It would be a mistake to imagine that, in advance of the invading Muslims, the entire Christian populace of Visigothic Spain had fled to the mountainous north of the country at the beginning of the eighth century. Most of the inhabitants stayed exactly where they were. The Muslims did not behave fanatically, and allowed both the Christians and Jews, regarded as 'People of the Book', to live their lives unmolested provided they kept the peace and paid their dues. Most of the country under Muslim domination accepted Islam without qualms. Recent research has shown that, whereas by AD 800 only about 8 per cent of the population of the peninsula was Muslim, the proportion had reached some 12.5 per cent by 850, 25 per cent by 900, 50 per cent by 950 and, by the year 1000, 75 per cent. They are eloquent statistics. The position changed over the following centuries, however, as the Christians conquered more and more territory from the Moors.

The linguistic situation in Islamic Spain was complex. The Christians continued speaking their native Romance and soon acquired command of conversational Arabic, at least in the cities and towns. In daily speech the Muslims used dialectal Arabic, Berber and even Romance, but classical Arabic was the norm in all official and administrative documents. As for the Jews, they assimilated Arabic and often wrote in it, knew Romance and used Hebrew for liturgical purposes.

The Muslims gave the name al-Andalus (not to be confused with the later, and more geographically restricted, term Andalusia) to all the territory they occupied in Spain. The word apparently derives from the Vandals, a Germanic tribe that had swept into and 'vandalized' Spain in the fifth century before crossing over to Africa. Al-Andalus, which in the early centuries of Islamic domination spread almost to the Pyrenees, was never a fully homogeneous unit. Emirates rose and fell; the powerful Caliphate of Córdoba, which occupied two-thirds of southern Spain and produced a civilization of extraordinary brilliance (someone once called tenth-century Córdoba 'the Athens of the West'), only lasted for just over a hundred years before splitting up into a series of rival *taifas*, or princedoms, in 1031; and fresh Berber incursions from Africa (first the Almoravids, then the Almohads) added more variations. These divisions and subdivisions paralleled those existing in the rest of the country, where the Christian kings tended to parcel out their territories on their deathbeds. It was little wonder that the 'Reconquest' took almost eight centuries.

Whereas the extant architectural monuments of Visigothic culture are far and few between, as well as off the beaten track (little more than a handful of churches, in fact), many of the fine buildings produced by Spanish Islam are still there for all the world to see and admire. Seville's soaring Giralda Tower and Alcázar, the Great Mosque at Córdoba, surely one of the most spiritually uplifting places of worship ever designed, the cool inner courtyards, the fountains and myrtle-enclosed pools of Granada's Alhambra (called by the young Disraeli 'the most imaginative, the most delicate and fantastic creation that ever sprang up on a summer night in a fairy tale'), the Aljafería Palace in the Aragonese capital of Saragossa . . . since the late eighteenth century these and other eloquent tokens of Spain's Islamic past have been firing the European imagination.

The Muslims who came under Christian rule over the centuries before the end of the 'Reconquest' in 1492 were known as Mudéjars. Among them were many skilled builders, who erected wonderful churches for their new masters. Fabulous examples of their art and skills can be found in the graceful towers of Teruel and Tarazona, Aragonese towns that had been thriving centres of Islamic culture before falling to the Christians.

There are many thousands of Arabic place-names in Spanish (Madrid among them) and the dictionary contains some 4,500 Arabic loan-words incorporated into the language during its long medieval development. Such a large surviving vocabulary shows to what an extent Islamic culture was a fundamental element in the forging of the Spanish spirit. The majority of these words are rarely encountered now, true, but hundreds crop up in daily speech, and many more hundreds in literature. The Muslims were expert farmers, gardeners and horticulturists, and in Spain the lexicon of irrigation, plants, fruits and vegetables is still substantially Arabic. Many of the latter were first brought to Spain by the Muslims, spreading from there to Europe along with their Arabic names – for example, artichokes, rice, aubergines, sugar, oranges, lemons and spinach. Don Quixote, in pedantic mood, informs Sancho Panza that *all* Spanish words beginning in 'al' are Arabic in origin. This is not true (as Cervantes must surely have been aware), although many hundreds are: words such as *alcázar*, 'castle', *alforja*, 'saddle-bag', *alféizar*, 'window-sill', *alcantarilla*, 'drain', and *aljibe*, 'well'. The most famous Arabic term in Spanish, universally recognized as such, is 'ojalá', 'perhaps', which means literally 'if Allah so will'. Richard Ford, always on the lookout for the survival of Moorish influences in the peninsula, believed that the extremely frequent use of 'ojalá' proved how greatly Spaniards had been vitiated by 'oriental fatalism'!

Between 711 and 1492 Spain was a land of three religions, with a unique cultural mix and, as a rule, an extraordinary degree of tolerance. Only very occasionally, during the almost eight centuries of Islamic domination, were the Christians (known as Mozarabs) and Jews harassed.

Most of the Jews of Sepharad (as they called Spain) were craftsmen, weavers, blacksmiths, dyers, armour-makers, cobblers and so forth. A minority were doctors, bankers, interpreters and businessmen. The Spanish Jews also produced some remarkable philosophers (Maimonides of Córdoba, twelfth-century author of *The Guide for the Perplexed*, is the most famous), writers, poets and artists.

Not uncommonly the Jews attained positions of great importance in the Muslim administration. In the eleventh century, to give just one example, Samuel ha-Nagid, a fine poet and expert on the Talmud, became vizier in Granada.

In the Christian kingdoms the Jews and Muslims were normally allowed to live their lives unhindered. However, the financial skills of some Jews occasionally caused problems at times of crisis, arousing the odium of their Christian debtors. Nor did it help that another of the professions in which the Jews specialized was that of tax-collector. The pogroms of 1391 in Castile, Catalonia and Valencia (echoing those perpetrated eight hundred years earlier under the Visigoths) left an indelible mark on the Sephardic mind. Such actions, though isolated, paved the way for the later persecutions which were to put an end to fifteen centuries of peaceful Jewish presence in the Iberian Peninsula.

In Castile and León, during the 'Reconquest', the king styled himself 'Monarch of the Three Religions', an indication that, between the eleventh and fourteenth centuries, there was no fundamental hostility towards the Jewish and Islamic communities living in the Christian kingdoms. The Castilian monarchs never forced the Jews to live in ghettos, as happened in other parts of Europe – until, that is, papal policy eventually obliged them to do so.

The cultural consequences of the coexistence of three religions and various languages were manifold and astonishing. At Toledo's School of Translators, for example, founded in the twelfth century, Jewish, Christian and Muslim scholars worked side by side, many of the most skilled and multi-lingual translators being Sephardim. The School played a role of extraordinary importance in European culture by rendering Arab philosophical and scientific treatises into Latin. The work was continued under King Alfonso the Wise (1225–84). Two hundred years before the fall of Constantinople (1453) led to a revival of Hellenic learning, this enlightened ruler and patron of the arts arranged for classical Greek works preserved by the Arabs, but not yet known to Europe, to be translated into Latin. They then circulated throughout the continent and helped to pave the way for the rebirth of learning we call the Renaissance.

In 1988 the West European Institute of Islamic Culture was set up in Toledo to promote research into Spain's Muslim heritage. In memory of the School of Translators, the archive and library of the International Federation of Translators is to be installed in the city during 1992. Perhaps as a result of this and related initiatives, Toledo, a dazzling cultural centre when Madrid was little more than a castle on a hill, will recover some of its former grandeur.

The fruitful coexistence of the three religions disappeared in tragic circumstances when the 'Reconquest' ended with the fall of Granada in 1492. A reign of terror against the Jews and Muslims was inaugurated by King Ferdinand and Queen Isabella, who had united the crowns of Aragón and Castile twenty years earlier and were bent on achieving national unity. If previously the king of Castile and León had been 'Monarch of the Three Religions', Ferdinand and Isabella were exclusively concerned with the well-being and propagation of Christianity. In return for their pains Pope Alexander VI bestowed on them the title of 'The Catholic Monarchs'. Initially the king and queen promised to respect the property and religious freedom of Granada's Jews, some 20,000 strong, but almost immediately they went back on their word. The Jews were given a choice: either conversion to Catholicism or banishment. They had four months in which to make up their minds. The expulsion order was then extended to the Jews throughout Spain, approximately half a million in number out of a total population of perhaps 7 million inhabitants. It is not known exactly how many Jews went into exile, but the figure usually proposed is in the region of 200,000. The victims had no option but to sell their houses, and most of their property, at rock-bottom prices. Twenty thousand are said to have died in their search for a new home.

When the four months passed, Granada's Jewish quarter was razed to the ground. The monstrous injustice of the diaspora caused a painful disruption to the society of the day, and left a permanent scar on the Spanish soul. The loss to culture was devastating and, in the field of science, led to an intellectual impoverishment the results of which have haunted Spain to this day. As for the economy, the Sultan of Turkey described as madness Spain's suicidal decision to deprive itself of its 'riches'. Soon Genoese and German businessmen stepped in to fill the gap left by the Jews in commercial and banking life, with the consequent re-export of the untold wealth which began to flow into Spain from America that same year as the Spaniards pushed ahead with the exploration and colonization of the New World.

The majority of the Sephardim who left Spain established themselves in North Africa (Tetuan, Tangiers, Oran, Morocco, Melilla, Casablanca...). Others made their way to Egypt, the Balkans, Greece, Syria, the Low Countries, Italy, Germany and England. Some 50,000 settled in Turkey.

The Sephardim never forgot their homeland, and to this day there are families who retain the keys of their forebears' houses in Toledo and other parts of Spain. The language the exiles took with them, known as *judeo-español*, is still spoken by some 150,000 people scattered throughout the world, and the Sephardim have also preserved an impressive repertoire of fifteenth-century songs, proverbs, folklore and recipes, of inestimable value to students of medieval Spain. Tel Aviv radio broadcasts special programmes in this strange, almost ossified tongue now in danger of extinction.

The Jews who, faced with a terrible decision, outwardly accepted conversion to Christianity and stayed on in Spain were known as *conversos*, converts, or New Christians. Many were really crypto-Jews, and lived and reared their children in an atmosphere of terror and secrecy. Four centuries later, George Borrow met some of their descendants on his Bible-selling travels around the country. Their secret religious practices were entirely unsuspected by their neighbours.

Any number of examples could be given of how the need for stealth among the Jewish converts to Christianity worked out in practice. I recently came across this one. By tradition the Sabbath began for the Sephardim on Friday evenings at the exact moment when the first three stars appeared. The faithful would keep a sharp look out for these and, on spotting them, point excitedly. 1492 changed all that. The *conversos* ordered their children never to point at the sky again, warning them that if they did so they might be seen by officers or spies of the Inquisition, and suspected of belonging to families still covertly practising Judaism.

So far we have been concerned almost entirely with the fate of the Spanish Jews, but what about the Muslims?

For seven years the 'Catholic Monarchs' kept their word to the Islamic population of Granada (estimated at 300,000 by some historians), respecting their property, religion and way of life. But in 1499 the fanatical Francisco Jiménez de Cisneros, cardinal-archbishop of Toledo and Queen Isabella's confessor, decided that the time had come to bring the infidels to heel. Many noble Muslim families, fearing the worst as forced conversions multiplied, fled to Africa. The cardinal worked fast. 'There is no one left in Granada who is not now Christian,' he was able to write to Isabella in 1500, 'and all the mosques have been turned into churches.'

In 1501 the *moriscos*, as the converted Moors were known pejoratively, staged a violent protest in Granada against this treatment. They were easily put down, and the insurrection gave Ferdinand and Isabella a perfect excuse for further repression.

Andrea Navagiero, Venetian ambassador to the Court of Charles I, Ferdinand and Isabella's grandson, has left us a fascinating contemporary account of a visit to Granada in 1526. A man of taste and sensitivity, he found desolation on all sides: the horticulture of the city's fertile plain, the Vega, so lovingly tended by the Muslims, was declining; the houses of the families who had fled into exile were falling down. 'The Spaniards, here as in the rest of Spain, are not very industrious, and take no pleasure in either cultivating or sowing the land,' Navagiero wrote in his *Trip Through Spain*; 'on the contrary, they prefer to go to war or to America and to make money this way rather than any other.'

In 1568, a full-scale *morisco* revolt broke out in Granada. Philip II, Charles I's son, was now on the throne. From his father, Holy Roman Emperor as well as king of Spain, Philip had inherited vast possessions in Europe and America, and commensurate ambition, boasting in later life that from his monastery-palace, the Escorial, at the foot of the mountains north of Madrid, he ruled half the world by jotting down instructions on scraps of paper. A religious fanatic, Philip was not going to tolerate trouble from Granada's rebel *moriscos*. They were quickly subdued in the city, but in the high valleys of the Alpujarras, between the Sierra Nevada and the sea, the fighting continued for two years. Finally, hopelessly outnumbered and no match for the well-equipped Castilians led by Philip's bastard brother, John of Austria, the insurgents were crushed. After the bloody defeat the *morisco* communities in the Alpujarras were dispersed to other parts of Spain, and the region resettled with Christians from the north.

In 1609 (the year in which Shakespeare's sonnets were published) Philip III devised a solution for dealing with the *moriscos*, inspired no doubt by the treatment his forebears Ferdinand and Isabella had meted out to the Jews. This was mass expulsion. Three hundred thousand men, women and children were ordered out of the country at cruelly short notice. Most crossed to Africa, where their descendants go to this day by the name of 'Andalusians'. As the distinguished anthropologist Julio Caro Baroja has written, the banishment decree signified 'a complete determination to extirpate every single Islamic element from Spanish society'.

The cruelty of this shameful episode in Spanish history is reflected by Cervantes in the touching account of the Moor Ricote in Part II of *Don Quixote*, published six years after the expulsion. Ricote has returned in disguise from Germany in order to recover some money buried hurriedly when he was banished, and happens upon his ex-neighbour, Sancho Panza. They embrace warmly. 'Wherever we are we weep for Spain,' the *morisco* laments; 'for after all, we were born here and this country's our true home.'

The Spanish Church of the Counter-Reformation was a harsh instrument for repressing the infidel, whether Jewish, Muslim or Protestant, and it is believed that the Inquisition tortured and killed almost a million people. Cultural repression became one of the hallmarks of the Spanish way of life. Cardinal Jiménez de Cisneros had the 80,000 books in the Arab University of Granada burnt, claiming they were all Korans, and the Inquisitor Tomás de Torquemada, a Jewish renegade, busied himself with winkling out Hebrew books in Seville. Cervantes, it must be presumed, parodied the book-burning proclivities of the Spanish Church in the famous scene in which the village priest commits to the flames those novels of chivalry in Don Quixote's library which he considers most responsible for the hidalgo's delusions.

In the atmosphere of terror consequent upon the fall of Granada in 1492, a new social type arose in Spain: the informer. He was not infrequently a Jew ready to denounce other Jews in order to save his own skin. Some of the worst Inquisitors were themselves *conversos* (Torquemada was a case in point) and posed a dire threat to their former co-religionists, whose minds they knew only too well. Suspicion and terror of one's neighbour became rife. Christians, Old and New alike, were to remain for centuries obsessed by the need to establish and proclaim the purity of their blood, often no easy task given the racial mix that had existed in Spain from medieval times. Imagine the bribes to the authorities, the pressing demand for false genealogies, the handsome payments to corrupt lawyers and scribes!

This obsession with purity of blood is well put by the protagonist of a seventeenth-century play by Lope de Vega, *Peribáñez and the Commander of Ocaña*. Peribáñez, a representative of the ordinary people, has a strong sense of his own dignity, as he makes clear (in the conventional terms of the day) when he has to stand up for himself against those above him:

> *Yo soy un hombre, aunque de villana casta,*
> *limpia de sangre y jamás de mora ni de hebrea*
> *manchada.*
>
> *I am a man, although of low estate,*
> *With clean blood untarnished by Moorish or Jewish*
> *female.*

Centuries later, National-Socialism copied from Spain the idea of 'clean blood'. According to Nazi-hunter Simon Wiesenthal, 'Hitler invented nothing. His racial problem and his hatred of the Jews was taken directly from the Spanish Catholic Church' (interview in *El Independiente*, Madrid, 10 February 1990).

Watered-down versions of Peribáñez can still be found in Spain today. Visit any Castilian or Aragonese town. They will show you the castle, the churches, the museum . . . but not, willingly, the remains of the Jewish quarter. All round the country linger reminiscences of the old terrors and suspicions connected with Jewish blood. Hardly anything is known by the local people of the suppressed Hebrew community. There is no historical memory. It is as if the Spanish Jews had never existed.

Exile, repression, persecution – from 1492 onwards Catholic orthodoxy was imposed brutally on the people of Spain, and the temptation to kill, imprison, banish or otherwise clamp down on ideological opponents became endemic. Philip II allowed Spaniards to study abroad at only three colleges in Italy and one in Portugal, which was then annexed to Spain. Everywhere else was too ideologically risky. 'Far be from us the dangerous novelty of thinking,' declared the authorities of the University of Cervera, in Catalonia, to Ferdinand VII three hundred years later. The opponents of the latter, one of the most odious of Spain's Bourbon kings, had to flee the country in their thousands. Another century passed and under the dictatorship of General Primo de Rivera (1923–30) troublesome intellectuals were still being forced into exile. When the Republic arrived in 1931, the

Fascists soon invented the lie that a 'Jewish-Masonic-Communist plot' was afoot against the 'traditional values' of the Spanish nation, and both the Left and Right censored the newspapers when in power between 1931 and 1936. General Franco's enemies, at the end of the 1936–9 Civil War, had no option but to cross the frontier into France in order to avoid reprisals. Four hundred thousand fled – with good reason, for the dictatorship continued executing prisoners right up to 1942. Only today, at last, has Spain recovered its true tradition of tolerance, forged over long centuries before the collapse of Granada in 1492.

One of the habitual results of such constant repression has been the need of dissident authors to develop great skill at writing between the lines, with irony and innuendo as the tools of their dangerous trade. Cervantes was a subtle practitioner of this technique, as he demonstrated with consummate guile in *Don Quixote*. So too, centuries later, were the rebel film makers who contrived to use their art to undermine the Franco regime. In Spain today everyone remembers Luis Buñuel's achievement with *Viridiana*, the country's official entry at the Cannes Film Festival in 1961 and winner of the coveted Golden Palm. The Spanish censors had failed to perceive that the script contained a very obvious parody of the Last Supper and, when the scandal broke, Franco's fury is said to have scaled epic heights. In the best tradition of Spanish intolerance, the police ransacked the producer's offices in Madrid and purging fire destroyed any copies of the film the authorities could lay their hands on. It is said that the *Viridiana* débâcle provoked the heart attack that shortly afterwards killed Gabriel Arias Salgado, the minister of Information and Tourism, who had been under the impression that Buñuel's film would afford great international prestige to Franco's Spain!

1492 was not only the year in which Granada fell to Ferdinand and Isabella and the Jews were expelled but of Columbus's discovery of the New World, a discovery that led to a revolution in mankind's thinking about itself and the universe as well as, more specifically, in Spain's economy.

Because the Jews, and then the New Christians (*conversos*), were often adept at commerce and money matters, the Old Christians reacted strongly against the skills connected with the acquisition of 'filthy lucre', although not, it need hardly be said, against lucre as such. The distinguished historian Américo Castro and his followers have argued that it was the atmosphere of distrust and suspicion surrounding all things Jewish (and, by extension, financial) that hindered the growth in Spain of what today we would call a middle class. Be this as it may, the immense wealth that, from 1492 onwards, flowed into the country from Spain's American possessions tended to be frittered away and not intelligently invested. Astronomical sums were expended on European wars and on the Armada that Philip II sent against England in 1588. The American gold and silver, seemingly inexhaustible, buoyed up the Spanish economy for a hundred years, giving a misleading appearance of great prosperity. But by the seventeenth century the country's bankruptcy, hastened by the exactions of foreign bankers, was plain for all to see.

It could be argued that Spain's imperial adventure was a disaster for the country (as well as for America's indigenous inhabitants, many of whose descendants object strongly to the notion that Spain 'discovered' America and, it may be added, to Expo 92). Right-wing Spaniards, however, have always considered the discovery and colonization of America Spain's greatest achievement, and revered Ferdinand and Isabella for their 'providential' backing of Columbus and their 'mission' as evangelists of the New World. In the 1930s the Spanish Fascists appropriated Ferdinand and Isabella's symbols of the yoke and arrows, and looked to the 'Catholic Monarchs' for inspiration in their self-proclaimed task of raising Spain once again to greatness – a greatness inseparable in their eyes from imperial power.

That power had slipped from Spain's grasp during the nineteenth century, as more and more American colonies broke loose. The process of dismemberment came to a brutal conclusion in 1898 with the loss of Puerto Rico, Cuba and the Philippines, the last vestiges (with the exception of a few tiny African enclaves and a strip of Morocco) of a once great empire.

When Spain woke up to the realization that it had now been stripped of all its American possessions it was profoundly shocked, particularly by the seizure of Cuba, where the US navy had disposed of the antediluvian Spanish opposition in an encounter as brief as it was decisive. Cuba had had a specially strong connection with Spain. Spaniards loved it for its music and gaiety and considered it virtually

27

another Andalusian province. Now it had gone. The scenes in Barcelona when the tattered troops disembarked (Spain had 70,000 soldiers in the island) were harrowing in the extreme. The historian Rafael Altamira has written of the profound depression that the events of 1898 provoked in all classes. They spelt not just the end of the American empire but inspired the feeling 'that it might be impossible for the Spanish people ever to rise again'.

The 'Disaster', as the 1898 calamity became known in Spain, and the introspection that followed it, made it impossible to deny that the country had fallen far behind the great European nations. If the reasons for the decline were open to dispute, its symptoms were ubiquitous. Spanish agriculture, which had flourished under the Muslims, was best symbolized by an antiquated wooden plough; there had been no mid-century industrial revolution; the middle class as such hardly existed; the level of education was appallingly low and a majority of the populace illiterate; land distribution was grossly unjust . . . It had been a century, moreover, of exhausting civil war. Spain in 1898 was a grotesque parody of its former imperial self.

Who are we? How have we managed to lose one of the largest empires the world has ever seen? Where have we gone astray? How can we become strong again? What do we understand by 'strong', in any case? These were the sort of questions the writers subsequently labelled 'The Generation of 1898' – men such as Miguel de Unamuno and the novelist Pío Baroja – put to themselves. Spain became the patient on the psychiatrist's couch, and the diagnoses of her condition varied as much as the cures proposed.

Three decades later the Spanish Fascists capitalized on the sense of failure attendant upon 1898, and began to preach the doctrine of a new imperialism. José Antonio Primo de Rivera, by 1933 Spain's principal Fascist leader (a little more about him in the next chapter), was deeply impressed by the fact that Columbus's discovery of America had coincided with the fall of Granada to Ferdinand and Isabella. 'That very same year of 1492 in which Spain completed its universal task of de-Islamizing itself,' he wrote, forgetting to add 'dejudaizing', 'it accepted the universal task of discovering and conquering a world.'

The Spanish Fascist publications teemed with nostalgic allusions to Spain's lost empire and with affirmations of the need to build another (presumably in Africa). I particularly like the following definition of 'Empire' and 'Anti-Empire' printed in the journal *J.O.N.S.* (June 1933). The reference is to Spain's recent, and pathetic, record in North Africa:

> EMPIRE: The Discovery of America. That is, the greatest example of expansive energy known to History. In the course of a single century we spread from California and Florida to Cape Horn. The 'conquistador' carries all before him. Space shrinks and almost disappears as men look on amazed.

> ANTI-EMPIRE: Text of a military despatch during the Spanish Monarchy's last campaign in Africa: 'We have succeeded in advancing from kilometre 48 to kilometre 49.'

With the victory of the Allies in the Second World War the Spanish Fascists' dream of a new empire vanished for ever, while the Franco regime soon relinquished any illusions it might have entertained initially on the subject.

Today, with Expo 92 just around the corner, there is a great deal of talk about Spain's relations with its former colonies, about commercial and cultural ties and, particularly, about the 'mother tongue' that unites them (when Mexico's Octavio Paz won the Nobel Prize for Literature in 1990 following on the heels of Spain's Camilo José Cela, the response of many editorials was to boast childishly that at last the world had recognized the 'excellence' of the Spanish language, and recently Puerto Rico has been awarded Spain's annual Prince of Asturias Prize for restoring the primacy there of Spanish). Much of this talk, however, amounts to little more than an alloy of sentimentalism and rhetoric: the truth is that the New Spain is more concerned about surviving, and hopefully succeeding, in the European Single Market than in investing its money and energies in far-off South America. Spain today is back in Europe and proud of it, as almost any Spaniard will tell you.

After centuries of amnesia about the expulsion of the Jews and

Muslims and the part played by Judaism and Islam in the shaping of Spanish civilization, it seems that we may now be beginning to witness what one historian has called 'a rebirth of the suppressed cultures'. A slow rebirth it is proving, however. The school curriculum does not yet make explicit provision for in-depth study of 'the three cultures', far from it, and the references in the standard history textbooks to the Jews and Muslims are still woefully inadequate. Almost twenty years after the death of Franco, school leavers still believe in the myth of the Christian 'Reconquest' of usurped 'Spanish' territories; that the eight centuries of Islamic and Jewish presence in Spain were fundamentally negative; and that the Cid was a kindly Christian soldier, which he certainly was not. The fact that Spanish popular ceramics or leather handicrafts are Arab in origin tends to be forgotten in the school textbooks; there is no reference to the wholesale destruction, after 1492, of synagogues, mosques and other buildings – of the fact that, for instance, the universally admired Giralda Tower in Seville is the only part still standing of one of the most splendid mosques in the world; the brutality of the expulsion of the Jews and, later, the *moriscos* is played down; and the presence of Arabic in the everyday vocabulary of Spanish not stressed. Personally it has come to me as a great disappointment that the Socialists, in power since 1982, have not done much more to improve the teaching of eight centuries of history fundamental to an understanding of Spanish civilization and the great buried tradition of religious tolerance.

The situation in the universities is little better. The study of Islam and Judaism remains very much a minority affair, and no specific courses on the Sephardim are as yet available. Serafín Fanjul, Professor of Arab Literature at Madrid's Autonomous University, is disconsolate about the abysmal ignorance of the first-year students entering his department, who know almost nothing of the geography of the Islamic world, let alone its culture. 'They haven't even grasped the fact that half the countries with Mediterranean coastlines are African and Asian,' he complains, musing that, if the *students* are like this, it needs little imagination to gauge the awareness of the nation at large. 'In the popular mind the "Moors" are still conceived of as absolute savages,' he adds, 'and, despite the Gulf War, you still have to explain every day that the terms Arab and Muslim are not synonymous.'

There is a heartening exception to the gloomy picture. In 1984 the

European Parliament approved the setting up, in Granada, of a Euro-Arab University for postgraduate students. Its four official languages were to be Spanish, French, Arabic and English. Not much progress had been made with the project when the Gulf War held matters up even further. It is still going ahead, however, and once the dream becomes a reality the new university may well play a prominent role in helping to forge links of understanding between the Arab world and Europe. One of its main aims will be to promote research into the scientific and artistic achievements of Muslim Spain, a meeting-place of cultures unique in European history.

Spain, it seems to me, should be seeking to become a bridge between the Muslims and Europe, between East and West. If such a vision had existed in 1990, the Socialist government would never, in my opinion, have involved the country in the Gulf War. By making the joint Spanish-US bases available for the massive bombing of Iraq, the government outraged many Muslim countries, not least the five nations of the Maghreb, Spain's neighbours to the south (Mauritania, Morocco, Tunis, Libya and Algeria), with which it is vital to maintain friendly relations.

Ceuta and Melilla, Spain's two cities on the North African coast (in reality, more military enclaves than cities), are lusted after by the Islamic fundamentalists of the Maghreb and, particularly, by Morocco. Their Muslim communities, which total some 40,000 souls, live in great poverty and came out unanimously in support of Saddam Hussein during the war. Some day Ceuta and Melilla might be attacked. There can be no question of *returning* them, since they were in Spanish hands centuries before the existence of Morocco as a nation, but an amicable solution could be reached, before there is bloodshed, about their future. It would be wise to do so as soon as possible.

Morocco today is a country of poverty, chaos and repression ruled over for three decades by a tyrant, King Hassan II. In recent years, not surprisingly, more and more Moroccans have flocked into Spain, their gateway to the EC, in search of employment. Millions pass through the country each year on their way to and from the rest of Europe. At the time of writing there are some 200,000 North Africans in Spain, mainly Moroccans, working illegally in agriculture, construction and as street vendors. Their brutal exploitation and their hardships have been exposed in an excellent film, *Las cartas de Alou* ('Alou's Letters

Home'), by the Basque director Montxo Armendáriz. Despite the introduction of visas in May 1991 (a measure imposed by the EC with Spanish government approval), illegal immigration is bound to continue – Morocco is a stone's throw across the Strait of Gibraltar and the Spanish coastline is vulnerable. It has been estimated that by the year 2000 the Maghreb will have a population of 160 million (while Spain's and Europe's will be ageing) and that 25 million North Africans will by then be knocking at the EC door. In such a situation it is in the best interests of Europe in general and Spain in particular to invest massively in the Maghreb's future, even if only as a self-protective measure, and meanwhile to do everything possible to improve the lot of the immigrant workers, who habitually live in appalling conditions.

The Spanish government, sensibly, is now stepping up its aid to the five Maghreb countries and seeking to forge closer cultural links. So, too, is the Andalusian regional government, a policy that makes sense given the history of southern Spain and its close physical proximity to North Africa. In July 1991 a new Treaty of Friendship, Neighbourliness and Co-operation was signed between Madrid and Rabat, and commercial ties are to be strengthened with Algeria. Spain already imports large quantities of natural gas from the latter, and this supply will be more than doubled when the new pipeline linking Algeria, Morocco and Seville comes into operation in 1995. All in all it seems possible that relations between Spain and the Arab world may now improve substantially, despite the country's involvement in the Gulf War.

Spain's relations with the Jewish world should also be a priority. As preparations began to go ahead for the celebration of the 500th anniversary of the discovery of America, an organization called 'Sefarad 92' was set in motion by a committee of Jews with the collaboration of the Spanish government. The aim was to ensure that, during the Seville Universal Exposition, the world should remember that 1492 was not only the year in which Columbus encountered America but also that of the cruel expulsion of the Sephardim. 1992, therefore, will not be just about man's ability to discover (the theme of the Exposition) but also about a *rediscovery*: that of the submerged Jewish component in Spanish culture and history. Since 1992 is also bound to provoke much invigorating debate about the persecution and final banishment of the *moriscos*, perhaps Spain's Great Year will stimulate a keener awareness of the imperious need to promote in every way possible, and particularly within the school system, a deeper understanding of 'the three cultures' and their interaction in the creation of Spanish civilization, undoubtedly the most complex in Europe. A civilization so complex, indeed, that no one person could ever hope to comprehend it fully.

Apart from the great cultural benefits bound to accrue, the fostering of such an awareness would be the best possible homage to the memory of the hundreds of thousands of Spanish Muslims and Jews who, centuries ago, fell foul of Christian intransigence.

−3−

The Republic, the Civil War and the Franco Regime (1931−75)

In Spain, when older folk gather to reminisce, you will hear them referring frequently to 'The Republic'. Some talk about it nostalgically, as if it had been a Golden Age; others with execration; many lament its mistakes and hope that the New Spain will learn from them.

The Second Spanish Republic was proclaimed on 14 April 1931, two days after municipal elections had decisively shown that Alfonso XIII, king since 1902, did not command the respect of the majority of his people. Polling had taken place with none of the violence forecast by some pundits on the Right. Suddenly, after centuries of monarchy interrupted within living memory only by the brief experience of the First Republic (1873−4), the possibility of a democratic, more just Spain was no longer a dream but a reality. It seemed little short of a miracle.

Newsreel film of those heady days shows jubilant crowds cheering, dancing, singing and waving improvised Republican flags in the streets of Madrid and Barcelona. The seven years of General Primo de Rivera's dictatorship (1923−30) had alienated popular support for a king who had appeared happy enough to go along with that authoritarian regime. After the general resigned and left Spain in January 1930, the demand for an end to the monarchy had grown apace.

34

Enough of the Bourbons! Republican meetings had been held up and down the country and a secret agreement reached on the composition of a provisional government to take over. Although a badly timed rising had been quickly put down in December 1930, the old order was clearly coming to an end. That it did so without bloodshed boded well for the future.

The young Republic was hampered by many difficulties, however. The economy, to start with, was in a run-down condition. Although Spain had benefited financially from its neutrality during the Great War, little creative investment of the profits had taken place. The situation had been made worse by the world recession of 1929, and unemployment was rife.

Then there was the agrarian question. Vast tracts of Spain (particularly in Andalusia) were in the hands of very few owners, and scandalously underexploited. The peasants, most of them day labourers living barely at subsistence level, were clamouring for land – and confidently expected the Republic to give it to them. Unless their understandable complaints were satisfied, serious trouble seemed unavoidable. According to the historian Gabriel Jackson, in 1931 the question of land reform 'bulked larger than any other single issue in the political consciousness of the public'. Any attempt at land redistribution, the Republicans knew, would infuriate the owners.

There were lots of other problems. For example, the hostility of an army overloaded with generals, accustomed to intervening in politics and deeply resistant to change. The leading Madrid monarchist newspaper, *ABC*, had warned five days before the municipal elections that, if the Republic were proclaimed, there was a possibility of 'imminent civil war'. Six days after the Republic's inauguration the Catalans had restored their ancient regional parliament, the Generalitat, and the conservative elements in the army were duly horrified, seeing Catalan autonomy as the first step on the road to independence and the destruction of the 'sacred unity' of Spain.

As well as all this there were bitter quarrels among the various democratic groups about the sort of Republic they wanted, while the Anarchists, who had grown very strong in Catalonia and Andalusia, were not prepared to truckle to any State whatsoever (their motto was 'No God, no owners, no private property'). Another deeply worrying factor was the lack of political expertise among the men who had now to guide the country on a democratic course through the troubled waters of extremism on both the Left and the Right, many of them academic Socialists with no grass-roots political experience.

Finally, there was the Catholic Church, which within days of the elections was already spelling out its misgivings about a lay Republic. A good idea of the Church's attitude to democracy at this time is provided by an official catechism in use in the 1920s, which included questions and answers such as the following:

> 'What does Liberalism teach?' – 'That the State is independent of the Church.'

> 'What kind of sin is Liberalism?' – 'It is a most grievous sin against faith.'

> 'What sin is committed by him who votes for a Liberal candidate?' – 'Generally a mortal sin.'

One of the Republic's greatest battles was undoubtedly going to be fought in the field of primary and secondary education. The progressives were determined to destroy the Church monopoly and create a State education system capable of meeting the huge challenge posed by widespread illiteracy (in 1931 Spain had 25 million inhabitants, of whom no less than 32.4 per cent were fully illiterate). It was estimated that 27,150 new schools were needed. The provisional government immediately drew up a five-year plan, undertaking to build 7,000 schools in the first year and 5,000 in each of the following four. They were to reach their goal for the first year, build 2,580 in 1932, and finish 3,990 in 1933 before the Right won the general election that November – an astonishing achievement. Over the previous thirty years only 11,128 new schools had been built; the Republic, in two and a half, was to create 13,570.

As well as building schools, the Republicans were determined to raise the status of the teaching profession, traditionally very badly paid. They especially improved the lot of primary school teachers: five thousand new posts were created, and salaries increased by 50 per cent. But this reforming zeal was not limited to education. Divorce and prostitution were to be legalized, Church and State separated, land redistribution initiated, the cemeteries and hospitals secularized and the number of religious orders reduced. An ambitious programme, and, from the right-wing point of view, highly provocative.

The Vatican did not immediately recognize the Republic, and the reaction of the Spanish Church to the provisional government's plans was hostile in the extreme. Scarcely three weeks after the proclamation of the new regime, Cardinal Segura, archbishop of Toledo and primate of all Spain, attacked the projected reforms in a virulent pastoral letter. He said the Republic was a serious threat to the rights of the Catholic Church, and asked the women of Spain to organize a prayer crusade to curb the regime. He recalled what had happened in Bavaria in 1919, when Catholics took to the streets to 'save' the country from a brief Bolshevik occupation, hinting thereby that the Spanish Republic was virtually Communist (nothing could have been further from the truth) and should be vigorously opposed.

These words had a literally incendiary effect. A few days later six convents and a Jesuit building were set on fire in Madrid. Catholic opinion was outraged. The failure of the police to intervene seemed to the Right proof that Cardinal Segura's apprehension was justified.

Undaunted, the provisional government pressed ahead with its educational and cultural reforms, creating an organization that was to influence Spanish life profoundly during these years, the *Misiones Pedagógicas*, or 'Teaching Missions', whose aim was to do something practical to help the underprivileged people of the country's lonely, isolated and often appallingly poor villages. They put on plays, performed concerts, encouraged local teachers, organized art exhibitions and talks, set up public libraries, showed films, and in general brought hope to folk who in many cases still lived almost in the Stone Age.

These were days of immense democratic enthusiasm, and the Teaching Missions fired the imagination of the country's best writers and artists, many of whom were to collaborate in the adventure of taking culture to the people. Among them was the charismatic poet and playwright Federico García Lorca, who became head of a touring theatre, 'La Barraca', set up with a government grant by the students of Madrid University. The Barraca's performances in the rural marketplaces and village squares have become part of the mythology of the 1930s.

June 1931 saw the Republic's first general election. It was won by a coalition of Socialists and 'Republicans' (for the latter the nearest English approximation would, I think, be 'Liberals'). Work got under way immediately to draw up a Constitution. It was produced in record time, six months, and proved one of the most progressive in Europe.

That October a parliamentary debate on the religious issue riveted the attention of the nation. It showed the depth of the divide separating the 'two Spains' – the Catholic and the lay. The speech by the Socialist minister of Justice, Fernando de los Ríos (a distinguished professor of International Law from Granada University), stands as one of the great documents of the Republic. Addressing himself explicitly to the Catholics in the House, De los Ríos spelt out the Republican attitude towards a Church that, he said, had been strangling the life of the nation since 1492. Recalling the abuses of the Inquisition he stated that the Republicans were 'the descendants of the followers of Erasmus, the descendants of those whose dissident conscience was stifled for hundreds of years'. The Church had persecuted, burned, maimed. It had expelled the Jews. It had consistently supported an oppressive monarchy and a corrupt financial establishment. It had stood for the suppression of human rights, and habitually misrepresented the views of those who disagreed with it. He was not calling for revenge, he assured the opposition benches. The Republic must not repay the Church in its own coin of intolerance. But it must be firm in the assertion of its rights. If it failed to do so it was lost. Above all, the Republic must stand for justice.

What the moderate Republicans wanted was some form of compromise that would enable the peaceful construction of a genuinely democratic and plural society. But it was not possible. The Left soon became impatient with what it saw as half-measures (De los Ríos and his colleagues were no revolutionaries), and the Right would continue to claim that it, and only it, represented the true Spain. If, on that October afternoon, the minister of Justice received a fervid ovation from the Republicans when he rounded off his long speech, the Right was equally delighted by the aggressive oratory of José María Gil Robles, the young leader of the Catholic Popular Action Party, who took it upon himself to reply. Before long Gil Robles proved to be one of the most fierce enemies of the new democracy, for which he expressed an 'invincible repugnance'.

By 1932 reactionary elements in the Army were plotting against the Republic, and in August General José Sanjurjo led an abortive monarchist coup in Seville. His death sentence was commuted to life imprisonment, but the Right gave the Republican government no credit for such clemency.

On 30 January 1933 Hitler became chancellor of the Weimar Republic, on whose Constitution that of the Spanish Republic had been based. The press followed the course of events in Germany closely. The burning of the Reichstag on 27 February; the dissolution of the political parties in March and the accordance of full powers to Hitler; the Concordat with the Vatican; the growing persecution of Jews and intellectuals; the destruction of the trade unions . . . all these developments received wide coverage in Spain. While the Catholic newspapers applauded, the Republican and left-wing columnists anxiously contemplated the vertiginous growth of Fascism in Germany and had no illusions about what was happening behind the scenes in their own country. Could anyone doubt that anti-Republican conspirators in the army, heartened by Hitler's success and in no way discouraged by the failure of General Sanjurjo's coup in 1932, were still busily plotting the collapse of Spanish democracy?

In November 1933 there was a general election after the Socialists, disillusioned with their moderate Republican partners, pulled out of the Cabinet. Convinced that growing popular dissatisfaction with the government headed since 1931 by the Republican Manuel Azaña favoured their chances, the Socialists decided to fight the election alone: 'No more collaboration with middle-class Republicans.' This was a fatal error in view of the provisions of the new Electoral Act, which encouraged the formation of coalitions. The Right was more astute, and all the conservative groups merged in a united electoral front. In the new Parliament the progressive Republicans and the Socialists found themselves on the opposition benches. The shock was traumatic.

At this time a book was being written by the recently appointed professor of Spanish at Cambridge University, John Brande Trend. Published the following year as *The Origins of Modern Spain*, it paid tribute to the group of European-minded Spanish educators who had arisen in the closing decades of the nineteenth century and could justly be considered the Fathers of the Second Republic – several of whose most outstanding politicians and supporters, including Fernando de los Ríos and the philosopher José Ortega y Gasset, had been their pupils. Trend had followed the events leading up to the proclamation of the Republic with intense interest. In the 1920s he had often stayed at the famous Students' Residence on the outskirts of Madrid, the closest approximation in Spain to an Oxbridge campus, and was on excellent terms with the composer Manuel de Falla and many leading contemporary writers. For the Englishman, the Republic signified Spain's coming of age. Trend agreed passionately with his Spanish friends that the Republic's principal duty was to raise the cultural level of society, particularly of the underprivileged classes. The 1920s had seen a dazzling artistic flowering, despite the rigours of the Primo de Rivera regime, but it had scarcely touched the populace at large. Now that must change.

Trend's book transmits a euphoric confidence in the future of the Republic. At last, after centuries of isolation, Spain was coming into its own and recovering the spirit of tolerance that had made it culturally great in the Middle Ages! No stormclouds disturb the picture. In the light of subsequent events, *The Origins of Modern Spain* makes painful reading.

The largest of the right-wing groups to emerge from the 1933 general election was the Confederación Española de Derechas Autónomas, or Spanish Confederation of Autonomous Right-Wing Groups, commonly known by its initials CEDA. The coalition was led by José María Gil Robles, mentioned earlier, who stated explicitly during the election campaign that in his view Spain now needed an authoritarian, corporative form of government. That is to say, some form of Fascism. Clearly he had Mussolini's Italy in mind. Over the next two years Gil Robles vindicated his reputation as the *bête noire* of the Republic. Although he never became prime minister, he was to exert a powerful influence on the course of events during what came to be known by the Left as the 'Black Biennium' (November 1933 to February 1936).

The biennium constituted a major setback for Spanish democracy, its succession of right-wing governments devoting most of their energies to dismantling the mass of enlightened legislation enacted between 1931 and 1933 (including, for example, co-education in the State schools). When, in April 1934, General Sanjurjo was amnestied, the Left felt sure that before long there would be another coup.

Tension came to a head at the beginning of October 1934, when three CEDA ministers (but not yet Gil Robles) entered the government. The Left, convinced that this spelt the beginning of a Fascist takeover in the footsteps of Hitler's, called a revolutionary general strike. This was supported massively in the Basque provinces, Catalonia and, above all, Asturias, the coal-mining region in northwest Spain. There, on 5 October 1934, 70,000 miners rose against the government. The insurrection was brutally crushed in a fortnight by colonial troops (the Moors and the Foreign Legion) from Spanish Morocco. There were almost 2,000 dead and 7,000 wounded among the miners and their supporters. Rigid press censorship ensured that Spaniards at large had no inkling of the magnitude of the tragedy.

Meanwhile, in Barcelona, the 'Catalan Republic Within The Spanish Federal Republic' had been proclaimed on 6 October. It lasted for only ten hours before being put down by the army.

As a result of these events some 30,000 political prisoners found themselves behind bars. Among them was ex-Prime Minister Manuel Azaña, who had happened to be in Barcelona when the trouble began. His totally unjustified detention, prolonged for several months, proved just how reactionary the government of the Republic had now become.

While the defeat of the 'Reds' in Asturias looked like a victory for the Right, convincing Gil Robles that he would soon be prime minister, it showed the workers what they might expect to achieve if they stood firmly together throughout the country. Asturias paved the way for the Popular Front of 1936 and, later, the resistance to Franco.

These events, particularly the Catalan separatist bid, played straight into the hands of the Right. José Antonio Primo de Rivera, son of the dead dictator and leader of the Fascist organization known as the Spanish Phalanx (Falange Española), founded in 1933, stated that Spain's 'sacred unity' was being threatened by a sinister Marxist-Jewish conspiracy organized from Moscow, and prepared his blue-shirts for action.

Spanish Fascism, stimulated by the progress of both the Italian and German regimes, was undoubtedly gathering momentum, although its militants were still numerically insignificant. The Catholic middle class, infatuated with Gil Robles, was not yet prepared to support a paramilitary organization that openly preached violence. In May 1935 Gil Robles became minister of War. One of his first moves was to appoint Francisco Franco, Spain's youngest general and a known conservative, chief of the Army General Staff. The Right breathed a sigh of relief. Franco had made a name for bravery during the campaigns against the Rif tribesmen of Morocco. His unflinching severity was proverbial. He was a military man through and through. Who better than he and Gil Robles to contain the Marxist threat? It was widely believed by the Left at this time that Gil Robles was preparing the ground to implant the corporate State to whose suitability for Spain he had so often alluded in his speeches.

In such an atmosphere the landowners, one of the most powerful pressure-groups in Spanish politics at the time, felt that they could treat the peasants as harshly as they pleased. The laws providing minimal job protection for the latter had been rescinded, and the conditions of work in the countryside were atrocious. As the conservative historian Ricardo de la Cierva has admitted, the behaviour of the Right in the provinces during the second half of 1935 engendered such hatred that it can be considered one of the main causes of the Civil War.

In February 1936 came the Republic's third (and last) general election. It was won by the Popular Front, a Republican and left-wing electoral coalition. Gil Robles, despite the advantage of a massive propaganda campaign that portrayed him as the Spanish Mussolini, failed signally to win the support he so confidently expected. His collapse had a shattering effect on his followers, many of whom now began to look for salvation to the extreme right-wing monarchist leader in the new Parliament, José Calvo Sotelo, who had done well at the polls. Particularly demoralized were the members of the youth organization of Gil Robles's coalition, some 15,000 of whom tore up their cards after the elections and threw in their lot with Primo de Rivera's Fascist-inspired Falange.

The Socialists now made the fatal error of refusing to rejoin the government, claiming that it was not in their interests to renew their previous collaboration with 'bourgeois' Republicans. Nor was there any other left-wing representation. As a result the new Cabinet was quite out of touch with the social realities of the country. Only truly great leadership, unity on the Left and a coalition government reflecting the composition of the Popular Front could have saved the situation in the strife-ridden Spain of 1936.

Meanwhile the army conspirators and the Fascists were plotting in earnest for the downfall of democracy. Chaos and violence increasingly gripped the country. Between the rival Socialist and Communist trade unions there was self-defeating friction and skirmishing as the spring advanced, while extreme right-wing gunmen brought terror to the streets. The almost daily assassinations were matched by scenes of great dialectical turbulence, and not infrequently brawling, in Parliament.

On May Day the recently created United Socialist Youth Movement (a fusion of the Communist and Socialist youth organizations) was out in strength in Madrid to show the Fascists what they were up against. By this time the Socialist Party was split between the moderates and the revolutionaries, dissipating its energies in what was practically a civil war within its own ranks.

On the evening of 12 June 1936 a group of gunmen assassinated Lieutenant Castillo of the Republican Assault Guard, a known anti-Fascist. Early next morning some of his colleagues-in-arms, accompanied by civilians, carried out a shocking reprisal, kidnapping and murdering José Calvo Sotelo, the extreme right-wing monarchist leader whose star had been in the ascendant since the elections of February. Here was the Right's ideal martyr. Many army officers who had hesitated to join the conspirators now threw caution to the winds. Among them was General Franco, stationed far away from Madrid in the Canary Islands since the victory of the Popular Front, but none the less dangerous for that.

The rising began on 17 July in Melilla, one of Spain's two enclaves on the North African coast, spreading to the mainland the following day. The rebels had underestimated their enemy, however: in Madrid, Barcelona and most of Spain's other major cities they met massive popular resistance and were crushed. What had been planned as a *coup d'état* then turned into all-out civil war – the most 'international' civil war in history.

Had there been unity among those fighting to defend the Republic it is difficult to see how the latter could have failed to reduce the insurgents soon after the rising began, despite the assistance given to the rebellious generals by Hitler and Mussolini. But vital time was lost in prevarication, and the Communists, the revolutionary and moderate Socialists, the Anarchists and the Republicans were unable to agree about what Spain they were fighting for, or about how to win the war.

Franco *did* know what Spain he was fighting for – and he made sure that everyone on his side knew so too. Implacable, cold ('disagreeable from the moment he was a cell', according to an acquaintance), ruthlessly ambitious and cunning, he realized that, if he was to prevail, all political discrepancies among his supporters must be ironed out, at least until the war had been won. His biggest headache was caused by the tension existing between the Falangists and the Carlists (an intensely Catholic monarchist organization whose stronghold was in Navarre). He solved the problem by forcibly merging them early in 1937, eliminating those who opposed the 'Unification Decree', as it was termed. From this moment on there only existed the 'Movement', a monolithic front for winning the war, with visceral Catholicism, hatred of the Republic and rabid anti-Marxism as its common denominators. Despite the 'Unification', however, it took Franco another two years to finish off the Republic.

The Civil War devastated the country. We will never know how many people died, although it appears that a figure in the region of 600,000 would not be far off the mark. Mass executions of prisoners were carried out on both sides with a ferocity that seemed to the world to confirm the Spaniards' reputation for fanaticism. Hundreds of foreigners gave their lives, and the exploits of the International Brigades became legendary. At the time, the war was believed by many to be a straight fight between Fascism and democracy; but the issues at stake were more complicated, as was later to become clear.

The Spaniards who escaped into exile as the war reached its closing stages in March 1939 included thousands of the country's best-educated men and women – doctors, architects, politicians, poets, writers, university professors, schoolteachers. It was an involuntary 'brain-drain' comparable to, and almost as definitive as, the expulsion of the Jews in 1492. Franco never forgave the exiles nor what they stood for, and their talents were lost to Spain.

General Franco behaved towards his vanquished adversaries with great cruelty. A 'Law of Political Responsibility' was passed to expedite the repression of those who had supported the Republic. At the stroke of a pen they became criminals, and could now be tried, imprisoned and even executed. The purge was carried out with a cold ferocity worthy of Franco. There were executions on a massive scale, and they continued until 1942. Franco resuscitated the inquisitorial Spain of the 'Catholic Monarchs', Ferdinand and Isabella, with the 'Reds' and the Masons (loathed by the Church) standing in for the Jews and Moors. Meanwhile the European democracies that had refused to help the Republic found themselves involved in a terrible war against Hitler and Mussolini, both of whom had used Spain as a practice run for their men, aircraft and weaponry.

Many of Franco's enemies, in and outside gaol, believed that the victorious Allies would overrun Spain and depose the dictator. Vain hope! The democratic countries merely shrugged their shoulders once again. To ease its conscience, the United Nations decided, in 1946, to ostracize Franco for a while. The embargo was lifted in 1950, thanks principally to US pressure. Three years later the Eisenhower administration reached agreement with the dictator about setting up American air and naval bases in Spain in return for substantial economic aid. The international tide had now turned decisively in favour of Franco.

Meanwhile the regime had begun to elaborate its own slanted historiography of the Republic and the Civil War. There was, of course, implacable censorship. Books and articles by Spanish exiles, foreign historians and men and women of other nationalities who had fought on the Republican side were banned, and draconian measures applied to anyone caught importing them. The accounts of the war published in Spain were tendentious in the extreme. For example, dozens of conflicting versions concerning the destruction of the Basque town of Gernika were put into circulation, and it was not admitted until the very end of the regime, and then only grudgingly, that the bombing had been effected by Hitler's pilots. The dictatorship encouraged and rewarded intellectual corruption, and Spain is still suffering the consequences.

Franco's victory gave enormous power to a Church which, except in the Basque provinces of Vizcaya and Guipúzcoa, had supported the anti-Republican cause fanatically during the Civil War. For the next three decades, inseparably wedded to the State, the Church renewed its traditional role as sole arbiter of Spanish morals and education. The

1953 Concordat set the seal on this privilege: Catholicism was ratified as the official religion of the State, the only one with the right to proselytize; the teaching of Catholicism was obligatory in all Spanish schools; the State undertook to pay, and periodically revise, the salaries of the clergy, who were guaranteed a considerable degree of tax exemption. In return, among other concessions, Rome empowered Franco to nominate archbishops and bishops (but not Apostolic Administrators or auxiliary bishops), and a grateful clergy committed itself to intone daily prayers imploring the Deity's protection for the country and its providential Dictator.

Spain under Franco was culturally hamstrung and, as had happened so often down the centuries, the dissident writers had no option but to resort to irony if they wanted to be published in their own country. Many of them preferred to go into voluntary exile, heading especially for Paris. The Franco regime lasted for much longer than anyone foresaw and, from the mid-1950s onwards, as the economic situation improved, the Generalissimo aged and tourists flocked to Spain, it gradually grew somewhat more liberal. But the dictator himself remained intransigent to the very end – and tried to ensure that his censors did, too.

Throughout those decades the question of Franco's succession was a constant topic of conversation, along with football, bullfighting, the latest American films (dubbed and carefully expurgated) and, from the early 1960s, female tourists. In 1947 Franco had promulgated a Law which defined Spain as a monarchy and provided that the dictator's successor be styled King. It contained no reference to the restoration of the Bourbons, however. In theory, if Franco had produced a son, it might have fallen to him to take over the reins. About one thing only the Generalissimo seemed determined: that the legitimate heir to the throne, Don Juan de Borbón y Battemberg, son of Alfonso XIII (who had died in Rome in 1941), would never be King of Spain.

Don Juan was thirty-four when Franco's Law of Succession was proclaimed, and had not set foot in Spain since his family went into exile in 1931. Like his father he had supported the rebel cause in 1936, asking to be allowed to fight against the Republic. But Franco had refused. Later, as the Generalissimo made it increasingly clear that he would never willingly relinquish his dictatorial powers, Don Juan developed a strong personal loathing for him and became convinced that only the return of constitutional monarchy could serve to heal the appalling scars left by the Civil War. At his modest home in Estoril, outside Lisbon, he listened attentively to the many Spaniards from all walks of life and of all political persuasions who made their way to the Villa Esmeralda.

To many people it appeared wildly inconsistent that, given his well-known opinion of Franco, Don Juan should have wanted his son Juan Carlos brought up by the dictator. But he did. It was a genuine obsession on his part that the boy should be educated in the 'Fatherland'. The urge was stronger even than Don Juan's prejudices against Franco, and so it was that, after difficult negotiations, Juan Carlos had travelled from Lisbon to Madrid in 1949 to begin his Spanish schooling. He was then eleven.

There was no commitment, when Franco undertook to educate the prince, that Juan Carlos would necessarily sit on the Spanish throne. Twenty years later, however, well pleased with the young man's progress and behaviour, the dictator did in fact decide to name him his successor, keeping in ambiguous reserve another candidate, Alfonso de Borbón Dampierre, who had married his granddaughter, Carmen Martínez Bordiú.

The designation of Prince Juan Carlos took his father by surprise. Don Juan had not been informed in advance and was outraged that he, the legitimate heir, should have been passed over so high-handedly. None of this friction received a mention in the Spanish press, nor were the newspapers allowed to provide Spaniards with detailed information about the young man whom Franco had named as his successor. Juan Carlos de Borbón was an enigma, and generally believed to be unintelligent. But might he be a democrat at heart, waiting for his moment? No one could say. As for his relations with his father, nothing at all was known about them. Luckily for Spain, Juan Carlos was neither unintelligent nor lacking in democratic convictions. Luckily, too, his father had profoundly influenced his thinking about the role the monarchy should play after the death of the dictator.

Installed in the Zarzuela Palace outside Madrid, the prince, then thirty-one, began to intensify his contacts with members of the opposition to Franco, with people in the world of business and culture, with foreign politicians and diplomats. Sometimes his private secretary smuggled visitors secretly into the palace, hiding them in the boot of his car.

To what extent did Princess Sofía, the sister of Constantine of Greece whom Juan Carlos had married in 1962, inspire her husband in his role as artificer of Spain's eventual return to democracy? It seems certain that her influence in this respect strongly enhanced that already being exerted by the prince's forceful father. People who know her have reported that Sofía, behind the charming exterior, is a woman of iron will. Certainly she is extremely shrewd, intelligent and cultured. No lover of military dictatorships, given what had happened to her own family, victims of the Greek colonels, it seems fair to assume that, from the moment she married Juan Carlos, she worked energetically with her husband for Spain's liberation.

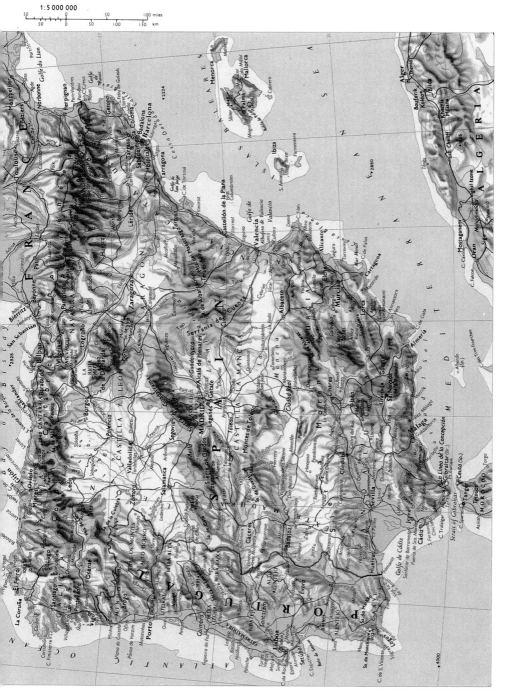

1:5 000 000

LEFT:
5 *Benjamin Disraeli rightly declared the Alhambra 'the most imaginative, the most delicate and fantastic creation that ever sprang up on a summer night in a fairy tale'.*

ABOVE:
6 *Philip II's Escorial at the foot of the mountains behind Madrid. From it he ruled half the world; it was at the Escorial that he received the news, in 1588, that the Armada had been destroyed.*

ABOVE:
7 Francisco Fernández Ordóñez was
responsible, as Minister of Justice, for
engineering modern Spain's divorce
legislation. Now the Foreign Minister,
he is one of the country's most respected
and well-liked politicians.

-4-

The Transition to Democracy (1975–82)

General Franco died in Madrid on 20 November 1975. He was eighty-three. Although for several years Spaniards had been able to contemplate his inexorable decline, when the end came they were stunned. It seemed impossible that, having maintained his grip on the country for almost forty years, the dictator could ever let go. But he had proved mortal after all. While those who loathed him and what he stood for quickly depleted the nation's reserves of *cava* (Catalan champagne) and his admirers mourned, the question uppermost in everyone's mind was, what would happen next?

On the morning of 22 November 1975, while the Generalissimo's body lay in state in the Royal Palace, Prince Juan Carlos was sworn in as King of Spain. He promised Franco's puppet Parliament to be loyal to the dead man and to uphold the principles and laws of his State. Then, in a brief and prudent speech, he said that a new era in the history of Spain was about to begin, and expressed his determination to work for a future in which there would be 'an effective consensus concerning national concord'. In terms whose ambiguity was surely deliberate, he went on: 'I hope to be capable of acting as moderator, as guardian of the constitutional system and promoter of justice. Let nobody fear that his cause will be forgotten, let nobody expect advantages or privileges. Together we will be able to achieve all if we give to all their legitimate opportunity. . .'

The King and his advisers knew that, for such a goal to be achieved, the political life of Spain must be brought into alignment with that of western Europe. The country was more than ready for democracy. Tourism had been booming since the 1950s, with the impact on mores this had entailed; the standard of living had improved; foreign investment had soared; and for years there had been a growing awareness that, once Franco was out of the way, it should be possible for Spain to join the European Economic Community (Brussels had said no to the Generalissimo) and break out of the isolation to which the survival of the dictatorship had condemned it.

There could be no doubt that the transition to democracy was going to be fraught with danger. As Franco's remains were taken for burial in the Valley of the Dead (the vast, megalomaniac pantheon excavated on the dictator's orders in the hills north of Madrid) it seemed that anything was now possible – army intervention, a mass rising, another civil war.

One of the King's main problems was Carlos Arias Navarro, Franco's prime minister since 1973. A sixty-seven-year-old lawyer who had acquired a sinister reputation during the Civil War as a merciless judge, Arias could not be expected to support any policy likely to alter the status quo that the King had sworn to maintain. Nonetheless, Juan Carlos decided to keep him on. Many people thought it a serious mistake, but almost certainly the King was playing for time. While the retention of the prime minister irritated progressive opinion throughout the country, it served to reassure the army and provided some breathing space in which the next steps along the road to democracy could be planned.

On 23 December 1975 Juan Carlos appeared on TV to deliver his first Christmas message to the nation. Nearly fifteen years later it emerged that the text of the speech, which had been prepared by the King's personal adviser, Joaquín José Puig de la Bellacasa (later Spain's charismatic ambassador to the Court of Saint James), had been tampered with by Arias Navarro, who since the very first day of Juan Carlos's reign had been undermining his policies. Thus, where the original version said 'May the Holy Year, soon to begin in Compostela, be one of advancement and progress down the path of reconciliation and Unity', Arias Navarro had struck out the word 'reconciliation' (a clear reference to the wounds left by the Civil War) and substituted for it the more anodyne term 'concord'. Where the King had used the word 'injustice' in referring to the financial and other problems of many Spanish families, the term 'difficulty' had been substituted. Injustice in Spain? Never! According to the journalist who discovered the emended text of the speech, the King had been highly irritated by all this meddling, and decided to get rid of Arias Navarro as soon as possible.

A few months later, on 4 May 1976, there appeared in Madrid the first issue of a new morning newspaper, *El País* ('The Country'), whose role in the making and consolidation of democracy in Spain cannot be sufficiently emphasized. Technologically the most modern daily in the country, with a team of outstanding journalists and a highly intelligent management, *El País* immediately became prescribed reading for Spain's progressives – and the bane of those who wanted to turn the clock back. Undoubtedly the incisive coverage of political events provided by *El País* during the first weeks of its existence hastened the fall of Arias Navarro, who resigned on 1 July.

From Franco the King had inherited almost dictatorial powers, and he now used these, extremely diplomatically, to give the democratic process the initial fillip it so badly needed. His first master move was to choose, as Arias's successor, a totally unexpected but eminently suitable candidate for the job of guiding Spain into a new era. This was Adolfo Suárez, a handsome and ambitious lawyer of forty-four from Avila, in Old Castile, who had been head of Spanish TV before his appointment as secretary general of the dictator's monolithic 'Movement' in 1975.

Suárez, whom diehard Franco supporters have never forgiven for what they consider his betrayal of the dead Generalissimo, quickly showed a democratic mettle that surprised those who had known him in his previous capacities. On 17 and 18 November 1976 a carefully prepared 'Law of Political Reform' was debated by Parliament, which revealed an unsuspected talent for political hara-kari by voting for its own abolition and proposing the establishment of an upper and lower house elected by universal suffrage. The twenty-man Council of the Realm, which formed the apex of Franco's political system and had the power to veto Parliament's decisions, was suppressed in the same session, thanks to the decisive influence of its head, Torcuato Fernández Miranada, one of the principal architects of the transition to democracy. Almost exactly a year had passed since the dictator's death. On 15 December 1976 the 'Law of Political Reform' was massively endorsed by the Spanish people in a referendum. It all seemed too good to be true.

The ultra-conservative and neo-Fascist forces in the country were aghast. Juan Carlos had already more than betrayed the trust placed in him by Franco, they argued, and Suárez was a blackguard. The great threat to the old values now lay in the setting up of free trade unions and the probable legalization of political parties, among them the Spanish Socialist Workers' Party (PSOE) and, worst enemy of all, the Communist Party. The extreme Right decided to act. On the night of 24 January 1977 an assassination squad murdered five left-wing lawyers in Madrid. It was an earnest of what the neo-Fascist bunker thought of the New Spain, and of the lengths to which the men of violence were prepared to go in hindering its progress. The killings were followed by a massive protest demonstration in Madrid in which half a million people took to the streets.

In March 1977 Franco's State-controlled trade unions were abolished; early the following month arrangements were made to allow for the legalization of political parties. The Socialists registered immediately. Then, on 9 April, Easter Saturday, with most of the army on leave, the government issued a decree legalizing the Communist Party. The worst fears of the extreme Right had been confirmed. The military establishment (some sectors of which, true to Spanish tradition, were already planning a *coup d'état*) was livid, and several Cabinet ministers resigned. It was one of the most dangerous moments in the whole transition to democracy.

These moves by the Suárez government were the result of pacts with the opposition elaborated in an atmosphere of compromise quite novel in Spain. The word *compromiso* exists in Spanish, but until recently it meant a binding agreement, an engagement. Over the last ten years it has increasingly taken on the English sense of the term, a further indication, surely, that political give-and-take is now the norm in a country where, as the veteran Communist leader Santiago Carrillo once told me, 'In the days of the Republic you would never have talked to anyone from "the other side."'

The Republic! In post-Franco Spain the memory of those five turbulent years, and of the terrible Civil War that followed them, has exerted great influence. Indeed, it is impossible to understand the nature of Spanish society today without taking into account the hopes, achievements and failures of that thwarted adventure in democracy. The new spirit of compromise shown by the politicians reflected the mood and wishes of the nation. It was decided by common consent that there could be no violent rupture with the previous regime, since such a break would be bound both to rekindle the old wartime hatreds and make army intervention almost inevitable. Spain might be plunged into another bloodbath, and that must be avoided at all costs. It was this same spirit that, a year later, was to inspire the makers of the 1978 Constitution.

Having legalized the Communist Party, the government proceeded to amplify the political amnesty conceded the previous summer, but which still left many hundreds of political prisoners, mainly Basque terrorist suspects, in gaol. This move further boosted the huge popular support now enjoyed by Prime Minister Suárez.

At the end of April 1977 I returned to Spain for the first time in six years. The atmosphere in the country had changed beyond belief. Stopping off first at Barcelona, I found the stalls along the city's colourful boulevard, the Ramblas, crammed with books banned under Franco – in particular, books on the Civil War. A roaring trade was being done in sex manuals and girlie magazines. Everywhere animated clumps of people were talking and gesticulating.

There was apprehension in the air, too, and the police inherited from Franco, known as the 'grises' on account of their grey uniform, were very much in evidence. In Madrid a few days later I witnessed a brutal baton charge against a student demonstration, while a helicopter buzzed the crowd. The police, long accustomed to beating and bullying, were obviously finding it difficult to adapt to the new political situation.

Things were not made easier at this time by the constant provocations of the Basque terrorists, whose murderous attacks on army officers and, particularly, the Civil Guard (Spain's long-standing rural police force, famous for its patent-leather three-cornered hats), were deliberately intended to goad the military into action.

A few weeks later, on 14 May 1977, the King's father, Don Juan, who had been following events closely and was proud of his son's efforts on behalf of democracy, formally relinquished his claim to the throne. This magnanimous gesture settled the last doubts that anyone could have entertained about the legitimacy of the reinstated monarchy. All was now ready for the first general election to be held in Spain since the victory of the Popular Front in February 1936. The date was set for 15 June 1977.

Four weeks of hectic electioneering generated intense excitement up and down the country. Victory went to Adolfo Suárez's hastily formed right-of-centre coalition party, the Unión del Centro Democrático (UCD), which obtained 165 of Parliament's 350 seats. The Spanish Socialist Workers' Party (PSOE) came second with 118.

If the UCD's triumph was logical in the circumstances, given Suárez's excellent track record and the publicity this had received on State television (there were as yet no private channels), the Socialist Party's outstanding performance needs more explaining.

During the campaign progressive Spaniards had been greatly impressed by the charisma, oratory and political intelligence of Felipe González, the Party's thirty-five-year-old general secretary, utterly unknown to the general public before the death of Franco. He and his young, European-sounding colleagues (many, like him, from Seville) projected an image of efficiency, enthusiasm, moderation and reforming zeal that was deeply attractive to millions of Spaniards who, despite Adolfo Suárez's great personal contribution to democracy, could not bring themselves to support his ideologically variegated coalition. In October 1974 the Socialists had held a congress in the little town of Suresnes, outside Paris, where their break with the survivors of the old, historical Socialist Party in exile, a survival from the Republic, was consummated. At Suresnes was born a new, pragmatic version of the Spanish Socialist Workers' Party intent on achieving power in Spain when the dictator died. At the time it had some 2,500 members.

One of the most interesting results of the June 1977 election was the relatively poor performance of the Communists, who only obtained twenty seats. Considering that it was they who had spearheaded the internal opposition to Franco during the long years of the dictatorship, bearing the brunt of police repression, they might have been expected to do much better. But the election was not a prize-giving ceremony, and it seems certain that some Communist sympathizers voted for the Socialists, fearing that the possibility of a military coup might be increased if too many Marxist MPs were returned. The results obtained by the right-wing Popular Alliance Party, led by Manuel Fraga Iribarne, were also poor: sixteen seats. In Catalonia and the Basque Country the parties appealing to regional sentiment carried all before them, not surprisingly after the cultural repression of these communities by the Franco regime.

Almost 80 per cent of the electorate had voted, and the results showed that an overwhelming majority of Spaniards were now in favour of parties promising moderate change. In this knowledge the first Parliament of the New Spain embarked on the formidable task of preparing a Constitution, despite the fact that no provisions for such an undertaking had been included in the 'Law of Political Reform' by which Franco's Chamber had abolished itself in November 1976.

Meanwhile, on 28 July 1977, the Suárez government applied for entry to the EEC. The negotiations were to prove long and arduous, due in large measure to initial French resistance to Spain's membership.

I referred earlier to the spirit of political compromise current at this time. In accordance with it the so-called 'Moncloa Agreements' between the government and the main opposition parties were signed on 27 October 1977 (the pact took its name from the Moncloa Palace, the Spanish equivalent of 10, Downing Street). Once again an admirable sense of give-and-take prevailed. The government succeeded in obtaining the go-ahead to freeze salaries, restrict credit, reduce public spending and increase taxes; in return it promised to legalize divorce and contraceptives, democratize the police and enact progressive laws governing strikes and the right of association.

Pending the promulgation of the Constitution, Prime Minister Suárez badly needed a stop-gap solution to the Catalan and Basque demands for political autonomy, daily more vehement. With Catalonia he was in luck. On 23 October 1977 the highly charismatic president of the Catalan government in exile, Josep Tarradellas, returned to Spain for the first time since the Civil War. He had sworn never to do so until the old Catalan Parliament, the Generalitat, abolished by Franco in 1938, was restored. The government appointed Tarradellas provisional head of the Generalitat until the Constitution should ratify the Catalans' right to their political freedom.

Unfortunately there was no corresponding Basque figure to hand.

The violence then being perpetrated by ETA (the separatist organization) made negotiations between the government and the Basque
nationalist MPs increasingly strained, and Suárez's failure to grant full
amnesty to the imprisoned terrorists probably strengthened ETA's
determination to carry on its war.

The drafting of the Constitution had been entrusted to a team of
seven brilliant lawyer MPs chosen by their respective parties. They
were Manuel Fraga Iribarne, the veteran conservative leader, former
Franco minister and now head of the Popular Alliance Party; Miquel
Roca i Junyent, of the Catalan conservative coalition; Miguel Herrero
de Miñón, a member of Adolfo Suárez's ruling UCD Party; José Pedro
Pérez-Llorca, a Suárez minister; another UCD representative, Gabriel
Cisneros; the Socialist Gregorio Peces-Barba; and Jordi Solé Tura, a
Catalan Communist professor (today minister of Culture). These men
later became known affectionately as 'The Fathers of the
Constitution'.

Manuel Fraga Iribarne has recalled that the memory of the Civil
War was never out of the minds of the team. This, for the first time in
the history of Spain, was to be a *consensus* Constitution, the result of
dialogue and compromise, with no bullying, no impositions and the
stress on national reconciliation. The word *consenso* could be heard on
everybody's lips in those days. It was accepted by all that the monarchist framework should be retained.

This is not to say that no disagreements took place during these
months between 'The Fathers of the Constitution'. They did – but
always the spirit of compromise prevailed.

The finished draft was debated by the Lower House for twelve hectic days in July 1978. Emended and approved, it passed to the Senate.
This stage completed, a mixed commission of MPs and senators
ironed out the discrepancies that had arisen, and prepared a final text.
After both Houses had given this the go-ahead, all was ready for the
grand finale.

On 6 December 1978 the Spanish people massively endorsed the
Constitution by referendum. On 27 December it was approved by the
King and promulgated.

Only three years after the death of General Franco, Spain was a full
democracy.

*   *   *

The great strength of the 1978 Constitution was the tact with which it treated the three areas that for centuries had most divided the nation: religion, education and the question of the 'historical autonomies', that is, Galicia, Catalonia and the Basque Country.

Only as the Franco regime drew to a close had the Church begun to distance itself cautiously from the dictatorship, influenced by the progressive spirit emanating from the Second Vatican Council (1962–6). The latter's pronouncement in favour of Church–State separation made a particular impression in Spain, where many young priests had grown sick of the apparently interminable identification of the Church with a system that scorned civil rights.

Among the hierarchy, too, there had been exceptions to the old, conservative stereotype. The most outstanding of these was Cardinal Vicente Enrique y Tarancón, appointed primate of Spain in 1969 and, in 1971, archbishop of Madrid and head of the Bishops' Conference. Tarancón admired Paul VI and proved himself his most effective Spanish apostle, vigorously supporting the Pope's view that the Vatican should now gradually dissociate itself from the ideologically discredited Franco regime and the Spanish Church move in the direction of disestablishment.

Tarancón, who once said that 'under less Catholic governments the Church lives better', received many anonymous death-threats. In those days the rhyming tag 'Tarancón al paredón' ('Tarancón to the Cemetery Wall') could be seen scrawled on hoardings, monuments and street-corners throughout Spain: the 'traitor' archbishop deserved, in the eyes of the extreme right-wingers, nothing short of execution by firing squad in the location traditionally reserved for this purpose.

With Tarancón at the helm and Franco dead, the hierarchy accepted without ostensible demur the inevitability that the separation of Church and State would be enshrined in the Constitution. Such resignation should not be seen as magnanimity, but rather as the recognition of a virtual *fait accompli*. In the new Europe which Spain so desperately wanted to join, the Church could not hope to maintain its privileged status. What it *did* hope to secure was some degree of special treatment. This it achieved. The definitive draft of the relevant clause (article 16.3) read:

No creed will have the standing of a State religion. The

> public authorities will take into account the religious
> beliefs of Spanish society and maintain, in consequence,
> the necessary relations of co-operation with the Catholic
> Church and the other religions.

After the long years of the Franco regime, under which the Church
had enjoyed immense privileges, this was indeed a turn-about,
although the loose wording of the clause was later to enable the
hierarchy to make life difficult for the Socialists.

As regards education, inextricably mixed up with the religious
issue, the Constitution sought to make everyone happy, endorsing the
basic right of parents to decide what education they wanted for their
children, and the obligation of the State to provide it. Here, too, as we
shall see, there were to be problems.

'The Fathers of the Constitution' had agreed from the outset that
the 'historical autonomies' should be allowed to have their own
regional parliaments and a considerable degree of devolution. They
also knew that it was imperative that the Constitution should explicitly foster the use of the Galician, Basque and Catalan languages.

It had been a mistake not to provide for Basque representation on
the committee that prepared the basic draft of the Constitution,
where Catalan interests had been carefully looked after by Miquel
Roca i Junyent and Jordi Solé Tura, and Galician by Manuel Fraga
Iribarne. This meant that, when the bill was debated by the Lower
House of Parliament in July 1978, the Basques were at a disadvantage
and failed to obtain the amendments they requested to the autonomy
clauses. As a result the Basque Nationalist Party recommended
abstention in the referendum. Despite this, 70 per cent of the Basques
who voted gave their approval to this, Spain's tenth Constitution since
1808.

As an example of the weaknesses in the Constitution arising out of
its fundamentally consensual nature we could take the heated issue of
the death penalty. To the Socialists, the retention of capital punishment for any reason whatsoever was abhorrent; Suárez's UCD was
divided on the question; and Manuel Fraga's party, considerably to the
right of Suárez, expressed itself in favour of such a penalty for terrorists proved guilty of assassination. The compromise? That capital
punishment should be abolished 'except in those cases which the mili-

tary laws may decide in time of war' (art. 15). As a direct consequence of this clause the new Military Code passed in 1985 includes more than thirty 'crimes' for which the death penalty can now be applied in wartime, among them acts of cowardice 'liable to cause panic or provoke serious disorder'. An indication of how far the Socialist Party had moved to the Right after eight years in power came in 1990 when its MPs ratified the death penalty clauses in the Military Code. MPs to the Left of the Socialists were outraged. It was one thing to have made concessions to the army in the 1978 consensus Constitution, said the spokesman for the United Left Party, Pablo Castellano. It was another to vote now for the retention of the death penalty clauses in the Military Code. Castellano announced that his party would press for the reform of the latter.

Another of the Constitution's unsatisfactory provisions, it can be argued, was the wording of article 8, which entrusts the Armed Forces with the duty of defending the 'territorial integrity' of Spain. Since, according to article 2, the Constitution 'is based on the indissoluble unity of the Spanish Nation', article 8 could be interpreted as sanctioning military intervention in Catalonia or the Basque Country should the army ever decide that these communities were moving too far in the direction of independence.

Once the Constitution had been passed, Adolfo Suárez, with his oddly assorted coalition party beginning to crack at the seams but his high personal reputation untarnished, decided that it looked like a good moment to go to the country again. The election was held on 1 March 1979. If Suárez hoped for an overall majority, he did not get it. For the third time in succession his party won, but the results were broadly similar to those of 1977. The UCD received 168 seats, the Socialists 121, the Communists 20, and various small parties a scattering ranging from three to nine. There had been considerable abstention, an indication that the gap between Parliament and voters was widening. The leaders of all the major parties agreed about one thing: that the end of the famous consensus was at hand. In the new House the UCD would not be able automatically to depend on the support of the other parties, so vital in establishing the Constitution.

One final exercise in democracy was about to take place: Spain's first municipal elections since 1933. They were held on 19 April 1979 and won decisively by the Socialists, who gained control of 42.5

per cent of the town councils around the country and 75 per cent of the large cities, including Madrid and Barcelona. Moreover, in those boroughs where neither the Socialists nor the Communists achieved an outright majority, they agreed to govern together. In the Basque Country and Catalonia the UCD did particularly badly. All told, the results were a great setback for Adolfo Suárez, and convinced the Socialists that they were going to carry all before them at the next general election.

On 27 January 1981, with the UCD showing unmistakable signs of disintegration, Adolfo Suárez resigned, exasperated by the divisions within the party but also, perhaps, in the belief that his political sacrifice might reduce the likelihood of a *coup d'état*. Everyone knew that feelings were mounting in the barracks over the murderous activities of the Basque terrorists.

The thousand rumours circulating in Madrid had a basis in fact. The conspirators were caught off-guard by Suárez's unexpected resignation, however. During February, as preparations went ahead for the investiture of his successor, Leopoldo Calvo Sotelo, they decided to precipitate matters. A leading plotter was Lieutenant-General Jaime Milans del Bosch, chief of the military region of Valencia and a man deeply loyal to the memory of Franco. The rebels felt confident that, once the coup succeeded, the King would lend his support to an authoritarian government presided over by his former adviser General Alfonso Armada, a fervent admirer of Charles de Gaulle. Perhaps the enemies of democracy, recalling how easily Juan Carlos's grandfather, Alfonso XIII, had accepted the *fait accompli* of General Primo de Rivera's seizure of power in 1923, thought that the King would react similarly.

Some high-ranking Socialists, apprised at this time of the possibility of a military coup, seriously considered that the only solution was a coalition government headed by a democratically-minded general. But events outstripped them.

The rebels struck at 6.25 p.m. on Monday 23 February 1981, when a contingent of Civil Guards commanded by Lieutenant-Colonel Antonio Tejero stormed into Parliament while MPs were voting the investiture of Leopoldo Calvo Sotelo.

The ceremony was being broadcast live on the radio, and the King was listening. Shocked by what he heard (was his first instinct, one wonders, to assume like so many others that this was an act of ETA terrorism?), he immediately contacted the Army General Staff HQ and, shortly afterwards, the heads of the eleven military regions into which Spain is still divided. Juan Carlos had been informed of the probable involvement of General Armada in a conspiracy, so when the latter now asked for permission to visit him in the Zarzuela Palace, he was refused point-blank. Later it transpired that Armada's failure to gain admittance to the palace had been a decisive factor in the collapse of the coup.

Soon after Tejero and his men occupied Parliament the radio went off the air. Unknown to the rebels, however, a camera which had been televising the investiture proceedings was still running. Over an hour passed before the guards discovered this and put it out of action. Too late! The following day, when normality had been restored, the video went round the world. The sudden irruption of the revolver-toting Tejero and his men, the stunned silence, the mustachioed lieutenant-colonel's raucous first injunction, 'Quiet everyone!', then the protests, the shouts of the guards, Tejero's stentorian command, 'All on the floor!', the long burst of submachine-gun fire aimed at the ceiling of the chamber, the MPs (with the notable exceptions of Adolfo Suárez and the Communist leader Santiago Carrillo) crouching behind their seats and then gradually re-emerging, the magnificent personal protest by the deputy prime minister, Lieutenant-General Manuel Gutiérrez Mellado, whom Tejero, despite his superior strength, failed to hurl to the ground . . . the brutality and the outrage had been captured for posterity, second by breathless second.

Once a semblance of calm had been restored to the Chamber an officer announced that soon the relevant authority, 'military, of course', would arrive to take charge of the situation. That authority never turned up – and a decade later has still not been identified.

With Tejero and his men holding Parliament, General Milans del Bosch now ordered his tanks into the streets of Valencia, and proclaimed martial law. Would the other ten military regions follow suit, as Milans hoped? Luckily they did not. Had the tanks rolled in Madrid all would have been lost, but in the capital Lieutenant-General Guillermo Quintana Lacaci remained loyal to the government and managed to curb his rebel officers. Quintana Lacaci was assassinated a few years later by ETA. A note found among his private papers showed that only one other of the eleven captains-general had immediately dissociated himself from the insurgents. The rest waited to see what happened.

As the minutes ticked by and we followed events on the Cadena SER radio, which provided inspired coverage all night long, the terrifying rumour spread that the King had thrown in his lot with the conspirators. Why had he not gone on television to explain what was happening? Was he waiting to see what course the rising took? In fact a group of soldiers had taken control of Spanish Television and Radio HQ, on the outskirts of Madrid, at 7.45 p.m., thereby preventing any possibility of a royal appearance. When they abandoned RTVE at 9.20 p.m. a mobile unit was rushed to the Zarzuela Palace, twelve miles away, where the King recorded a message to the nation that was broadcast at 1.13 a.m. the following morning, 24 February, and played a major role in defusing the conspiracy.

Juan Carlos, who had taken the measure, essential for the occasion, of wearing the uniform of Head of the Armed Forces, explained that he had intervened personally to order the rebels to desist from their illegal attempt to overthrow the Constitution. The message lasted for one minute twenty-five seconds. The King's voice was firm:

> In addressing myself to all the people of Spain, with brevity and concision, in the unusual circumstances through which we are living at this moment, I ask from all of you the utmost serenity and confidence and inform you that I have issued the following orders to the Captains-General of the Military Regions, Maritime Zones and Aerial Regions:
>
> > 'Given the situation created by what has been happening in the Parliament, and in order to avoid any confusion whatsoever, I confirm that I have ordered the Civil Authorities and the Junta of Chiefs of Staff to take whatever steps are necessary to guarantee constitutional order within the legal framework currently in force.
> >
> > 'Whatever military measures may have to be taken

in due course must have the approval of the Junta of Chiefs of Staff.

'The Crown, symbol of the permanence and unity of the Fatherland, cannot possibly tolerate actions or attitudes by persons hoping to interrupt by force the democratic process determined by the Constitution which, in its day, the nation endorsed by referendum.'

The King's appearance and message provided immense momentary relief, but it was not yet clear to what extent his instructions had been obeyed by the rebels. Only several hours later, in the knowledge that no other garrisons had risen and that Tejero was completely isolated in Parliament, were we able to collapse into our beds confident that democracy had prevailed, thanks to the common sense of most of the army and to the King's magnificent stand.

The occupation of Parliament was not yet over, however. It lasted for eighteen and a half hours in all. Tejero surrendered at 12.05 p.m. on 24 February, and shortly afterwards the bleary-eyed MPs emerged into the sunlight, where they were acclaimed like heroes by the waiting crowd.

On 27 February the inhabitants of Madrid celebrated the failure of the coup by taking part in the largest political demonstration ever seen in Spain. More than a million people flocked into the streets and, headed by the leaders of all the democratic political parties, paraded slowly down the Carrera de San Jerónimo (the site of Parliament) and the Paseo del Prado. In Spain this century only the joy that greeted the arrival of the Republic in April 1931 could possibly have matched, for democratic fervour, the scenes that took place that day. It was an unforgettable occasion. Freedom had survived! We would never let it be threatened again! There were tears and smiles, kisses and hugs; singing, slogans and dancing. 'El 23-F' ('23 February'), as it soon became universally known in Spain, had helped us all to grow up.

During the military trial of the thirty-two officers arrested in connection with the failed coup, Tejero, who, with General Armada, was sentenced to thirty years, went on record as saying: 'I wish someone would explain to me what happened on 23 February 1981.' If he, of all people, had difficulty in understanding what lay behind the momentous events in which he had played so conspicuous a part, one can imagine the perplexity of the nation at large. Ten years later many aspects of the conspiracy not satisfactorily clarified during the trial remain obscure – in particular, the extent of the non-military involvement in the plot. That it was considerable is beyond doubt. Only one civilian was sentenced, and he died not long after his release. Perhaps we shall never know the identity of the other conspirators.

Alberto Piris, a retired Artillery general and expert on defence, has written that one of the positive effects of the attempted coup was to make many democratically hesitant officers deeply ashamed of what had happened and, in particular, of the gross behaviour recorded for posterity in the famous video. In his view, the débâcle produced 'a catharsis, a collective sense of shame that spread imperceptibly in all directions'. The trial did not help to relieve such feelings. Many of the accused spoke with an arrogance, scorn and, at times, vulgar insolence that did the military no credit. Once the trial was over, according to Piris, the idea took root that never again must the army be involved in such antics. The only hope now was resolutely to enter the modern world.

The King emerged from '23 February' with immensely enhanced prestige: during those dangerous hours he had kept his head, repeatedly ordered Milans del Bosch to desist, and given his approval to a provisional government composed of secretaries of State and subsecretaries which, during the night, issued forceful instructions to the Army General Staff and symbolized the maintenance of democratic legality

One of the consequences of '23 February' was that the UCD government decided to speed up negotiations for Spain's entry into NATO, initiated the previous summer in the hopes that, once the country was a member, France would reduce its opposition to Spain's joining the EEC. Clearly the government now felt that NATO entry would have the added advantage of taking the army's mind off politics and making it more outward-looking. Spain entered in June 1982.

The Socialists had fiercely opposed NATO membership from the outset, insisting that it was the government's obligation to hold a referendum on the issue. They now announced that, if they won the next general election, as the opinion polls were predicting, *they* would hold such a referendum, recommending the Spanish people to vote for withdrawal.

The election was held on 28 October 1982, after a campaign in which the NATO issue predominated. As well as the referendum, the Socialists promised a new, ethical style of government. 'Cambio', 'change', was their motto, NATO withdrawal, EEC entry and the definitive modernization of Spain their goal.

The Socialists obtained the biggest landslide victory in Spanish electoral history, and the first overall parliamentary majority since the advent of democracy. They have been in power, almost unchallenged, ever since. The ethical revolution they promised never materialized as thousands of job-hungry opportunists flocked to join the party and 'pragmatism' became the order of the day. As for NATO, the referendum was not held until 1986, after Spain was safely in the EEC. The government had changed its mind, and Felipe González succeeded in convincing the necessary majority of voters that leaving the organization would bring dire economic consequences. Spain stayed in NATO.

As regards their achievements, the Socialists can legitimately claim completion of the EEC negotiations (Spain became a full member on 1 January 1986), industrial reconversion, many advances in human rights and the most stable period of democratic government ever known in Spain. Looking back, one can see that their electoral triumph on 29 October 1982, whatever reservations one might have about their decade in office, marked the end of the transition to democracy and the beginning of a new era.

— 5 —

Church and Army in Transition

How are the Church and army, traditionally the bastions of reaction in Spain, faring today? How do they feel about the new liberties? About their changing roles since the death of Franco? About the fact that the Socialists have been in power now for almost ten years? About Spain's place in the modern world?

Despite the Church's acceptance of disestablishment, and its decision, in line with the Second Vatican Council, not to sponsor the creation of a Christian Democrat confessional party after Franco's death, it was obvious to the Socialists when they won the 1982 general election that relations with the hierarchy would be fraught.

Little effort of imagination is required to grasp to what an extent the older rank-and-file members of the Socialist Party dislike the Catholic Church. No Socialist over sixty-five can forget its role during the Civil War – the priests blessing Franco's soldiers or giving the Fascist salute, the open-air masses for Nationalist troops, the 'Collective Letter' of the Spanish hierarchy in 1937, addressed to all the bishops of the world, in which Franco was portrayed as the heroic leader of a Holy Crusade against Communism...

Nor can people forget the attitude of the Church in the immediate postwar period. What protests were made by the bishops about the thousands of executions being carried out by the regime? Too mindful of the priests assassinated by the 'Reds' during the war, the Church held its tongue. Then, prayers were offered at every mass for the dictator, who on certain ecclesiastical occasions was even carried under a canopy, a privilege normally reserved for the Sacred Host and the Pope. How can the Socialists be expected to forget that gross servility?

One of the many miracles of modern Spain is that, despite the generally wretched showing by the hierarchy under Franco, most Spaniards today are not violently anti-clerical but simply determined that the Church should be put firmly in its place and kept there – and equally firmly removed from those areas it has habitually usurped.

At times subterranean, at times out in the open, a tremendous struggle has been taking place between the bishops and the new moral order represented by the Socialists. There can be little doubt about which side is winning. The international tide is running against the Catholic Church, Spain is a freer, more permissive country than even before, there has been a sexual revolution, attendance at Mass has dropped to an all-time low, vocations are down, and hardly anyone goes to confession. In 1976, a year after Franco's death, a survey conducted by the Spanish bishops showed that 64 per cent of Spaniards claimed to be 'very' or 'fairly' constant in their attendance at Mass. Only 9 per cent said they did not go. In 1986 the number who admitted they no longer practised the Catholic religion had risen to 30 per cent. The 'very church-going' category had shrunk from 22 per cent to 14 per cent, and the 'fairly regularly' one from 42 to 26 per cent. Catholic baptisms plummeted from 501,836 in 1980 to 380,502 in 1986, and Catholic marriages from 202,752 to 160,833 in the same period. Hardly figures to gladden the bishops' hearts.

As might be expected, it is in the area of secondary education that there has been most friction between the bishops and the Socialists. Under the system inherited by the latter, agreed in 1979 between the UCD government and the Vatican (without the support of Socialist MPs), Spain's many thousands of private Catholic schools received State aid and it was compulsory for pupils in State schools to take either Religion (i.e. Catholic doctrine) or Ethics. When, in 1990, the Socialist government announced its determination to introduce a new Education Act which, among its many other provisions, would drop Ethics from the curriculum and relegate Religion to the status of a non-core, optional subject, the bishops were beside themselves. The new Act, according to the hierarchy, would have the effect of undermining the moral health of the nation. Fewer and fewer pupils would bother to take Religion, preferring a free period in the playground. It would be a national disaster. The government insisted that, in a State without an established Church, you cannot force children to study Religion, much less indoctrinate them in Catholicism. As for Ethics, the government felt that it should not figure as just another subject on the curriculum: in all areas of school life pupils should be encouraged by their teachers to think responsibly about themselves and society.

In 1990 the bishops were no longer headed by the broad-minded Cardinal Vicente Enrique y Tarancón, but by a very different sort of man, Monsignor Angel Suquía Goicoechea, archbishop of Madrid since 1982 (the year of the Socialists' victory), a hardline conservative known to be close to the reactionary Opus Dei movement and absolutely faithful to Pope John Paul II, who had made him a cardinal in 1985. In February 1990 Suquía was re-elected president of the Spanish Bishops' Conference for a further three years. The latter's fierce opposition to the Education Act was therefore inevitable.

The first attack came in a virulent pastoral by one of Madrid's four auxiliary bishops, Javier Martínez, which the priests of the archiepiscopacy were instructed to read out during Mass on Sunday 25 March 1990. The letter accused the Bill of being 'confessional' in reverse, and claimed that it would 'destroy young people, who will be brought up with neither morals nor feelings'. Martínez insisted that the Bill was but part of a general campaign to debase human nature.

Members of the group of progressive young Madrid priests known as 'The Three Hundred' (about a third of all those employed in the capital) refused to read the pastoral to their parishioners, thereby incurring the wrath of Archbishop Suquía. 'We are being supported by society but abandoned by a Church that is busily engaged in retreating to its pre-Vatican-II winter quarters,' said one of the group's spokesmen. 'Suquía is like a eucalyptus tree,' he added wittily; 'in his proximity nothing else can grow. The only way to avoid being dried up by him is to flee from his shadow.'

The government lost no time in reacting to the Church's attack on the religious, moral and social implications of the Education Bill. The director-general of the Ministry of Justice's Department of Religious

Affairs, Luis María de Zavala (a highly intelligent, diplomatic ex-Jesuit and latterly successful businessman), commented: 'When the Church accuses from the pulpit, it should do so with facts, not mere points of view.' A few days later Zavala added that, in his opinion, 'A lay State is under no obligation to impose a curricular subject touching on transcendent aspects of the individual.'

Many people felt that the Socialists were missing a golden cultural opportunity by not creating, in place of Religion and Ethics, a new compulsory subject such as 'Comparative Religion' or 'History of Religion' which would encourage pupils to compare and contrast different religious beliefs. 'Such a subject could play a vital role in the regeneration of Spanish life,' the distinguished liberal Catholic theologian, Enrique Miret Magdalena, commented to me. 'Spain was once a country of three religions, but nowadays the young know nothing about Islam or Judaism, let alone Catholicism, and their part in the making of Spain. What an opportunity we are missing!'

The Bill, with Ethics suppressed and Religion optional, was enacted in September 1990, leaving most of the details to be hammered out later.

One focus of controversy was the fate of those pupils who did not take optional religious studies. Should they be 'let off' the hour in which Religion was taught, usually at the beginning or end of the school day? The government's response, that the 'free' hour would be a supervised study period, dismayed many teachers who saw this as a form of detention, a punishment in disguise. Alternatively, why should some pupils be granted time for study within school hours that the students of Religion must do without? Left-wing teachers felt that Religion did not belong at all on school premises: Catholic parents should indoctrinate their children outside school.

Whatever the final outcome of the polemic, the compulsory teaching of Catholicism has now disappeared from Spanish State schools, a logical consequence of the separation of Church and State enshrined in the Constitution. Here again Spain, where the Church has traditionally had such power to control the minds of the young, is embarking on a new era.

If the question of the teaching of Religion in State schools has alarmed the Spanish Church, so too have the issues of abortion and divorce, which will be discussed in chapter 6, and of birth-control.

In November 1990, shortly after the new Education Act was passed, the government launched a birth-control campaign that caused the Bishops' Conference once again to accuse the Socialists of destroying the moral fibre of the nation. A joint venture by the ministries of Health and Social Affairs, the campaign was intended to persuade young people to use the sheath. The reasons given for the initiative were Spain's increasingly disturbing AIDS statistics, among the worst in Europe; the high numbers of unwanted pregnancies (30,000 annually in the under-twenties group) and abortions (3,500 each year in the same group); and the fact that the young were not using the family planning clinics. The researchers had discovered that three out of every four Spanish adolescents were having full sexual relations before nineteen but that 50 per cent of the females and 75 per cent of the males interviewed had on occasions taken no contraceptive precautions whatsoever. It was no wonder that there were so many adolescent pregnancies (47.69 per cent of the nineteen-year-olds who obtained legal abortions in 1988 had never used birth-control), nor that AIDS was spreading so alarmingly.

For their campaign the two ministries came up with the neat motto 'Póntelo. Pónselo,' 'Put one on. Put one on him,' which was widely propagated on TV and radio to the accompaniment of some famous pop songs whose lyrics had been specially adapted for the purpose. Across the land tens of thousands of posters conveyed the urgent prophylactic message, while 1,600,000 attractively packaged condoms were distributed free to adolescents. 'We say "Put one on" in an attempt to exorcise the boys' fear of being observed, naked, as they put on the sheath,' a government spokeswoman explained. 'The second half of the motto is intended to involve the girls in the use of this contraceptive method, and to modify the "naughty" image still projected by girls who take the precaution of carrying condoms when, curiously, many *boys* are happy to confess as a matter of prestige that they have one in their pockets – even though they rarely use them.'

The 'Condom Campaign' profoundly offended traditional Spanish Catholics, who now rounded on the minister of Health, Julián García Vargas. He explained that the government did not particularly like the idea of a campaign to promote the use of the condom among the young, but that it had come to the conclusion that, given the failure of other agencies, and of the family, to provide adequate sex education, there was simply no alternative. It was the government's absolute duty to take measures to protect the population against AIDS and to preclude unwanted pregnancies.

As for the Catholic hierarchy, a week before the publicity campaign got under way the secretary general of the Bishops' Conference, Monsignor Agustín García Gasco, a man dismayed by the increasing secularization of Spanish society, issued an angry statement in which he called for Catholic parents to organize co-ordinated protests. The campaign, he alleged, 'was a political, materialistic, agnostic and atheistic project aimed at depriving human beings of their transcendent dimension', at reducing sexuality to 'a biological function', love to 'the mutual attraction of bodies', and at establishing sexual pleasure as 'the fundamental thing in life'. García Gasco's outburst was soon echoed by other Church dignitaries, while the Vatican co-operated by issuing a statement condemning Catholic chemists who sell contraceptives – a statement which, if largely disregarded in the Spanish cities, made an immediate impact in the more traditional rural areas, where it became increasingly difficult to obtain the sheath.

The initial reaction to the 'Condom Campaign' on the part of the conservative Partido Popular, the main opposition party, was to ratify an epoch-making decision taken a few months earlier to back free, NHS, birth-control. 'The government's initiative is opportune,' commented the PP's spokesman on health, 'because it's intolerable that at the end of the twentieth century thousands of Spanish women should still be having unwanted pregnancies.' Behind the scenes, however, there was virulent rejection of the campaign and anger over the party leadership's stand on birth-control. During the following weeks these differences of opinion were to grow more acute as the PP's Christian Democrat wing became increasingly vocal.

Bishop García Gasco, ever combative, was much in the news at the time. In one statement he claimed that, if the government had consulted the Church first, 'more effective solutions' could have been found to the sexual problems of the nation. He did not say what these solutions were, although presumably abstinence was to the fore. He went on to make the damaging allegation that 'AIDS is an excuse the government is using to promote its birth-control campaign', and maintained that the minister of Health had told him that he hoped the bishops' protest would be a success! Meanwhile, the Vatican expressed its approval of the Spanish bishops' position.

Blas Piñar, leader of the extreme right-wing National Front, also took a hostile line: the minister of Social Affairs, Matilde Fernández, was an unashamed pro-abortionist and the purpose of her campaign, he alleged, to degrade the young people of Spain. Probably as a result of this tirade, neo-Fascist thugs in the Castilian city of Valladolid (traditionally a breeding-ground of right-wing extremists) began to smash up public telephone booths carrying the 'Put one on. Put one on him' posters.

Then, at the end of November 1990, the bishops produced a long document on public morality entitled *The Truth Shall Make You Free*. It revealed clearly the extent to which the Spanish Church was now feeling its loss of power. While the hierarchy made no direct attack on the Socialist government as such, there could be no doubt about who was responsible for 'the grave ethical crisis' afflicting Spain. The bishops, appalled by society's current permissiveness, particularly in sexual matters, expressed their conviction that, without belief in God and Christ, there could be no genuine altruism. Mere humanism, they said, was not enough. Only a return to true Catholicism could guarantee the 'recomposition of the moral fabric of our society', 'the necessary moral regeneration of our people', 'the ethical reconstruction of our society', 'the moral rearmament of our people'.

The language of the bishops' document was more restrained than had been expected. Not so that of Monsignor García Gasco, who a few days after its publication stated that the Spanish 'democratic system' was 'rotten to the core' ('podrido').

The immediate reaction of the Socialist Party and several government ministers to these attacks was to suggest that the bishops had lost contact with contemporary reality. 'Aberrant', 'profoundly antidemocratic', 'utterly out of touch with society', 'unjust', were some of the comments. The prime minister himself observed, with his customary diplomacy, that the bishops 'have every right to say what they want, but perhaps wouldn't be so ready to listen to what I'd like to tell them, although maybe it would be more responsible on my part not to engage them in polemics.' The most outspoken Socialist was the newly appointed head of the party's Women's Department,

Josefa Pardo, who told a journalist: 'We're not afraid of the Church . . . It's an unescapable fact that young people have sexual relations, and that therefore they need to be well informed. Chastity, abstinence (which is basically the recommendation the Church is transmitting), is the enemy of maturity and human nature.'

While undoubtedly the episcopal protest had pointed up some real ills in contemporary Spanish society (inordinate consumerism, for example), it was clearly misguided to blame everything on the Socialists. In the case of birth-control, moreover, the bishops could no longer count on the unanimous support of the faithful. According to a survey published earlier in the year, 37 per cent of Spanish priests were unhappy about the hierarchy's conservative attitude on the subject, 24 per cent indifferent and 39 per cent in sympathy. The bishops were fully aware, therefore, that even among the clergy there was strong opposition to the Vatican line on this crucial issue.

Every 6 December Spain celebrates the promulgation of the 1978 Constitution, and a reception is held in Parliament. For twelve years the president of the Bishops' Conference, the archbishop primate of Toledo and the papal nuncio had each accepted the invitation to be present. But not in 1990. All three made an excuse. Never had the relations between the Socialist government and the Church been so strained.

Three days after this snub the results of an opinion poll carried out by the Sociological Investigation Centre were published. They indicated that eight out of every ten Spanish Catholics, practising and non-practising, disagreed with the Church's stand on abortion, and that four out of every ten Catholics habitually attending Sunday Mass were now using the pill or condom. More than half of those interviewed expressed themselves in favour of euthanasia. Clearly the Church was profoundly out of touch with its own people.

Alive to its poor image among non-Catholics, the Church pours much energy into propaganda, running a host of bulletins, weeklies, diocesan magazines and publishing houses. In an effort to counteract the enormous influence of the daily *El País*, close to the Socialist government and often highly critical of the bishops, it has strengthened its ties with the long-established conservative daily *ABC*, since the disappearance of the Church-controlled newspaper *Ya* virtually the mouthpiece of the Bishops' Conference as well as being the paper

most widely read by the Spanish Right in general and by army officers. The Church has an 80 per cent holding in an extensive radio network, the COPE (*Cadena de Ondas Populares Españolas*, literally
'Network of Popular Spanish Radio Waves'), with 111 stations (45
medium-wave and 66 FM); and, although it possesses no television
stations of its own, has space on State and private TV. The COPE
often expresses extreme hostility to the Socialists. In 1989 it made a
pre-tax profit for the Church of some £12,000,000.

Another highly polemical aspect of Spain's relations with the
Vatican since the promulgation of the 1978 Constitution has been the
new arrangements for the financing of the Spanish Church. According
to an economic agreement drawn up in 1979 between the hierarchy
and Prime Minister Adolfo Suárez's government, it was decided that
the State would no longer pay the Church directly, as had been the
practice under Franco. Rather, the government now undertook to
allow taxpayers to apportion 0.5 per cent of their dues to the Church
if they so desired and itself to make up the difference, if this should be
necessary. In return the Church pledged itself to work conscientiously
towards full self-financing. The new system was to go into operation
from the tax year 1987.

It did so, with the Socialists now in power. From 1987 onwards
Spaniards had the option of instructing the Inland Revenue to transfer
precisely 0.52 per cent of their income tax either to the Church or, for
'social ends', to the State. All they had to do was to place a cross in the
relevant box on their tax returns. Where they failed to do so the
money was to go to 'social ends', not to the Church, although probably very few taxpayers indeed realized this. The assignation became
known popularly as 'the religious tax'. In 1987, 35.11 per cent of taxpayers gave to the Church, 11.85 per cent to the State. The rest failed
to indicate either box. A year later, in 1988, 39.08 per cent assigned
their 0.52 per cent to the Church, 20.45 per cent to the State: the
public was getting the hang of the system.

Then, in 1989, there was a tremendous outcry from the Right
when the minister of Social Affairs, Matilde Fernández, announced
that she was preparing a campaign to persuade taxpayers to give their
percentage to 'social ends'. She argued that, if the hierarchy was using
the press and radio (particularly the COPE network) to push its
claims to the 0.52 per cent, the State had the right to do so too. Was

this not a free society? Such were the Church's objections at this point that Felipe González intervened and Matilde Fernández was forced to climb down. The prime minister, prudent as always and presumably concerned not to alienate the Socialist Party's many Catholic supporters, had decided that it was the moment to make a conciliatory gesture. The Right now called for Matilde Fernández's resignation, claiming that, given her openly admitted agnosticism, she could not be trusted to apportion fairly the 0.52 per cent for 'social ends', and would probably favour non-Catholic charities and organizations. By 1990 things had calmed down, however, and the minister successfully reinitiated her frustrated campaign to persuade taxpayers to tick the 'social ends' box on their returns.

The progressives were intensely dissatisfied with the new arrangement. In a non-confessional State, they argued, no public money whatsoever ought to be made available to any religion. Why should the State allow Catholics to apportion a percentage of their State taxes to the maintenance of a Church traditionally hostile to democracy, and whose current hierarchy was daily proving itself intensely reactionary? With memories of the Franco regime's police files of 'dissidents' still fresh in everyone's minds, how could the Socialists, of all people, dream of asking taxpayers to put themselves on record as having wished *not* to contribute to the Church? It was an 'anticlerical census', wrote the liberal Catholic philosopher José Luis López Aranguren, and probably an infringement of article 16.2 of the 1978 Constitution, which declares: 'No one will be obliged to identify his or her ideology, religion or beliefs.'

Foremost among the critics was the diplomat Gonzalo Puente Ojea, Socialist ambassador to the Vatican until sacked in 1986 after the Spanish hierarchy brought pressure to bear on the government. Puente Ojea's crime was threefold: he was a declared atheist; in the process of obtaining a divorce; and, most offensive of all, cohabiting in Rome with his new partner. The ambassador's dismissal delighted the Spanish Right.

Not surprisingly, in view of his fall from favour, Puente Ojea had strong views about the Socialist government, beginning with Felipe González. The latter, as the ex-ambassador reminded readers in a magazine interview, had studied at Louvain with the help of a grant from a Catholic Youth Organization, and had been seriously attracted by Christian Democracy before opting for Socialism. Felipe González could be relied on not to offend the bishops more than was absolutely necessary.

When, in September 1990, the foreign minister, Francisco Fernández Ordóñez, paid a visit to the Pope in Castelgandolfo, Puente Ojea followed events closely. The trip was designed to announce yet more financial concessions to the Spanish Church, he stated – concessions for whose resolution there was already an established diplomatic channel through the Papal Nunciature in Madrid, so that really there was no need for Fernández Ordóñez to see His Holiness at all. It was outrageous, at all events, that the Socialists should maintain the policy of financing religious education, and therefore Church influence, in the State schools (the teachers of Religion are chosen by the bishops in each diocese). Did the Constitution not clearly declare that Spain was a non-confessional State?

It was true that the minister had gone out of his way to put the Vatican's mind at rest. He told journalists that the government would continue to spend 11 billion pesetas a year (some £55 million) on the teaching of religion in State schools, and 40 billion pesetas (approximately £200 million) on helping to finance the private, Church-run schools. In Italy, by way of contrast, he pointed out, the Christian Democrats, in power for forty years, had never made a single lira available to privately run Catholic schools. The inference was that the Vatican should be positively delighted with the Spanish government's spirit of co-operation and religious tolerance.

What will happen when the present arrangement is phased out at the end of 1991 and the State no longer makes up, as it has been doing since 1987, the difference between the taxpayers' contribution and the financial needs of the Church? It seems likely that the 0.52 per cent assignation will be raised to 0.8 or even 1 per cent, thereby allowing Catholic taxpayers to come to the Church's aid more effectively while at the same time redoubling the progressives' despair at what they consider far too indulgent an attitude towards the Church on the part of the Socialists. Probably other moneys will increasingly be made available to the Church by granting tax exemption on donations to Church organizations, as is the pattern in the United States (where there is 50 per cent relief on such transactions) and elsewhere.

The Catholic hierarchy, disgruntled by what it considers unfair treatment at the hands of the Socialists, has retaliated by promoting the canonization of priests and nuns killed by the 'Reds' during the Civil War. More recently, it has been pressing for the reopening of the case of Queen Isabella 'the Catholic' in the hope that her beatification will coincide with the 500th anniversary of the discovery of the New World (her examination was begun by the Vatican in 1958 but stalled by Pope Paul VI, no friend of Franco, in 1974). Given that Ferdinand and Isabella have gone down in history, not only for financing Columbus in 1492 and initiating the 'evangelization' of South America but for the expulsion of the Jews and forcible conversion of the Moors, the thought of the Queen's elevation to sainthood is repugnant to those who are working to revive a tolerant Spain reminiscent of pre-Inquisitorial days. And all the more so since Isabella was venerated as a symbol of 'the true Spain' by the Spanish Fascists and, later, the Franco regime.

Isabella's beatification was reanimated by Pope John Paul II, a man who, according to Archbishop Suquía, 'reads the Spanish press daily and is much disturbed by the country's spiritual decline'. When Wojtyla visited Spain in 1989 he talked of the need for a 'New Reconquest' – a less than diplomatic allusion to the myth of the eight-centuries-long Christian 'reconquest' of Muslim Spain and to the enforced religious orthodoxy that followed it. As Queen Isabella's case was being pressed in Rome, the dissident Jesuit Pedro Miguel Lamet, religious correspondent of the Madrid newspaper *Diario-16*, observed: 'Would it not now be better to promote the elevation of candidates who unite rather than separate?'

The Jewish Anti-Defamation League of the United States has declared that, if Isabella is raised to sainthood, relations between Jews and Catholics will be irremediably damaged internationally. As for the Sephardic Jews, particularly those who have returned to Spain, their outrage at the proposed beatification knows no words. The Vatican, it now seems, has decided to shelve the matter until after 1992, influenced by the French hierarchy, which has come out strongly against the canonization, and by increasingly adverse world opinion.

Naturally there is more to the Spanish Catholic Church today than its narrow-minded bishops or older, traditional, clergy. Particularly in the big cities there are modern priests, such as Madrid's celebrated

'Three Hundred', mentioned earlier, who are grappling with the related problems of drugs (very widespread in Spain), unemployment and lack of hope that now affect a considerable segment of the young population.

One of these enlightened priests is Enrique de Castro, a charismatic, chain-smoking man from northern Spain whom we filmed in Entrevías, an underprivileged housing estate on the southern fringe of Madrid.

When he began to work with young people in the early eighties, Castro was horrified to discover how much torture was still being used in the police stations, five years after the death of Franco, as part of normal daily routine. Some stations even had what was termed euphemistically a 'catharsis cell', an isolated, padded cubicle in which youthful offenders were being forced to spend long periods. Castro also found that the quality of work in the juvenile courts left much to be desired. No one really seemed to care. So he and some like-minded fellow priests decided to take action.

First they set up a free legal advice service. Then, houses in which young people thrown out of home, or living on the streets, could take refuge. Today Castro shares one of these with a floating population of youths beset with problems, not least drug addiction. 'We've become used to death here,' he told me. 'Over the last few years twelve or eleven kids have died, some from AIDS, some from heroin overdoses, one from a police bullet, one stabbed; one or two have commited suicide. What I try to do is make this house a secure base for them. I can't stop them taking drugs or stealing cars, but I don't allow drugs on the premises, and, if they steal a car, it has to be parked a few blocks away.'

While Enrique de Castro talked I found myself thinking that, unless the Spanish Church can produce more priests like him, its days may be numbered.

How, indeed, is the Church likely to evolve over the next few years? Little change can be expected in the mood of the Bishops' Conference unless Angel Suquía's place is taken by a more liberal man, and it seems unlikely that such a person will be elected soon.

But whether the bishops become more liberal or not, one thing is clear: the place of the Church in Spanish society has changed beyond recognition since the Franco days.

That of Spain's armed forces has also changed, although perhaps not so obviously. Made up at the moment of 56,000 officers and over 200,000 young conscripts doing military service, the army is currently going through a major identity crisis.

The principal role of Franco's army, in practice little short of an army of occupation, was to repress opposition to the dictator and maintain the status quo. Distributed throughout Spain in eleven military regions, with no apparent prospect of ever having to defend the country against outside enemies, it grew increasingly indolent and self-satisfied. Franco consistently gave military men portfolios in ministries regarded in other countries as civilian preserves, or awarded them top posts in State-controlled companies. All of this made the brass hats feel important and essential to the running of the nation. The army under Franco was a clique apart, with its own exclusive clubs, schools, shops, housing enclaves, prejudices; inter-marriage between military families became normal practice. It comes as no surprise to learn, therefore, that approximately half the officer cadets in the Saragossa Military Academy are still today the sons of regular soldiers – soldiers trained under Franco and often nostalgic for the good old days of the dictatorship, when the army was the backbone of the regime and had a clearly defined role. Like father like son: where Spanish army officers are concerned, this tends to be only too true.

The failed coup of 1981 demonstrated the degree of dissatisfaction with the New Spain in the most reactionary quarters of the army. Since then, though ten years have passed and democracy is firmly established, Franco's presence continues to pervade the military establishment. Take the Infantry Academy at Toledo, which I visited in 1990. I found the central patio still named 'Plaza del Generalísimo'; the dictator's portrait, as well as hanging in the Head of the Academy's study beside that of the King (chief, remember, of the armed forces), was on view in many other parts of the buildings; the dictator's sayings were inscribed on the walls; and, in a prominently displayed roll of honour listing Infantry officers killed during the Civil War, there was not one single Republican. Only Franco's officers died for Spain. As well as all this specifically military and political symbolism, crucifixes hung in every classroom and office, a reminder that, to the traditional military mind, if you are not Catholic you cannot be a true Spaniard, nor, of course, a good soldier.

The situation in the Infantry Academy is no exception. Franco's portrait is endemic in the barracks, so much so that in May 1990 Joseba Azkárraga, parliamentary spokesman for one of the Basque nationalist parties, asked the minister of Defence to order the immediate removal of 'Franco symbols' from military buildings. Their prevalence, he said, 'is a faithful reflection of the convictions and ideologies that persist among certain sectors of the armed forces, who refuse to accept that the maintenance of such symbolism represents the most "tragic" aspect of the history of Spain.'

In his cautious reply, Narcís Serra, the minister of Defence, made the astonishing statement that, in a stable democracy, such issues have little importance. 'It seems unbelievable that a government calling itself Socialist could allow such abuses to continue year after year, or seek to minimize their importance,' Azkárraga said to me recently. 'The mentality of the officer corps has hardly changed since Franco, and the maintenance of the old symbols fosters it.'

It is a fact that the Socialists have been very careful indeed not to move too quickly in their attempts to wean the army from its Franco fixation, clearly feeling that to insist on the suppression of the dictatorship's emblems in military buildings would be to ask for trouble. Where this delicate matter is concerned the government has decided that sleeping dogs should be let lie.

The Socialists have been careful, also, not to meddle too overtly with the view of modern history transmitted in the Saragossa Academy, where the previous regime is still mythified by teachers nostalgic for the old values. Presumably the feeling is that here too, in tune with society, things will change of their own accord, little by little, whereas direct intervention would only make matters worse.

Where the Socialists *have* acted is in the modernization of the army's promotion system, an initiative that has caused tremendous disgruntlement in some quarters. Previously the officers knew exactly when they would be promoted, because the system depended merely on seniority. If you were number 17 on your year's list, you knew that you would be upgraded after number 16, and that was that. Not now. Under the new arrangement promotion depends on ability as well as age, so that younger, more able men often overtake their seniors. This has caused great resentment.

As a rule the army chiefs avoid hinting publicly at what they think

8 Spain has a bewildering array of traditional festivities and local holidays. The Rocío is one of the most famous. From throughout Andalusia, pilgrims flock at Whitsun to the edge of Doñana National Park to do homage to the Virgin of the Dew.

9 *In contemporary Spain there are
many non-practising Catholics. Most,
however, will have taken their First
Communion, an occasion still invested
with great social importance.*

10 *The funeral of General Franco.
The old dictator groomed Prince Juan
Carlos de Borbón as his successor, but
in the event the present king
contributed vitally to the country's
peaceful transition to democracy.
Today he is deeply admired by almost
all Spaniards.*

ABOVE:
13 *The Franco regime paid scant attention to the environmental problems caused by industrial pollution, but EC membership is leading to a growing awareness of 'green' issues. Before long even Bilbao, which has Spain's heaviest concentration of industry, should be considerably cleaner.*

about post-Franco, democratic Spain. Those recently retired, however, are only too happy to voice their opinions, as are some of the men who, imprisoned for their implication in the Tejero coup, have now been released. Among the latter is ex-navy commander Captain Camilo Menéndez Vives, who sprang from anonymity to dubious fame in February 1981. A close friend of Tejero, Menéndez turned up in Parliament when it became obvious that the rebels had lost, and received a year and a half's imprisonment for his presumed part in the conspiracy. When I interviewed him for the BBC outside the Parliament building in Madrid he expressed forceful views on contemporary Spain, exclaiming that the situation was even more disastrous than the one Tejero and his fellow conspirators had 'so nobly' sought to remedy. Were not terrorism, crime, immorality and drugs destroying the country? Was it not a fact that MPs, ostensibly the representatives of the people, rarely turned up for debates? 'Spain is in a very bad state,' Menéndez insisted. 'I am completely convinced of it, a very bad state indeed.'

The officer corps of the Spanish army is today in a quandary. Brainwashed into thinking of itself as a bulwark against Marxism, the ultimate guarantor of the 'traditional values of the nation', it is bemused by the complete breakdown of Communism, both in and outside Spain. The enemy has disappeared! Moreover, the diluted Socialism of Felipe González and his successive governments, whatever Camilo Menéndez may think about it, has posed a threat to no one. In such a situation the army cannot avoid musing on its future. Nor, in a free society, can it avoid knowing how the Spanish people feel about it. Its morale, to put it mildly, is low.

How *do* Spaniards rate their armed forces? Above all there is massive rejection of military service, still obligatory (it lasts for a year), and growing support for the creation of a much smaller army, purely, or largely, professional. Such support grew even stronger as a result of the Gulf War, to which raw conscripts were sent on board three warships as part of Spain's 'logistical support'. At the beginning of March 1991 a comprehensive opinion poll found that some 64 per cent of Spaniards were against conscription.

Since 1984 conscientious objectors have been allowed to substitute social work for the 'mili', as it is known. While 5,438 submitted their claims to the National Council for Conscientious Objection in 1986, the number had risen to 13,508 in 1989. A 'punitive' element in the law lays down that those accepted for social service, which is regulated by the Ministry of Justice, have to put in six months longer than other conscripts, presumably because such work is held to be a softer option (a similar system pertains in all the NATO countries with military service).

The Gulf War has had the effect of making young Spaniards facing military service increasingly aware of the moral and practical issues involved. Recent figures show that growing numbers of youths are not only opting for the alternative, social service (there were 4,000 applications in January 1991, more than double those for the same month the previous year), but are prepared to break the law by refusing point-blank to do either. 'No service, neither military nor social' is the motto of the 'insumisos', 'unsubmissives', as they are known. Particularly tricky is the situation of those who, having started their military service, decide suddenly to desert. For them there is no legal loophole. At the time of writing some 2,000 young people are in the 'insumiso' category, while eleven are paying for their stubbornness by imprisonment.

During the courts martial at which the 'insumisos' are tried it is not uncommon for the military judges to call the lads in the dock cowards, unmanly and so on. Many of the older Spanish judges are conservative enough, but the military variety are ultra-conservative. A handful of conscripts failed to turn up when summoned to embark for the Gulf. A military judge termed them 'a disgrace to their country and their families'. But should cases of 'non-submission' and desertion in peacetime properly be tried by court martial at all? (Spain was not technically at war with Iraq, but simply lending 'logistical support'.) The Constitutional Court, asked for a ruling, decided in March 1991 that they should. Its decision baffled, and disappointed, many people.

Despite the public rejection of military service, the Socialist government has consistently argued that the 'mili' should be retained, albeit pruned down and modernized, Felipe González asserting quaintly that only conscription from all levels of society can guarantee the 'democratic character' of the armed forces. One person not convinced by the prime minister's reasoning is Colonel Amedeo Martínez Inglés, who was dismissed from the army in 1990 for his criticisms of both the military establishment and the Ministry of Defence. In his controversial book *España indefensa* ('Spain Undefended'), published in November 1989, Martínez Inglés expressed his conviction that the government's real reason for not dispensing with military service altogether is fear of offending those officers opposed to the introduction of a professional army and, more generally, to a modernization that might deprive them of their cushy jobs.

Like Martínez Inglés, General Alberto Piris, the retired Artillery general and expert on defence and ecology mentioned in chapter 4, is strongly in favour of professional armed forces. In the foreseeable future, he argues, Spain is not likely to be called on to take unilateral aggressive action of any kind, the only possible threat on the horizon being Morocco, with its claims to Ceuta and Melilla – a threat which Piris trusts can be defused in time (on this, see pp. 31–2). This highly respected general is adamant that the Spanish army, in view of the new world situation, should now be modernized along essentially *defensive* lines. In his view, a fully professional army of this kind would need only some 40,000 men as against the present 250,000. The money saved would be astronomical, and some of it could usefully be spent on the reduction of environmental pollution.

Another distinguished defence expert and ecologist, Vicenç Fisas Armengol, proposes an 84,000-strong professional army, with 24,000 officers and 60,000 volunteers who would enlist for a minimum of three years. By Fisas's calculations, such a structure would save the country a sum in the region of £600 million per year.

As this book goes to press, the government has just introduced its new Military Service Bill, which will be debated by Parliament after the 1991 summer recess. Since its main provisions have the support of the Partido Popular, the leading opposition party, there is no doubt that it will become law. The Bill reduces military service from twelve to nine months and envisages that, by the year 2000, the Spanish armed forces will be made up of between 170,000 and 190,000 men, 50 per cent of them professionals. As regards 'unsubmissives' and deserters, the Bill provides that they will be tried by civil, not military courts – a notable advance in human rights, surely. Until the very last minute the Bill included a harsh clause barring 'unsubmissives' definitively from entering the civil service, but in its final draft it states that *preference* for civil service posts will be given to those who have done their military or social service. This aspect of the Bill is bound to be attacked fiercely by the Left.

One final question will remain in some people's minds. Could there be another army coup, or will the 1981 débâcle turn out to have been the last effort by nostalgic officers to put the clock back? With the country fully integrated in Europe and a member of NATO, with the collapse of the Warsaw Pact and the new *entente cordiale* between the USA and the Soviet Union, with the business and banking communities far from displeased with the Socialists, it now seems impossible that Spanish democracy can be forcibly overturned.

The only remaining danger is the problem of separatism. The 1978 Constitution entrusts the army with guaranteeing the 'territorial integrity' of Spain. If ever Basque or Catalan separatists overreach themselves, the military could in theory intervene – and the results might be catastrophic. But such a contingency is almost unthinkable. It comes as a relief, therefore, to be able to report that the army, at long last, no longer poses a threat to the Spanish people.

−6−

Women's Rights

Spaniards are equal before the law, and there can be no discrimination based on birth, race, sex, religion, opinion or any other personal or social condition or circumstances whatsoever.

Article 14, 1978 Constitution

Etched deep into the Spanish unconscious, male and female, is the belief that women are inferior to men, second-rate citizens. Such a notion persists in other European countries, of course, despite advanced social legislation, but nowhere so tenaciously as in Spain, not only owing to five centuries of dogmatic Catholicism but, more immediately, because of the Franco era. Enormous progress has been made in the matter of women's rights since the death of the dictator, however, due in no small measure to the country's new European involvement and obligations. To appreciate the situation of women in Spain today, a brief review of their previous tribulations is, I think, called for.

On the evening of 4 May 1931, three weeks after the proclamation of the Second Republic, a largely female audience crammed the imposing, portrait-lined lecture hall of Madrid's famous liberal club, the Ateneo. The crowd had come to hear the first of five talks on the subject of Spanish women and the Republic by the combative feminist writer and teacher María Martínez Sierra, a fine orator. The atmosphere was electric – and the speaker responded. She praised the ordinary people of Spain for the common sense and magnanimity they had shown in achieving the transition to democracy without bloodshed; recalled the jubilation in Madrid when the election showed that support for the monarchy had collapsed; pointed out that the middle-class women of Spain had never done a stroke of work in their lives, and must do so now; voiced her conviction that, for the first time in Spanish history, the emancipation of women was at hand; and begged those present to give their support to the provisional government in the run-up to the general election.

María Martínez Sierra waxed eloquent on the appalling problems facing the majority of Spanish families (many with six, seven or eight children) at a time of dire economic recession. Under the previous regime birth-control had not been available. Now there was talk of introducing it but, of course, the Catholic Church was already flinging its arms to heaven at such an immoral proposal. María Martínez Sierra had little time for the Spanish hierarchy.

When the lecturer tackled the subject of women's rights in general and married women's rights, or lack of them, in particular, she came fully into her own. Brandishing copies of the Civil and Penal Codes in force under the monarchy, she demonstrated that married women in Spain had been little more than the chattels of men: slaves in the home, deprived of dignity. She adduced one particularly telling example. Among the 'legitimate grounds' for divorce the Civil Code included adultery 'by the woman in every case and by the husband when it occasions a public scandal or scorn for the woman'. That is, the husband could philander to his heart's content, but unobtrusively. There were special provisions for husbands who discovered that their wives were misbehaving. 'The husband who, catching his wife committing adultery, should kill her in the act, or the man, or should wound both of them severely, will be punished by banishment,' read the relevant article, without specifying either where, or for how long. It went on: 'Should he cause them only lesser wounds, there will be no legal sanctions,' adding: 'these rulings are applicable in similar circumstances to fathers with respect to daughters under twenty-three years of age and to their corruptors, provided that the former be still living under the paternal roof.' Mere banishment too, then, for an outraged father who should take it upon himself to murder his wayward daughter and her lover.

Conducting her audience step by step through these and other articles of the two Codes, María Martínez Sierra concluded that, under the monarchy, married women in Spain had enjoyed no legal protection whatsoever. But now, at last, things were about to change, and it was up to women to fight for their rights. Had not the provisional government already proved its good intentions by appointing an outstanding women lawyer, Victoria Kent, as director of prisons? In fifteen days, María Martínez Sierra exclaimed, the provisional government of the Republic had done more for women than all the monarchist governments together since the thirteenth century! And given the fact that women now far outnumbered men in Spain, she felt certain that, if they stood together, they would prevail.

On 28 June 1931 the Spaniards elected a Parliament whose specific brief was to draw up a modern Constitution. It was promulgated on 9 December 1931. María Martínez Sierra's faith in the men who had ushered in the new Republic (many of them distinguished intellectuals, university teachers and lawyers, the best brains of a brilliant generation) was justified when in January 1932 Parliament passed Spain's first-ever divorce law, prepared at record speed and in several respects in advance of legislation in other European countries. As well as receiving the right to divorce by mutual consent (a provision not introduced in Denmark until 1970 and in Britain until 1971), men and women were treated on an equal footing with regard to adultery, and exquisite attention was given to the problem of the children of broken marriages.

Despite the Church's dire prognostications (the reactionary press had furiously opposed divorce legislation) there was no stampede to the courts. From March 1932 to December 1933, 88.6 per cent of the 3,546 divorces granted applied to married couples who had been living apart for several years. Half the petitions came from women.

During the two years of progressive rule that ended when the Right won the general elections of November 1933, the position of women in Spain improved notably in other respects, at least in the statute books, and the Republic introduced the female vote. From November 1933 until the electoral victory of the Popular Front in February 1936 there was no advance in women's rights. Then, six months later, came civil war, almost three years of it, followed by the decades-long dictatorship of General Franco.

Given the fury of the Church when the Republic had dared to sponsor divorce legislation, it was not surprising that the Catholic Franco, the self-appointed head of State, should have decided to rescind the Act. This he did by decree on 2 March 1938, a year before the Civil War ended, and the ruling was ratified by the nationalist government on 23 September 1939. It declared null and void all divorces obtained under the provisions of the 1932 Act, and restored the marriage clauses in the Civil Code that the Republic had abolished. As a result, the remarriages of those who had obtained divorces under the Republic were considered null and void, and their fruits illegitimate. The tragic history of those unions illegalized by the Franco regime has never been told, nor that of their 'bastard' offspring.

Thus was initiated a period of forty-two years in which divorce was unobtainable. Annulments by the ecclesiastical courts were available for the rich. Legal separation was a possibility, but required the display of so much dirty linen that only the brave, and again, the wealthy, were prepared to go through with it. Meanwhile the regime encouraged large families and instituted a fecundity prize for the most prolific. Characteristically, most of the credit went to the father, not the mother.

The dictatorship introduced other laws that made life miserable for married women, who had to obtain their husbands' explicit permission for a whole range of activities: to travel alone, get a job, open a bank account, start a business, buy a house . . . Where their children were concerned, women were allowed no *patria potestad*, or legal authority; they had no control over the property acquired jointly during the marriage; and they even had to obtain their husband's permission to dispose of that which they had brought to the union.

As regards the marriage bed, there was no sexual education in Franco's Spain and no acknowledgement of the female orgasm. I was amazed by the frankness with which middle-aged women in a Seville sex seminar, in 1990, were prepared to talk to camera about their recent discovery of the clitoris and the new happiness they were beginning to find with their husbands. 'Under the dictatorship no one told us anything,' one of the women explained to me. 'You had to ask your friends, and even that made you shy. And the men were shy too. All they cared about was proving themselves. Now it has all changed. Couples talk to each other, tell each other what they like sexually, how to do it. The shame has gone.'

There were many other ways in which the Franco regime disabled women. They were virtually debarred from higher education and, accordingly, from a whole range of occupations; they were expected to find fulfilment exclusively in the old stereotyped roles of mother, domestic worker and helpmate; courtship was a painful, secretive business, with chaperones and prying neighbours; all public demonstrations of affection were forbidden. One finds disillusionment, indignation and sometimes great bitterness among many middle-aged and older women today. They feel that they have been cheated. In the Andalusian hill town of Ronda, elderly female pensioners spoke sadly to me about their married lives, the drudgery in the home, the endless children, the impossibility of escape.

María del Consuelo Alcalá was luckier than most of the women who found themselves unhappily married in the sixties. Coming from a good family, and married at the age of sixteen to one of Spain's most flamboyant bullfighters, Jaime Ostos, she obtained a legal separation in 1969. When I interviewed her she was scathing about women's lack of rights under Franco. 'After I obtained the separation from my husband,' she said, 'people were extremely hostile. Some turned away when they saw me, others refused to talk to me. Men looked at me as if I were the very image of sin. And, of course, there was scorn, too. They did their best to ostracize me.' Despite all the difficulties and all the odds, María del Consuelo decided to fight for her survival in what was then almost exclusively a man's world. She succeeded. Today, after twenty years of effort, she has turned a large inherited olive grove in Utrera, near Seville, into Europe's biggest organic fruit farm. She employs mainly women, convinced that they have a deeper feeling for life and nature than men, and finds it difficult to believe that Spain could have changed so radically in so short a time. But one of the reasons it has evolved so fast is precisely because women like María del Consuelo made a stand for their rights at a time when it required immense courage, and great will-power, to do so. They were the pioneers of the new liberties, beginning with divorce.

Article 14 of the 1978 Constitution, quoted as the epigraph to this chapter, states categorically that, in the New Spain, women and men have equal rights. As regards marriage and divorce, article 32 reads:

> 1. Men and women have the right to marry on the basis of complete equality.
>
> 2. The law will regulate the forms of marriage, the age and capacity to contract it, the rights and duties of the partners, the causes of separation and the dissolution of marriage.

The artificer of the divorce law elaborated as a consequence of these provisions was the Social Democrat Francisco Fernández Ordóñez, who became Adolfo Suárez's minister of Justice in the summer of 1980 and who, as his first contribution to the new democracy, had reformed the Inland Revenue. Fernández Ordóñez, one of the most likeable, courageous and liberal-minded politicians to emerge in the post-Franco period, was determined that his divorce Bill should not make concessions to the more conservative elements in the uneasy coalition that had been governing the country since 1977. Accordingly the highly restrictive draft drawn up by his ministerial predecessor immediately following the promulgation of the 1978 Constitution, after a point-by-point negotiation with the Church, was withdrawn and a much more radical one prepared. Fernández Ordóñez's Bill allowed for divorce by mutual consent, as its Republican archetype had done fifty years earlier. The intensely hostile Christian Democrats in the UCD coalition, following indications from the Vatican, blocked its progress through Parliament, and it was only in June 1981, after Suárez's resignation and Tejero's attempted coup, and amid vitriolic argument, that the Bill completed its passage through both houses.

Fernández Ordóñez said later that the coverage given to the divorce issue during those turbulent months by the influential daily newspaper *El País* had been vital. In 1982, after leaving the party, he stated that in his opinion 'it was not so much an Act promulgated *by* the UCD coalition as *despite* the UCD – despite, that is, the opposition, at times subtle and at times direct, of the ruling party.'

Fernández Ordóñez's Act was the very best that could have been achieved in the circumstances. It set out two ways in which a divorce could be obtained. The first provided that, without the necessity of having to go through the procedure of legal separation, couples in mutual agreement could obtain a divorce after living apart for two years; in the absence of such an agreement, it had to be established that they had been apart for five. The other way was to obtain a legal separation, a year after the granting of which either party could then petition for a divorce.

Fernández Ordóñez's Bill became law on 7 July 1981, a historic date in the annals of human rights in Spain. Many petitions for divorce were immediately submitted, a considerable proportion by couples who had obtained legal separations under the previous regime and had long been waiting for this liberating moment. From July to December 1981 there were 9,483 divorces and, in 1982, 22,578.

During the months leading up to the passing of the Act, the Church and its supporters had echoed their opinion of 1931, that divorce would spell the breakdown of the family. A year later, Fernández Ordóñez said that he had received the impression, as the first divorce figures came in, that Catholics opposed to the Act were positively disappointed: perversely, they had hoped that the numbers would be far higher.

Ten years after Fernández Ordóñez's Bill became law, divorce is accepted as a *fait accompli* in Spain, even by a Church which, to judge from its prudent silence on the subject, has recognized that this battle, at least, has been definitively won by the opposition.

The ruling UCD party tackled the question of divorce, and flinched from that of abortion. It did, however, make some timid progress on birth-control. Under Franco both the sale and use of contraceptives had been crimes, and their clandestine distribution a major subterranean industry. Only in the latter years of the regime were a minority of privileged women with complaisant doctors able to obtain the Pill, alleging that they needed it to regulate their menstrual cycles.

With Franco dead and Spanish society desperate for change, the

UCD had no alternative but to modernize the law. Accordingly, in 1978, it revoked the articles in the Penal Code banning the sale of contraceptives. Fearful of Catholic reaction, however, the government made no attempt to get birth-control to the people. This initiative was left to the local authorities: depending on their political composition, family-planning clinics were or were not set up.

In 1985, three years after the Socialists gained power, an inquiry into the birthrate was carried out by the National Statistics Department. The researchers asked women: 'Was your last child planned?' No less than 27.07 per cent replied that it was not; 52.51 per cent said that they used no contraceptive methods whatsoever; and of the 47.4 per cent who stated that they did, 12.97 per cent were still pinning their faith on *coitus interruptus* – almost as many, that is, as the 13.95 per cent who said they were using the Pill. More than 60 per cent of the women questioned had never been to see a gynaecologist.

Clearly, there was still massive ignorance about birth-control.

In July 1990 observers of the Spanish scene were presented with an eloquent indication that the country's conservatives were no longer quite so . . . conservative. This was the decision by the right-wing Partido Popular, now under the leadership of Manuel Fraga's young successor, José María Aznar, to propose the availability of free contraceptives through the Social Security service. That such a line could be taken by a party that had inherited the Catholic values of traditional Spain came as an intense shock to many people. The PP's spokeswoman on the issue explained that, given the party's opposition to abortion, it was natural that they should support sex education in school and contraception. Asked about his views on birth-control, Carlos Robles Piquer, former head of Spanish Television and today a Partido Popular Euro-MP, replied: 'The proverb says "prevention is better than cure". I accept that the Partido Popular should propose prevention in order to preclude abortion, and search for ways of avoiding the creation of an unwanted life.'

The PP's about-turn on birth-control provoked mixed reactions among its political adversaries as well as in its own rank-and-file. For one newspaper, it was simply a sensible ploy to ensure that the PP did not begin to lose the support of its female voters, more liberal than their male counterparts. Whatever the motives, one thing appears certain: the PP's 'official' acceptance of birth-control helped to ease the conscience of many of its Catholic supporters.

Birth-control is now openly available to those who want it, and can be obtained on the Social Security, although some gynaecologists refuse to prescribe contraceptives on religious grounds, and some chemists refuse to sell them. Social Security contraception is not yet completely free, moreover. Some family-planning clinics run by local councils make no charge, but the problem remains of connecting with the socially and economically deprived women who need such services. In addition, there is still frontal resistance by the Spanish Church to birth-control. The bishops' reaction to the government's controversial 'Condom Campaign' in the autumn of 1990 has already been reviewed (pp. 70–3).

When the Socialists won the general election in October 1982 they undertook to implement the constitutional requirement of equal opportunities for men and women in every sphere of life. They therefore set up a commission that led to the foundation, a year later, of the Instituto de la Mujer (literally, Women's Institute, but Women's Welfare Department would be nearer the mark) under the auspices of the Ministry of Culture (in 1988 it moved to the newly created Ministry of Social Affairs). The Department's mission was to collaborate closely with the other ministries in every relevant area, and generally to work for women's participation on an equal footing with men in political, cultural, economic and social life.

True to its brief, the Department has played a major role in bringing Spanish women's rights into line with Europe. Since 1983 a great deal of research into the position of women in Spain has been carried out, and Parliament has passed legislation recommended by the Department's *Plan of Action for Equal Opportunities for Women, 1988–1990* (see below, p. 99). Training courses have been run for women throughout the country and a huge number of publications issued. Among the latter, a detailed report on the social situation of women in Spain made a particularly strong impact early in 1990. So too has its *Guide to Women's Rights*, first published in 1984 and recently revised. Much still remains to be done, however, as the Department's head, Carmen Martínez Ten, recognized in 1990. 'Verbally, Spanish women and men today are super-modern, super-progressive,' she told me, 'but when you scratch the surface you soon find the traditional Spain – for example, the view that, if a woman has been raped, she must have "done something" to encourage the man. Our task now is to make the new legislation an integral part of society's awareness of itself, so that the old, deep-rooted attitudes can be finally eradicated.'

Those attitudes are not going to disappear overnight, but the Women's Welfare Department has done more than any other body to hasten their demise.

Education, too, is vital if the final eradication of machismo is to be achieved. The old attitudes must be patiently undermined at school, and in this respect a tremendous effort has been made since the Constitution was passed in 1978. But widespread latent sexism remains a problem.

Recent research has shown that in Spain – even more than in the rest of Europe – men are still associated by both boys and girls with strength, ambition, power and authority, women with emotion and weakness. Boys put their hands up in class, and intervene in school assemblies, twice as often as girls. They dominate the playground while the girls congregate in corners. The traditional patterns are repeated. When the moment for specialization comes at the age of fourteen, very few girls opt for Technical Training ('Formación Profesional'), and those who do so tend to choose such time-hallowed 'female' subjects as Health, Hairdressing and Domestic Science rather than go for, say, Electronics, Draughtsmanship or Metalwork. Inevitably, the curricular division established at school is maintained when girls enter further education.

Feminists are harsh in their criticism of the educational system. 'What has been done is to incorporate the girls into an educational model designed for boys,' a spokeswoman said in 1990; 'every effort is made to ensure that they accept male values in order to survive in a male world, or that they acquire a cultural conditioning that turns them, simply, into educated housewives.' She went on: 'Why is it always the girls who have to change and not the boys? What we need is to rethink the feminine model and not be constantly conforming to the male one.'

Feminists are also angry about the sexist use of language in textbooks, often unconscious. Spanish, like other descendants of Latin, has masculine and feminine nouns and adjectives and the rule has always been that, where males and females are indicated together as a group, the masculine form takes precedence. This the feminists are no longer prepared to swallow. Thus, if anyone wants to address himself or herself to the Spaniards as a whole, they should now say 'los españoles y las españolas', not simply 'los españoles'. No doubt the feminists are pleased that, as far as the professions are concerned, there is a growing proliferation of analogical female forms where, previously, these would have been unthinkable. 'Juez', 'judge', for instance, now has a female counterpart, 'jueza'. 'Doctora' and 'profesora' have long existed but as women move increasingly into hitherto male preserves we are bound to find more and more terms like 'fontanera' (female plumber), 'bombera' (firewoman), 'albañila' (female bricklayer) and so on.

But it is not just a matter of the male gender taking grammatical precedence over the female. What about the blatantly sexist definitions in the dictionaries? Luz Méndez de la Vega, a member of the Guatemalan Academy, caused an uproar in 1990 by declaring that it was the Spanish Royal Academy's absolute duty to eliminate from its famous dictionary, considered the authority throughout the Spanish-speaking world, the literally thousands of definitions based on assumptions of male supremacy. She gave one particularly telling example. In modern Spanish the verb 'gozar' is a popular term for 'to have sexual pleasure', with orgasm implied. The most recent edition of the Academy dictionary, however, retains the definition 'to have carnal knowledge of a woman'. As Señora Luz Méndez de la Vega observed, this not only reduces women to the level of objects but denies the possibility that they too are capable of orgasm.

As regards school and university textbooks, the Women's Welfare Department has placed their revision high on its list of priorities, with the aim of eliminating male bias from their grammar, content and illustrations.

In September 1990 a comprehensive new Education Act included equality of the sexes as one of its principal aspirations. 'The Act gives us the framework we've being waiting for,' the head of the Women's Welfare Department told me; 'now it's a question of making the constitutional right to equal opportunities a reality. I'm optimistic. The Act opens up fascinating new ground for progress, including rigorous, scientific sex education.' Listening to Carmen Martínez Ten I found myself thinking, as I so often do, about the very different Spain I had first known back in the summer of 1957, a Spain in which legal abortion, for example, was unthinkable.

Under Franco abortion was a heinous crime. As a result, many thousands of women (including the present minister of Social Affairs, Matilde Fernández) were forced to terminate their pregnancies abroad, London being the favourite destination. These 'extra-territorial' abortions were considered illegal in Spain, and several women arrested on returning from England and Portugal, both before and after the death of the dictator, were subjected to humiliating trials and awarded prison sentences. The operative article in the Penal Code was not revoked by the Constitutional Court until 1984, two years after the Socialists won the general election.

The Socialists had pledged themselves to introduce abortion legislation if returned. No sooner were they in power than they reaffirmed this intention and got to work on a draft Bill which was made public in March 1983. The progressives found it much too restrictive, arguing that, given the Socialists' overall majority in Parliament, they could have afforded to be far more radical: their hesitancy proved their fear of offending the Church and of alienating their Catholic supporters. The Right thought the Bill too lenient.

The Abortion Act was passed by the Lower House on 6 October 1983 and the Senate on 30 November. Then came the bombshell. On 11 December the Constitutional Court decided to admit the opposition's appeal against the Act, which alleged that it violated article 15 of the Constitution ('All citizens have the right to life and to physical and moral inviolability, and in no case whatsoever can they be subjected to torture or to inhuman sentences or treatment. The death penalty is abolished except in those cases which the military laws may decide in time of war'). As a result of the Court's decision to examine the appeal, the Act was held up for a year and a half.

Meanwhile, Spanish women were continuing to abort in London, maintaining an average of some 22,000 terminations a year. In 1984 the operation in any of London's thriving private clinics cost between £115 and £140, depending on the length of pregnancy. The income of the English practitioners was swollen each year by almost £3 million.

In April 1985 the twelve-man Constitutional Court pronounced against the text of the Socialists' Abortion Bill, thanks to the casting vote of its president, on the grounds that it did not provide sufficient constitutional guarantees. The government made some minor changes in the Bill and reintroduced it. It was passed by the Lower House on 28 May 1985, after a heated debate, and by the Senate shortly afterwards. The opposition decided not to appeal for a second time to the Constitutional Court, and on 2 August 1985 the Abortion Act became law. It remains in effect.

The Act allows for abortion in three contingencies: when pregnancy is the result of rape, when the woman's life or health (mental or physical) is in danger, and when the foetus is deformed.

From the outset a majority of Catholic doctors and nurses in the Social Security hospitals refused to perform abortions, or to participate in them, while the anti-abortion campaigners made life miserable both for the women who sought to obtain terminations in such centres and for those involved in the operations. As a result, middle-class demand for private clinics grew hugely, while abortions became increasingly difficult for the less privileged to obtain.

On 25 July 1988, the third anniversary of the Abortion Act, the weekly Madrid magazine *El Globo* published the startling results of an investigation which showed that, of the approximately 105,000 women who had aborted since 1985, only 18,000 had done so legally. Of these, a mere 5 per cent had attended Social Security hospitals. The magazine provided details of the harassment to which women seeking legal abortions, both Social Security and private, had been, and were still being, subjected.

The situation was particularly serious in the autonomous community of Navarre, where a Catholic pressure group had brought abortions to a two-year standstill. In 1990, the 1,100 Navarrese women who decided to abort had to have the operation performed either in the Basque Country (Bilbao) or across the frontier in Biarritz.

By October 1990 there was widespread dissatisfaction among progressives about the provisions and working of the Act. Right-wing judges had recently passed several harsh, and highly questionable, sentences for alleged infringement of the law by abortion practitioners, and militant feminists were virulent in their criticism of the Socialist Party and, in particular, of its women MPs, who in their view had done nothing constructive since 1985 to press for reform. The 1985 Act, the feminists concurred, had had the effect of 'normalizing' the subject of abortion in Spain, of removing it from the list of taboo subjects. But now radical overhaul was necessary. 'The only solution is a system similar to the British,' the leading feminist writer Lidia Falcón told me at this time, 'with abortion on demand up to, say, four months. The government knows this but is afraid to act for fear of offending the Church. If they merely add a "socio-economic" provision it won't solve anything either, because the judges will still have the power to decide who can afford another child and who can't. Once again, women will be deprived of taking the decision themselves.'

In November 1990 the Socialists' 32nd Federal Congress was held in Madrid. The journalists pressed the minister of Social Affairs for her views on abortion reform. Matilde Fernández's polemical birth-control campaign, already discussed (see pp. 70–3), was then in full swing, and she seemed loath to get involved in another polemic. A parliamentary report on the working of the present Act was pending, she explained, and any future modifications would be linked to the new Code of Civil Law, currently being elaborated.

Four months later the abortion issue came to a head again when a gynaecologist from Málaga, Germán Saénz de Santamaría, a dissident Socialist, was imprisoned for having given an abortion in 1984, *before the passing of the Act*, to a fourteen-year-old who, since the age of eight, had been consistently raped by her cousin, a man of over fifty, who had threated to kill her if she told anyone. Felipe González had gone on record as saying that, while he was prime minister, nobody would be gaoled for performing an abortion. Now it had happened. Saénz de Santamaría was reprieved after four days by the government, but the fact that he had been locked up at all shocked the country. On his release the doctor was scathing in his criticism of the judges involved (so much so that within a few days he was back in prison for contempt!), and even more so of a political party which, by failing to pass adequate legislation in the first place and now dragging its feet over the reform of the Act, had made it possible for some judges to behave as if Franco were still alive.

It is impossible at this point to say whether the government will dare to legalize abortion on demand up to three or four months, or whether it will be content, once again, to compromise, adding a 'socio-economic' category to the existing Act. During the Saénz de Santamaría scandal, Matilde Fernández at last made her personal position on the subject clear: she was, she said, in favour of abortion on demand and felt that, in the Welfare State her ministry was working towards, no 'socio-economic' clause should be necessary.

If, despite the opinion of the minister of Social Affairs, the government should now settle for such a clause (and it is perfectly capable of doing so) it will be just one more instance of how far the Socialists have moved to the right since 1982.

While the present abortion law does not satisfy the progressives, only the government's harshest critics on the Left would deny that, in the field of equal rights, considerable advances have been made since the Socialists took power. The *Plan of Action for Equal Opportunities for Women* elaborated in 1987 by the Women's Welfare Department was an ambitious document. Divided into five areas (Legal Equality, Education and Culture, Work and Labour Relations, Health, International Co-operation and Political Participation), it set out thirty broad objectives for putting Spanish women on an equal footing with men, and made no fewer than 122 recommendations.

By the end of 1990, when the Plan expired, more than 90 per cent of its objectives had been satisfactorily achieved, according to the minister of Social Affairs. Among the few exceptions were the failure to achieve the hoped-for agreement with Spanish State Television on the elimination of female stereotypes in advertising; various measures concerning procuration and sexual harassment, held up by the government's slow progress on the reform of the Code of Civil Law; and regulations about female miners.

There had been two major breakthroughs: the 'Ley de Infracciones y Sanciones' ('Law of Infractions and Sanctions'), under which fines of up to 15 million pesetas (approximately £75,000) can be imposed for sex discrimination at work, and the 'Ley de Bases de Procedimiento Laboral' ('Law Concerning the Bases for Labour Procedure'), which puts the onus on the employer, not the employee, to prove that there has been no infraction in such cases.

The minister announced that, in 1991, a second Plan would come into operation. One of its aims would be to increase the proportion of the female working population to 40 per cent of the total (the

European average is 41 per cent), a feasible objective given the great progress already made under the first Plan (whereas in 1987 the proportion had been 27 per cent, in 1990 it reached 33 per cent). Another objective would be to help those mothers who had never worked to join the labour force.

Despite the advances made by 1990, some of the problems were proving more tenacious than expected. 'Women in Spain today have opted for a higher level of education and culture,' Carmen Martínez Ten commented, 'but they are finding that the old system of values still persists along with a family situation based on traditional models. This creates dysfunctions and a completely different way of life for many women, who have to take on a double workload.'

That workload is largely a result of the fact that, in the home, Spanish husbands have traditionally been extremely loath to participate in routine domestic tasks, probably because of excessive maternal pampering not only in their youth but right up to their wedding day. Men from such a background are bound to expect that their wives will provide the same exclusive service as their mothers. Research carried out by the Women's Welfare Department in 1989 came up with some interesting findings in this respect. Of the males interviewed, six out of every ten over the age of eighteen stated that they never helped at home in any way; those who said they did turned out to be referring to such 'masculine' tasks as putting out the refuse, washing the car and executing odd repair jobs. None admitted to involvement in the boring, repetitive business of cleaning, cooking, washing and generally helping in the organization of the house. All of which means that, when the married working woman gets home in the evening, she is usually expected to settle down alone to her 'domestic duties'. Things are changing gradually, however, and many women marrying today make sure before they do so that their husbands-to-be realize that they will be expected to play their part in the household.

Is the day almost upon us when a married Spanish male might conceivably stay at home, prepare meals, do the shopping and look after the baby, while the woman earns the income? The possibility is hard to imagine but none the less real for that, as a brief sketch in the satirical TV series 'We're European Now', starring the Catalan comedian Albert Boadella, hinted recently. In this, two husky males, one of them with a baby on his arm, are seen pushing their trolleys around a supermarket (we must assume that their partners are out working). The men collide, the inevitable aggressive reflex is quickly stifled, chivalrous apologies are proffered – and the new-style Spanish males continue on their domestic way.

Inmaculada Sánchez, whose marriage in Seville we filmed for the 'Fire in the Blood' series, is a modern Spanish woman with a clear idea of what she wants and expects from life, and from her partner. She was careful not to get married too soon, leaving it until she reached thirty, and even then there could be no question of beginning a family immediately (liberal Catholics, both Inmaculada and her husband Pepe expressed themselves opposed to abortion, but not to responsible birth-control). Inmaculada's views on being a housewife? 'The very idea horrifies me,' she assured us. There could be no question of giving up her work, either: motherhood would only interrupt this temporarily. Luckily, in the run-up to the wedding Pepe had developed an interest in cooking and shopping, so it seemed that in this marriage at least the division of household labour would be equable.

And what about higher education? In her series of lectures in 1931, María Martínez Sierra had joked that, thanks to a blatant case of grammatical discrimination, Spanish females were at least not prevented from embarking on university studies. The case in question concerned the word 'españoles', Spaniards, which, as I mentioned earlier, is automatically taken to include females. Thus, 'españoles' being allowed to attend university, women could not legally be excluded. Those who, under the Primo de Rivera dictatorship, took advantage of this possibility were very far and few between indeed. With the advent of the Republic the educational situation of women improved considerably, but then came the Franco dictatorship.

In 1940, immediately after the Civil War, only 13 per cent of Spanish students entering university were women; by 1979, four years after the death of Franco, the figure had reached 37 per cent; by 1984, 50 per cent; in 1989, 61.6 per cent of the students registering at Madrid's Complutense University were female, at its Autonomous University 59 per cent and at Alcalá de Henares, twenty miles from the capital, 53 per cent. No more startling indication of the changing situation of women in Spain could be adduced than this progression.

But the situation is not yet quite as rosy as the figures suggest. The women attending Spanish universities have habitually gone for arts courses, following the pattern set in school, and this tendency still predominates today. Fine Arts, Languages, Geography, History, Pharmacy and Medicine (there are now more women than men in the medical faculties) – these are the subjects they go for most. In the words of María Antonia García de León, a sociologist and teacher at the Complutense, 'the subjects chosen by women show that the old stereotypes that classify her as educator, nurse or chemist persist'. Despite this the number of female Law students is growing and women are moving steadily into the Sciences, Economics and Architecture and new technologies such as Telecommunications and Computer Studies. In the academic year 1986–7 women accounted for 43.95 per cent of the students enrolling for Economics and Business Studies at the Complutense, and 31 per cent of those beginning Architecture at the same university. There can be no doubt about it: Spanish women are on the move.

It is one thing for women to obtain university degrees and quite another, of course, to be allowed to compete on equal terms with male graduates for university jobs. Here there is still widespread discrimination. Thus, while in 1990 women occupied some 28 per cent of university posts, very few indeed, only 8 per cent, had professorial status. As I write, none of Spain's thirty-two public universities has a female Rector, and out of 169 Vice-Rectors, only twenty-one are women.

As regards women in politics, progress has been steady if not spectacular. After the municipal elections of 1987, there were 247 women mayors out of a total of 7,980, and 3,652 women town councillors out of 44,193. The forthcoming elections seem likely to show a further rise in the number of women town councillors.

The 1989 general election saw a marked increase in the number of female MPs, mainly as a result of the recent decision by the Socialist Party that 25 per cent of its important posts should be held by women. Among the new MPs was Carmen Romero, wife of Prime Minister Felipe González. In the election as a whole, one out of every three candidates was female as compared to 21 per cent in the 1986 elections. Today forty-six MPs (out of a total of 350), twenty-seven Senators (out of 208) and two Socialist Cabinet ministers are women. This is a breakthrough, but not yet a major one. In the seventeen regional assemblies, with female MPs averaging a mere 6 per cent, the situation is far less satisfactory.

In the job market as a whole, women earn on average 18 to 19 per cent less than men, mainly as a result of the fact that, given the stereotyped educational pattern that has been described, the majority do not have the training to go for the more highly paid professions. But even where they obtain the same qualifications as men, and do the same job, they still tend to get lower salaries, despite the new legislation. Also there are far more women than men out of work, and they find it extremely difficult to obtain part-time employment. Despite these residual inequalities, the increasing incursions by women into traditionally 'male' jobs are more in evidence every day. While women police and taxi drivers have been familiar for some time, recently it has become commonplace to have a new washing machine fitted by a female technician or a special letter delivered by a young woman on a motorbike. There are even female Civil Guards and pilots – something undreamt of a decade ago. With this growing work-force behind them, the Women's Welfare Department and the dozens of associations and agencies now fighting for women's rights around the country are likely to find the going easier.

There will still, however, be plenty of work for these organizations, not least on behalf of women who find themselves at the receiving end of macho brutality and arrogance. According to the Association of Separated and Divorced Women, some 300,000 Spanish women are the victims of male violence every year. In 1989, eighty-four women were murdered by their husbands or companions, while 17,738 reported mistreatment at the hands of their partners. Those engaged in women's rights work in Spain seem to agree that only a tiny minority of such cases, perhaps 10 per cent, have been coming to the notice of the authorities.

In October 1990 the government launched a campaign to persuade women to report cases of battery and sexual assault to the police. There are several reasons why the victims are reluctant to do so. In the first place, Spain has long been a country where the fear of what the neighbours say has strongly influenced social behaviour and encouraged the hushing up of 'domestic problems'. This conditioning, gradually losing its grip in the cities but still potent in country areas, has worked particularly against women, given, until very recently, their inferior legal status. Then there is a profound conviction that the police will not help much (a conviction not without some basis, unfortunately), a justifiable terror of reprisals, and most women's sheer ignorance of their legal rights.

Under Franco no provision was made for the protection of battered women. By 1990, 131 'centros de acogida', or 'reception centres', had been created throughout the country where women and children could be taken in and advice given. It was a good beginning, but today there are still not enough such centres to cope with the demand.

The location of these refuges is kept as secret as possible to avoid retaliations. It was to one of them that twenty-four-year-old Isabel de la Rocha, whom we interviewed in Seville for the 'Fire in the Blood' series, fled with her little girl in terror and despair after having been frequently beaten up by her husband. At the refuge Isabel met other women in a similar position and was counselled about the possibilities open to her. She started a training course in TV lighting and took the opportunity to remake her life. While Franco was alive such an outcome would have been unthinkable.

Another great disincentive to reporting cases of battery has been the administrators of justice themselves. The European Parliament has repeatedly requested the governments of the Community to be punctilious in the elaboration of sexual aggression legislation, not least in order to reduce to a minimum the subjective appreciations of judges, all too often tinged by sexism. Where Spain is concerned, such admonitions are particularly necessary in view of the fact that there is not yet a jury system (experiments are being made) and that many of today's older judges, survivors from the Franco days, are intensely conservative.

In recent rape and sexual harassment cases there have been some very dubious, and much publicized, sentences clearly biased in favour of the male aggressors involved. Far too many Spanish judges still consider that the way women dress can 'provoke' attack, or that the victims of rape fail adequately to resist their assailants. In one case, in which a secretary was raped by her employer, the judge decided that the girl was to blame for having excited the man by wearing a miniskirt.

In June 1990 the militant feminist lawyer Cristina Alberdi, then the only woman member on the General Council of the Judiciary (a body elected by Parliament to ensure the fair application of the law), was asked by a journalist if Spain still had reactionary judges who were failing to act in the spirit of the Constitution. 'The judges accept the Constitution,' she replied diplomatically; 'what happens is that they reflect the mentality of the society to which they belong.' 'A society that continues to act in accordance with *machista* assumptions?', the journalist prompted. 'Yes,' Cristina Alberdi agreed. 'That's why we must make a concerted effort to change that mentality.'

If women are still very hesitant to report rape, cases of sexual harassment at work are being increasingly brought to the notice of the authorities. However, in early 1990, despite the new legislation, it was calculated that a third of the female work-force in Madrid was still being molested in one form or another, ranging from catcalls and bottom-pinching to threats from bosses that, if they did not comply sexually, they would be fired. Here, as in other areas, it is not the law but society itself that is behind the times.

Although they may concede that considerable progress has been made in the field of women's rights, feminists still have much to complain about – and to work for. Spain remains the country in the Common Market with the lowest percentage of working women (and the highest ratio of housewives). And feminists tend to insist that, until women occupy commanding positions in banks and businesses as a matter of course, not just as token exceptions to the rule, there can be no talk of real equality with men, given that in this society, as elsewhere in Europe, the power is where the money is.

One of the reasons for Spanish women's hesitation to vie for such positions of power, in the view of economist María Vega de la Cruz, is that for centuries they have been brainwashed by men to believe that women are literally incapable of understanding money, an assumption that grew stronger under the Franco regime. A contemporary reflection of this attitude is the fact that, when a woman asks for a loan to set up a business, particularly an unconventional business, the male-dominated financial bodies tend to prove extremely unhelpful. So strong is the bias that business women who are successfully running their own concerns often put up their husbands' names as a front.

It must be said at the same time that many Spanish women with more than adequate business acumen and talent decide freely that struggling to the top of the male world against all the odds is simply not worth the effort. 'Men feel obliged by the "social imperative" to compete and win, but women don't,' writes businesswoman Lucila Gómez-Baeza, adding: 'A man can reach the top and still have a family life, but it's much more difficult for women. Despite this, it's happening. The history of women is about to begin!'

How would María Martínez Sierra, with whom I began this chapter, feel about the place of women in Spain today? That great battler for women's rights under the Republic (who died in exile in 1974, almost a hundred years old) would probably be reasonably satisfied with what has been achieved since the collapse of the old order, although I imagine she would have expected more of the Socialists. But she could not deny that Spanish women today are in a stronger position than ever before in their history. Most of the basic legal spadework has been done to put them on an equal footing with men; the battle is on to eliminate the remaining pockets of discrimination; they are more educated and their confidence is running high. For me their progress symbolizes, more than any other achievement of post-Franco Spain, the degree to which this country has changed for the better.

− 7 −

Wild Spain: Conservation versus Development

For anyone who loves scenery, flowers, sun, birds, sky, animals and walking (in short, the outdoor life), Spain is a truly marvellous country, a naturalist's and hiker's paradise replete with variety, interest and surprises. A hundred brown bears still roam in the isolated uplands of Asturias, although their future is threatened by illegal hunting; there are wolves in the forests of Galicia; by night lynxes prowl in some central and southern parts of the country; in the highest mountains you may be lucky enough to catch a glimpse of the Iberian ibex, now less rare than it used to be. For the botanist, Spain harbours hundreds of endemic flowers and plants, as well as thousands of species not often found elsewhere, including, on the high slopes of the Sierra Nevada in Andalusia, the Alpine gentian. For the ornithologist the country unfolds a dazzling array of bird life. Around the Gallocanta lake in Aragón, for instance, gathers Europe's largest wintering population of common cranes. On another lake, this time near Málaga, nest 3,000 pairs of flamingos. The Coto Doñana, south of Seville, is one of the world's great wildfowl sanctuaries, while Spain as a whole qualifies as Europe's birds of prey reserve, thanks to its predominantly mountainous configuration. In the Pyrenees the lammergeyer, or bearded vulture, almost extinct, can still be seen dropping bones onto rocks from a great height in order to get at their mar-row, while more common species of vulture abound among the country's crags and precipitous cliffs, as do many different sorts of eagle, falcon and hawk. Who would believe that, only ten miles from the heart of Madrid, imperial eagles circle slowly above the oak groves?

Spain now has ten National Parks covering more than 300,000 acres: one each in the Pyrenees (Ordesa), the mountains of the Cantabrian Range (Covadonga), Catalonia (Aigües Tortes), New Castile (the Tablas de Daimiel wetlands), Andalusia (the Coto Doñana) and the Balearic Islands (Cabrera), and no less than four in the Canaries. All more than repay a visit. The National Parks are managed by the central government (Ministry of Agriculture) and should not be confused with the *Natural* Parks, administered by the seventeen autonomous regions. At the moment there are some 200 Natural Parks in Spain (sometimes called by other names), and plans exist to open many more. Then, there are thousands of hunting preserves where many species are protected, while various Royal Demesnes, such as El Pardo near Madrid, afford cover to innumerable birds and animals. No country in Europe can boast such natural riches.

The term 'Wild Spain', appropriated in the heading of this chapter, is the title of a book published in 1893 by the naturalist Abel Chapman and his friend Walter J. Buck, British consul in Jeréz de la Frontera, mentioned briefly in the first chapter. In their preface the authors explained that, while many works were currently available in English on the history, antiquities and architecture of Spain, hardly anything had yet been published to interest the 'sportsman-naturalist'. It was this gap that they had set out to fill, drawing on their more than twenty years' experience of shooting and bird-watching up and down the country.

Chapman and Buck made the point that no part of Europe had been so largely abandoned to 'nature in wildest primeval garb, untouched by man, untamed and glorious in its pristine savagery'. Such abandon they ascribed not only to the inaccessible, mountainous character of most of the country but also to a 'certain sense of insecurity and a hatred of rural life inherent in the Spanish breast'.

That last statement needs some qualification. In the mountains and bleak plains of Castile or Aragón, where human survival has until recently been a terrible struggle, you would not expect to find people enthusing about birds or flowers. One will look in vain for detailed descriptions of the Castilian tableland in *Don Quixote*. This is not because Cervantes had a biological aversion to nature, however, but because the endless wastes through which the Knight of the Doleful Countenance wanders in search of adventures offer very little 'country-side' in the English sense of the term. Other regions of Spain are much more benign than the Meseta (the lush lowlands of Murcia and Valencia, for example), and here people feel themselves closer to the earth. It is not true, in other words, that *all* Spaniards have the 'inher-ent' hatred of rural life to which Chapman and Buck allude.

That in most of Spain there has traditionally been considerable indifference to nature is, however, undeniable. The Franco regime was notorious for its lack of environmental sensitivity. The notion that you could build where you pleased and do what you wanted so pervaded the consciousness of businessmen and speculators that most of the coastline was ravaged as the tourist boom escalated in the 1960s. The rivers suffered too, and many other ecological outrages were committed.

Since the dictator's death in 1975 environmental awareness has grown apace, especially as a result of EEC entry in 1986, and today there are many conservationist associations up and down the country. Tremendous battles are being fought between environmentalists and developers, and these receive wide coverage in the newspapers. Here again Spain is changing.

Of these conflicts, the bitterest by far concerns Spain's most inter-nationally famous National Park, the breath-taking Coto Doñana.

While Chapman and Buck had ranged widely in their Spanish expedi-tions (trout-fishing in the glens of Asturias, ibex-stalking in the Gredos Mountains, not far from Madrid, fowling in Valencia's Albufera, great bustard shooting in the plains of Andalusia), they were at their happiest in the Coto Doñana, situated at the mouth of the River Guadalquivir, south of Seville. In *Wild Spain* and a later work, *Unexplored Spain* (1910), they provided a detailed account of the astonishingly varied natural life of this vast tract, 80,000 acres in area, which, fringed along the Atlantic shore by a wide barrier of sand-dunes, is believed to cover the silted-over remains of the ancient city of Tartessos (in Hebrew, Tarshish), whose fabulous wealth is men-tioned in the Bible.

The Coto Doñana takes its name from Doña Ana de Silva y Mendoza, daughter of the notorious Princess of Eboli and wife of the Duke of Medina Sidonia, admiral of Philip II's failed Armada in 1588. The dukes of Medina Sidonia were owners of the estate for almost five hundred years. It became a National Park in 1969. That it did so was due mainly to the efforts of the Spanish naturalist José Antonio Valverde, aided and abetted by a group of European ornithologists led by Guy Mountfort, co-author of the famous *Field Guide to the Birds of Great Britain and Europe*. When Mountfort read Chapman's *Wild Spain* in the 1930s he dreamt of seeing the Coto one day for himself. He did so in 1952, recording his experience of that and two later expeditions in his *Portrait of a Wilderness* (1958), profusely illustrated by nature photographer Eric Hosking. The book brought the wonders of Doñana to the attention of a new generation of British readers, and provided strong arguments for its preservation. Today it is recognized as one of the most important National Parks in the world, and has been classified by UNESCO as a 'Biosphere Reserve'.

A few statistics will give an idea of Doñana's uniqueness. The wintering birds that throng the *marismas*, or marshes, include, in round figures, 80,000 greylag geese (which arrive here each autumn from their breeding grounds in the far north of Europe – not all greylags make for the Severn!), 170,000 teal, 120,000 widgeon, 80,000 shovellers, 20,000 pintails, 40,000 coots and 40,000 black-tailed godwits. The habitual breeding population includes gadwall, whiskered terns, pochard, black-winged stilts, avocets and purple gallinules (some 1,500 pairs). Several extremely rare species in danger of extinction also breed in Doñana: the marbled teal, the bittern, the black tern, the crested coot, and, above all, the imperial eagle of which, as I write, there are at least ten breeding couples out of a total Spanish population of between 120 and 150 pairs.

If we turn to animal life, Doñana's rarest and shyest denizen is the Spanish lynx, of which there are some fifty individuals (perhaps a fifth of all those in the country). The park also has many deer, rabbits and an engaging furry mammal belonging to the mongoose family and going by the name of ichneumon (in Spanish, 'meloncillo').

One of the most moving wildlife spectacles in Europe is the morning flight of Doñana's greylag geese, which wing up in their thousands from the marshes at dawn to eat sand on the highest point of the dunes that border the reserve along the sea. (They feed on sedge and need to swallow sand to make the digestion of this tuber easier.) A hundred years ago Chapman beheld the ancestors of today's greylags flying in 'serried ranks' to the dunes at first light. As I crouched one freezing January morning waiting for the geese to arrive, that phrase, and that vision, came back to me from my schooldays.

Doñana's survival is a fine achievement, but its future is not yet assured. Since the Park's inception in 1969 it has continued to be threatened by a mixed bag of property dealers, rice-growers, practitioners of intensive under-plastic horticulture, and holiday-makers. The latter, some 300,000 of them, are attracted each summer to the tourist resort of Matalascañas, built on the very edge of the sanctuary, with its splendid Atlantic beach. It was begun, almost without planning permission, under Franco – and has gone on expanding ever since.

Among Doñana's many other problems is the number of different bodies involved in the area's management, which occasions administrative chaos. Spain's National Parks are run by the central government, and more precisely by ICONA, the Institute for the Conservation of Nature, a department of the Ministry of Agriculture inherited from the Franco regime. Under the latter ICONA elaborated a disastrous reafforestation policy, replacing indigenous species such as the ilex with pines and eucalyptus. As a result, it earned for itself the nickname of Institute for the *Destruction* of Nature.

Nowadays, while some conservationists still do not trust it, ICONA is more enlightened. But if it controls the Doñana National Park proper (minus the Biological Reserve, run by Madrid's Higher Institute for Scientific Research), the 'Pre-Park', or surrounding protected area, which has the status of a Natural (not National) Park and is essential to Doñana's survival, is the responsibility of the Environment Department of the Andalusian government. Here already is a potential source of conflict between the central and regional authorities. Then, the Andalusian Institute for Agrarian Reform is the body responsible for monitoring the agricultural development of the neighbouring area (where the widespread use of herbicides, fertilizers and pesticides among rice and strawberry growers is affecting several of the surface water inputs to the Park). As regards the water supply, the most vexed question of all, we find involvement by the Guadalquivir Basin Authority, the Spanish Mining and Geological Institute (responsible for the groundwater in the Park) and the Almonte Town Council. The latter controls the provision of water to Matalascañas, which is pumped in its entirety from beneath the adjoining sand-dunes. Between all these uncoordinated groups there is bound to be friction.

In 1989 Doñana became the centre of an international debate with the announcement of an ambitious private project, widely advertised in Europe, to build a new luxury tourist complex, cunningly baptized 'Costa Doñana', just beyond Matalascañas, with beds for 30,000 people. The fact that Prime Minister Felipe González likes to spend his summer holidays in the old palace of Doñana (HQ of the Biological Reserve) was by this time well known in Europe, and added subliminal publicity to the project, as did an utterly unauthorized reference by the promoters to the approval of King Juan Carlos himself.

The launching of the 'Costa Doñana' scheme coincided with the publication, in May 1989, of a report by the World Wildlife Fund in which it was stated that any further pressure, for irrigation and tourist purposes, on the Almonte-Marismas aquifer underlying the Park could seriously threaten Doñana's survival. The document also pointed out that there was a very real danger that heavy pumping would eventually cause salt water intrusion into the wells surrounding the Park, and perhaps even into the sanctuary itself. The construction of 'Costa Doñana', the WWF experts felt sure, would exacerbate all these problems.

Spanish and European ecologists and environmentalists (among them British naturalist and TV personality David Bellamy) decided to fight 'Costa Doñana' to the death. It has proved a bitter struggle, not least because the projected development was aggressively supported by Rafael Díaz, until June 1991 Socialist mayor of Almonte, the town within whose municipal area the Park falls. When, in March 1990, some 10,000 ecologically-minded people from throughout Spain, myself included, arrived to take part in a protest march against 'Costa Doñana', this man claimed that our travel expenses had been paid by rival tourist resorts intent on discrediting Matalascañas!

The mayor of Almonte was not the only Socialist in favour of the new development. So too were certain members of the Andalusian government in Seville. And neither Felipe González nor his then

112

deputy prime minister, Alfonso Guerra (at the time chairman of the Board of the Doñana National Park), made any statement condemning the project. Luckily the protests reached such magnitude, with strong pressure brought to bear by the European Commissioner for the Environment, Carlo Ripa di Meana, that the Andalusian government delayed granting the necessary planning permission. Meanwhile the would-be developers changed the name 'Costa Doñana' to 'Dunas de Almonte', equally offensive to conservationists because the dunes in question, on which it is planned to build the new tourist complex, have some unique features and stand on one of the last stretches of virgin coast left in Spain.

In the autumn of 1990 elections were held in Andalusia. The Socialists won again. Manuel Chaves, the new head of the regional government and a former Felipe González minister, had been prudent during the campaign in his references to the 'Dunas de Almonte' project, promising that he would reconsider the matter 'from scratch'.

In March 1991 Chaves announced that the central and Andalusian governments had set up an eight-member 'commission of experts' to evaluate the development. Conservationists were incensed to discover that the chairman of the commission was Manuel Castells, a Seville sociology professor and member of the federal committee of the Socialist Party, who in 1988 had called the 'Costa Doñana' development 'one of Andalusia's most attractive tourist projects'. His appointment was obviously political, conservationists claimed, and so too was that of several other members of the group, which comprised two ecologists, a geographer, two economists, a hydro-geologist and an expert on regional development. The latter and one of the ecologists had been nominated by the EC.

Unperturbed by these criticisms, Chaves insisted that the committee would not be subject to political pressures, and that it had the full support of the European Commission. No time limit had been set for the completion of the team's report, and to date it has still not been made public.

Given the many vested interests involved in Doñana, the tangle of responsibilities, the constant threat represented by the speculators, poachers, farmers and horticulturists and the drain on the Park's water resources, no one can yet be too sanguine about the survival of Spain's Camargue. It does seem, however, that the increasing attention being paid to the Doñana issue by the EC, whose Environment Commission recently visited the Park, may help to tip the balance. If so, one of the world's greatest nature reserves may yet be saved for humanity.

The situation in Doñana reflects that pertaining throughout a country torn between all-out development and conservation. Much of the Wild Spain that Chapman and Buck loved has survived to our own times. But that survival is now threatened, not least because recent legislation is not being respected.

The 1978 Constitution showed great sensitivity to the issue of conservation, and, between the lines, a sensibly pragmatic awareness that, once Spain joined the EEC, the country would be required to adapt its environment legislation to Europe's. The first two paragraphs of article 45 read:

> 1. Everyone has a right to an environment suitable for the development of individual potential, and a duty to protect it.

> 2. The authorities will implement the rational use of the country's natural resources in order to protect and improve the standard of living and defend and restore the environment, counting for this on the indispensable support of society.

The final paragraph of the article provided for the enactment of legislation penalizing the infringement of these environmental norms. This was not introduced into the Penal Code until 1983, by the Socialists, who had promised during the election campaign that catapulted them to office the previous year that they would bring in a comprehensive Environment Act. They never did, and in practice their position on conservation issues has been ambiguous. The 1983 addition to the Penal Code proved utterly inadequate. The only infractions envisaged concerned industrial waste and pollution, which ignored perhaps 95 per cent of everyday environmental damage. The heaviest fine that could be imposed was a million pesetas (about £5,000), the longest period of imprisonment six months. Spanish conservationists have been insisting since then that the article needs to be extended to cover a far wider range of ecological offences.

Within a year of the Socialists' accession to power, conservationists were already seriously alarmed. Responsibility for the environment (with the exception of the National Parks) had been transferred to the seventeen autonomous regions, and most of these had as yet no bodies capable of even beginning to deal adequately with ecological matters.

Meanwhile, negotiations were going ahead for EEC entry. They took longer than expected, but on 1 January 1986 Spain became a full member of the Community. From this moment the country was subject to European rulings on conservation. In June the government began to introduce the Community's 'environmental impact' legislation, which, however, did not become law until the autumn of 1988 – until, that is, the huge road and infrastructure upheavals called for by the Seville 1992 World Fair were well under way.

On 27 March 1989 a new Law for the Preservation of Natural Spaces and Wild Flowers and Animals was promulgated in implementation of article 45 of the 1978 Constitution, quoted on the previous page. It seemed to conservationists that the Law's elaboration had taken an excessively long time – a decade! – but it was an ambitious document in a country where, until recently, interest in nature has been negligible.

'This looks wonderful on paper,' I thought as I first perused the text, 'but how will it ever work out in practice?' For example, the Act stated that the 'administrations' would undertake to make conservation part of the educational system, so that children would grow up with a love and understanding of nature. Would the authorities *really* get down to this essential task? And would it ever be possible for the seventeen autonomous communities to plan a co-ordinated approach to the multiple problems affecting the environment? It was one thing to pass enlightened legislation, brimful of good intentions, but quite another to put it into effect.

As regards encouraging the young to respect nature, there has been progress since then: the new Education Act (1990) laid down explicitly that, from 1992 onwards, children beginning their primary schooling were to be taught environmental awareness.

A key provision of the Law for the Preservation of Natural Spaces was the establishment of a Plan for the Ordering of Natural Resources, according to which the authorities of each regional community would have to draw up a report on the state of the resources and eco-systems in the area of its responsibility, and then decide what should be done by way of protection and improvement. Under the Plan, each administration would also be expected to decide which development projects in its area (building, tourist resorts, agricultural innovations, etc.) should be subject to the recently introduced 'environmental impact' legislation. If the Plan could be made to work, there might still be time to save much of Wild Spain from destruction: it would no longer be a question simply of caring adequately for the National Parks and other protected areas, but of thinking of Spain, globally, as a territory in which the interests of Nature and Man should be reconciled.

The Spaniards have a proverb corresponding to Britain's 'There's many a slip 'twixt cup and lip.' It runs: 'Entre dicho y hecho, buen trecho' – 'Between saying and doing, there's a good distance.' And so it has proved in this case. The Plan for the Ordering of Natural Resources remains largely a chimera.

Spain today is one of the few countries in the European Community that does not have a full Ministry of the Environment. Even more anomalous, the secretary general for the Environment is directly responsible to, of all bodies, the Ministry of Public Works and Town Planning (since the Cabinet reshuffle of March 1991, Ministry of Public Works and Transport). The conflict of interests can be imagined. When, early in 1990, the Secretariat for the Environment replaced the earlier State Office for the Environment, Cristina García-Orcoyen, head of the Spanish branch of the World Wildlife Fund, confessed her 'astonishment and surprise' at a decision that implied a minor upgrading on paper (presumably to impress the Europeans) but none in practice. It was easy to understand her dismay. The Spanish minister of Public Works, mainly concerned with building motorways and dams, sitting down in Brussels to discuss his country's conservation issues with Europe's ministers of the Environment!

'Spain has the richest natural heritage in western Europe and the great challenge is to preserve it,' Cristina García-Orcoyen said. She now feared greatly for such preservation. Moreover, she insisted, Spain particularly needed a Ministry of the Environment in view of the division of the country into autonomous regions, each with responsibility for its own conservation, an arrangement that impaired co-ordination and wasted resources.

Why had the government decided not to create a Ministry of the Environment? To conservationists the answer was obvious: Felipe González, hell-bent on material progress, believed that such a body, with power to meddle in the projects of other ministries (particularly Industry, Economy, Public Works and Agriculture), might be disastrous for his plans to turn Spain into a leading industrial power. In May 1990 a Ministry of Economy spokesman put the matter very frankly: no European country had shown much interest in the environment while undergoing intense development, and Spain could simply not afford to act differently now that it was in the EC and up against stiff competition; unless Europe provided more finance, conservation must remain a secondary concern; nonetheless, the spokesman went on, every effort was being made to introduce adequate legislation.

Notwithstanding the obvious lack of precedence given in Spain to environmental matters, the government was pressing at this time for the establishment in Madrid of the EC's European Environment Agency. This seems to conservationists a gross example of what Spaniards call *caradura*, or 'brazenfacedness', both in view of the government's refusal to set up a Ministry of the Environment and, even more important, because Javier Sáenz de Cosculluela, the then minister of Public Works, had been consistently vetoing the EC's proposed Directive on the Protection of Natural Habitats ever since 1988, using the argument that its implementation would cost far too much.

This Directive, if it were to become law, would radically improve the chances for survival of Wild Spain by the creation of hundreds of Special Protection Areas, under EC supervision, for birds, animals and plant life. As this book goes to press the good news is that the new minister of Public Works, Josep Borrell, has formally dropped Spain's opposition to the project after receiving guarantees from Carlo Ripa di Meana, the Community's Environment Commissioner, that Brussels will make adequate finance available to help set up and run the Special Protection Areas in Spain.

As a result of this momentous decision it seems that there is now the possibility that Madrid may after all be chosen as seat of the European Environment Agency. Such a hope had received a further setback when the European Department for the Environment published a report in February 1990 stating that Spain was the least adapted of all the member countries to EC legislation on conservation. The allegation was hotly contested, naturally, by the Ministry of Public Works, but the Europeans were not convinced, and the decision about the siting of the Agency (for which Copenhagen is another candidate) had been deferred. Were Madrid now to receive the Agency nothing but benefits could accrue: the Europeans would be closer to Spain's very real conservation problems, and therefore more able to help; and the Spanish ecological movement would feel itself stimulated to greater efforts and acquire a deeper understanding of environmental issues in the rest of Europe.

Europe: it's an obsession in a Spain intent on 'modernization', whatever the ecological consequences. By the time this book appears the 300 miles of Spain's first high-speed railway line will have been constructed at astronomic expense between Madrid and Seville, and tests will be taking place to ensure that the service is ready for Expo 92. The train is just one more consequence of the determination to prove to the world that, as we near the year 2000, Spain is in the top league of technologically advanced nations.

Work began on this, modern Spain's most ambitious engineering undertaking, in October 1987, nine months before the new 'environmental impact' legislation came into force. As a result, massive destruction of the landscape was effected with little concern for the ecological consequences. It is widely felt that the legislation in question was delayed precisely in order to avoid infringing the EC rules. After June 1988, 'environmental impact' reports had to be obtained before the work continued, but doubt has been cast on their objectivity.

The authorities racked their brains for months in search of a name which would not merely echo that of the French version, the TGV (Train de Grande Vitesse). Opinion polls showed that Spaniards identify the high-speed train with self-assertion, masculinity, competitiveness and other similar qualities. In order to soften such an aggressive image it was decided to devise a 'poetic' name. Finally the experts came up with the word AVE, which means 'bird', the initials standing at the same time for Alta Velocidad Española, Spanish High Speed. The idea was to suggest speed, yes, but also grace and . . . silence! To

118

ecologically concerned Spaniards, incensed at the grave damage to natural habitats (including ornithological ones) occasioned by the project, it came as a blatantly cynical gesture.

Conservationists believe that the damage has been irreparable in several areas through which the new tracks pass. More than 75 million cubic metres of earth were moved during the excavations, and huge slices of rich arable land lie stifled under the mountains of rock and other dead material extracted from the tunnels. At Getafe, just south of Madrid, a mile of the fertile valley of the River Manzanares has been ravaged, and the province's most outstanding Neolithic remains were obliterated after a makeshift investigation. Further south, the din and disruption caused as the machines hacked their way through the Hills of Toledo devastated one of the most important lynx territories in Europe.

The worst devastation, however, has taken place in the Sierra Morena, south of La Mancha, where giant 45-foot oaks, some of them 200 years old, have been destroyed, thousands of other trees cut down and whole hillsides defaced. The line cuts in two the Alcudia Valley, between Ciudad Real and Badajoz, and important colonies of deer, eagles (golden and imperial) and black vultures have been disturbed. The town of Brazatortas and its surroundings have suffered a cataclysmic upheaval.

Only in January 1990 was there an official announcement about the way the environmental damage caused by the AVE was to be 'made good'. Acoustic screens, underpasses for the animals, reafforestation . . . the huge sums about to become available for this meritorious work of 'restoration' would soon put everything right. Few people were convinced.

A few months earlier conservationists had organized a gathering in Brazatortas to coincide with the delivery of a document of protest to the European Commission in Brussels. In this they demanded that the EC Regional Development Fund, which had provided 40 per cent of the cost of the AVE's infrastructure, should now ask for its money back. The project was injuring the landscape cruelly. Had the bureaucrats in Brussels forgotten that the Fund should only correctly be allocated to finance regional projects that provided explicit environmental guarantees?

The conservationists raised many other objections to the AVE.

They pointed out, for example, that, while the train was bound to make money during Expo 92, there was no certainty that it would do so afterwards. Experience in other countries had shown that the high-speed train is only viable when there is a great deal of traffic, as in Japan or on the Paris-Lyon Line. There were no grounds for thinking that this would ever be the case between Seville and Madrid. A far better argument might be put, if there had to be an AVE, for a line connecting Madrid to Barcelona and the French border.

The conservationists maintained, moreover, that if the existing railway lines were improved, Spain's own advanced train, the popular Talgo, would be able to reach speeds of up to 220 kilometres an hour, only slightly slower than the AVE. Why not forget all about the high-speed train, built with foreign technology, and improve the home product? Moreover the government had decided that the AVE was to run on European-gauge lines, not Spain's wider ones (designed to lessen the possibility of foreign invasion by rail!), thereby ensuring that the country's conventional rolling stock would never be able to use them. Might this not turn out to be very short-sighted?

Bluntly, was it justifiable to get people to Seville a bit faster at the price of defacing the countryside and doing untold harm to wild life?

Where the Madrid–Seville line was concerned, nothing could now be done. But the conservationists calculated that, as a result of their protests, and given the growing public awareness of 'green' issues, the government would have to think very hard indeed before embarking on a prolongation of the AVE, especially at a time when Great Britain, Italy and Japan have decided not to go ahead with further high-speed train plans, but to improve their existing lines. If the AVE is to be extended from Madrid to Barcelona or the north, as the Socialists intend, 'environmental impact' reports will be required along all the length of the lines, and conservationists, European and Spanish, will be watching every yard. A protracted battle, as in the case of the 'Costa Doñana' project, can be confidently predicted.

Such a battle has been raging over the last few years in Anchuras, a village that, before 1988, was almost totally unknown even in Spain. Some 100 miles south-west of Madrid among the Hills of Toledo lies Cabañeros, a vast, 62,000-acre estate declared a Natural Park in 1988 by the government of Castile-La Mancha. In private hands since the

Middle Ages, Cabañeros was used mainly for hunting over the centuries. It has been called 'the Spanish Serengeti'.

Cabañeros only became a Natural Park by the skin of its teeth. In October 1981 it transpired that the Ministry of Defence was thinking of acquiring the estate in order to turn it into a target practice range for the bombers and fighter planes of the Spanish air force. The government headed by Leopoldo Calvo Sotelo, successor to Adolfo Suárez, was just about to hurry Spain into NATO, and rumour had it that the range would be made available to Spain's new allies.

A Socialist spokesman attacked the project in the Senate, pointing out that the estate had unique ecological value. When the Spanish Workers' Socialist Party attained power in October 1982, however, the new government decided to press on, and such objections were hastily forgotten. The journalists did not forget, though. Numerous articles appeared on the natural riches of the site, and by mid-1983 public opposition to the practice range was growing.

Certainly there could be no doubt that Cabañeros mattered. It boasted thousands of acres of splendidly preserved Mediterranean maquis, an immense tract of savannah and, nesting in its thickly wooded valleys, more than a hundred pairs of black vultures – the world's second largest colony (the biggest is not far away in Extremadura's Montfragüe Natural Park). Other species included Spanish lynx, jennet, mongoose, the very rare black stork, white stork, imperial and golden eagle, eagle owl and little bustard. The place positively teemed with deer. To use it for target practice, with supersonic aircraft and exploding bombs, would be a major ecological crime.

Numerous foreign naturalists, alerted by their Spanish colleagues, were soon assailing both Felipe González and King Juan Carlos with letters of protest. Michel Terrasse, a world authority on birds of prey, informed the prime minister that he considered Cabañeros 'one of the richest eco-systems in Europe'. How could the Spanish government possibly think of using it for *bombing practice?*

It was also pointed out that Cabañeros would be extremely hazardous to pilots on account of its black vulture colony. When scanning the countryside for carrion these giant birds circle high into the sky on upward thermals in groups of thirty or more. A plane colliding with one of them, or sucking a bird into its engines, could crash with fatal consequences, as had already been demonstrated at the Las

121

Bardenas practice range in Navarre. To make Cabañeros really safe for pilots, the black vultures would have to be destroyed. And that was unthinkable.

By now the Ministry of Defence must have been waking up to the fact that, along with the black vultures, it had inherited a white elephant from its predecessors in government. But it maintained a tight-lipped silence, declaring the matter a 'military secret'. Only in October 1987 did the ministry admit officially that it had bought two thirds of the estate.

In 1988 José Bono, the Socialist candidate to the presidency of the autonomous government of Castile-La Mancha, within whose territory the estate falls, promised that, if elected, he would press for the declaration of Cabañeros as a Natural Park. Clearly this was an electoral ploy agreed with a Cabinet now resigned to the fact that, given public opinion at home and abroad, it had no option but to climb down over Cabañeros. The Socialists were successful at the polls and, on 11 July 1988, Cabañeros became a Natural Park.

A jubilant José Bono announced immediately that the bombing range would probably be located somewhere else in the vicinity. He already knew where. Only nine days later, on 20 July, the inhabitants of Anchuras, an isolated town of 517 inhabitants situated a mere thirteen miles from Cabañeros, were horrified to learn that the government had decided to re-site the range virtually on their doorstep.

The government declared that the area had 'no ecological value', which, on the face of it, seemed impossible in view of the fact that it belongs to the same eco-system as Cabañeros. Moreover, despite the fact that the European 'environmental impact' legislation had just come into force in Spain, no report on the ecological consequences of siting the range in Anchuras had been requested by the Ministry of Defence, which later sought to justify this omission by pointing out that for national defence projects such reports are not mandatory.

A six-page document had been hastily prepared for José Bono, however. The main author was his friend Manuel Peinado, a plant ecology researcher in the Biology Department of Alcalá de Henares University. A shoddy affair for which the university quickly disclaimed all official responsibility, the document set out to demonstrate, on the basis of aerial photographs, that Anchuras was indeed ecologically unimportant. This finding was completely discredited

122

two months later in a detailed report on Anchuras drawn up by the joint Ecology Department of Madrid's Complutense and Autonomous Universities, which demonstrated that the surroundings of Anchuras were rich in plant and animal life.

Moreover, the conservationists insisted, it was not just a question of Anchuras itself but of the disruption that would be caused by the manoeuvring of supersonic aircraft to the whole area – an area affording cover to protected species, some in danger of extinction, and with hundreds of thousands of migrating birds passing through annually, including great flocks of cranes. It was also pointed out that vultures and other large birds of prey from the surrounding countryside fly over Anchuras frequently (a pair of golden eagles, which I myself have seen, breeds in the vicinity).

The target range was to be situated only a mile from the town. Such proximity would not only guarantee a tremendous deterioration in the standard of living of the inhabitants, but would spell constant danger. Nor was this all. Less than fifteen miles away stood the nuclear power station of Valdecaballeros. Work on it stopped when the Socialist government imposed a nuclear moratorium in 1983, but might soon be renewed (in the event, the government decided in 1991 to extend the moratorium for a further ten years). To think of siting the practice range so close to Valdecaballeros was utterly irresponsible. Then there was the risk that a stray bomb might fracture the huge Cijara dam six miles south of Anchuras. If this happened there could be a terrible disaster; the released flood waters might reach as far as Portugal.

The argument grew more bitter when, two months after the government's statement that Anchuras had 'no ecological value', the State Office for the Environment produced a report making some specific recommendations for the preservation of the area's wildlife once the range was installed. One suggestion was that there should be no practice flights during the migration of cranes in autumn and spring. The government's own experts were now admitting, in effect, that Anchuras had ecological importance after all.

At this time the then minister of Defence, Narcís Serra, explained in the Senate that bombing ranges are 'privileged spots for the preservation of eco-systems' because they are never tramped over by human beings. Moreover, he added, only blank ammunition and bombs are used. This was to miss the point completely. What about the crash of the explosions, the deafening noise of the big jets coming in low? How could birds and animals be expected to survive in such an environment? And what about the damage to the hearing and way of life of men, women and children? (Human beings can adapt to living with consistent noise – the relentless drone, say, of a motorway – but this would have been different, the sudden roar of aircraft and the crash of the detonations coming at any moment between 5 a.m. and 5 p.m.)

Led by their twenty-five-year-old mayor, Santiago Martín, who, as befits a man of La Mancha, looks like a younger version of Don Quixote, the inhabitants of Anchuras decided to fight the Ministry of Defence. The sixty-seven local landowners told reporters that they would refuse to sell their land to the government at any price. They would have to be expropriated.

In October 1988 an appeal against the government's decision was lodged with the Spanish Supreme Court by the Anchuras town council. The Court immediately requested from the government a copy of the dossier on which its decision had been based. The government refused to comply, alleging that the matter was 'a military secret'.

Meanwhile the European Commission, after receiving a detailed complaint from the Spanish branch of the Friends of the Earth, decided to look into the situation at Anchuras.

The Ministry of Defence now sought to buy off the owners of estates in and around Anchuras by offering to exchange them for land held by the Ministry elsewhere, in the generous ratio of roughly three acres for one. The land they offered was in Cabañeros National Park, of all places, and complaints went to Brussels about the legality of such transactions. The largest of these estates, 'El Rosalejo', lay inside the town boundaries of Anchuras, and the whole town turned out to keep military surveyors away from the place. Outside the estate of 'El Cijaral' protesting townspeople were brutally attacked by a contingent of Civil Guard riot police in August 1989. An outcry ensued, and the military left the area. They have never returned. Later the *anchureños* formed a co-operative society to till 'El Rosalejo'. There was no intervention by the police.

Anchuras's young parish priest, Rafael Galán, is one of the most outspoken opponents of the bombing range, and proud that his bishop is, too. 'It's an odd position to find oneself in,' he told me over a glass of beer. 'The Socialists say, "Look, in Anchuras all the opposition to the bombing range is right-wing and Catholic, with the parish priest, the Partido Popular town councillors and even the Bishop of Ciudad Rodrigo against us. It's an anti-Socialist conspiracy." I say it's an odd position for me to be in because, quite frankly, I consider myself more left-wing than they are.'

And there the matter rests for the moment. The environmentalists who fought to save Cabañeros, and now, following in their footsteps, the people of Anchuras, are giving a lesson in peaceful 'green' protest to the whole of Spain. They have shown up the ignorance and duplicity of the Socialists in matters of nature conservation. They have demonstrated what can be achieved when people stick together. Whatever the final outcome of their resistance to the power of the Ministry of Defence (and they seem likely to win) things can never be quite the same again in this country where, until recently, organized group protest has been the exception rather than the rule.

Respect for animals is also scarce, and Spain is the only EC country that has not yet introduced specific national legislation against cruelty to animals. Catalonia, however, has recently become the first autonomous region to do so. This comes as no surprise, because the Catalans are probably the State's most ecologically-minded community. It is no coincidence, either, that Catalonia is the region most opposed to bullfighting, which many Catalans consider a barbarous 'Spanish' practice. While Tossa de Mar on the Costa Brava has closed down its bullring, in 1990 a polemic raged in the correspondence column of *La Vanguardia*, Barcelona's leading newspaper, over the mayor of Figueres's determination to *reopen* his.

Bullfighting apart, around the country there are many barbarous fiestas involving outright cruelty to animals. When any attempt is made to interfere with these the locals always furiously defend their 'rights', adducing the usual arguments about protecting the 'traditional way of life of the people'. With increasing EC pressure, and as the number of Spanish conservationists grows, such customs are bound to die away gradually.

As regards the butchery of Spain's wild creatures, the figures are horrific: 200,000 are poisoned each year, vicious illegal traps are still used for catching wolves and rabbits, and no less than 22 million animals are killed by hunters and poachers in a country where the rule has always been that, if it moves, you shoot it.

Then there is the annual slaughter of protected migrant birds. According to the Spanish Ornithological Society, 400 million of these arrive in Spain each autumn from Europe on their way to winter quarters in Africa. At least 20 million never reach their final destination. They belong to the 64 million small birds trapped illegally in Spain each year. In 1988 it was estimated that 250,000 people were involved in this trade. Most of the birds caught are munched as diminutive *tapas*, called *pajaritos fritos* ('little fried birds'), in bars. Many are exported to France and turned into *pâté d'alouette* (only a small proportion of which, despite its label, is made from skylarks). The rest end their days in cages, and each Sunday morning you will see wild songbirds being sold openly but against the law in the Rastro, Madrid's famous fleamarket. The authorities have not dared to intervene forcibly to put an end to a practice sanctioned by custom, and the situation is further complicated by the fact that the seventeen autonomous regions have their own conservation rules, or lack of them. Several of the regions, indeed, have been quite explicit in their determination *not* to outlaw the time-hallowed trapping of migrant birds. The reasons are probably mainly electoral: to prohibit the practice would be to court disaster at the polls.

Understandably there is fury in Europe at Spain's massive annual destruction of birds born beyond its frontiers and protected by EC legislation. (Italy, it must be said, is almost as bad a culprit.) Fury not only at the proportions of the holocaust, but at the methods used. Before joining the Common Market Spain had already signed the Berne Convention, by which it committed itself to outlawing the use of traps, snares and nets for the hunting of birds and animals. Yet today these methods are still almost universal. The feeling in Europe is that, having pressed so tenaciously to join the Community, Spain must now abide by all the rules, including the ecological ones, that bind its members. The Europeans have shown that they understand the problems involved (for example, that the Spanish government cannot force people to change their habits overnight), but they do not believe that the authorities, central and local, are doing all they could to improve the situation.

126

Doubtless they are right. In a country where concern for the environment is a novelty, one would not expect either local or national officials to be particularly sensitive about conservation issues. After all, they were born under the Franco regime – a regime notable for its lack of concern over pollution and the effects of rampant land speculation. But little by little attitudes are changing for the better.

As Spain becomes increasingly environment-conscious, polluting industries will be obliged to take the conservation legislation much more to heart. For the moment there is little indication that they are doing so. When the National Plan for the Control of Industrial Waste was drawn up in 1990, for example, the 250,000 industries on the Ministry of Industry's files were invited to supply details of their effluent. Co-operation was minimal, and the ministry received very few replies.

According to José Joaquín Pérez de Gregorio, one of Spain's first prosecutors specializing in ecological infringements, at the end of 1990 the country was still disregarding the majority of the EC's rulings on the environment. Pérez had recently been involved in the only 'green' issue fought in court since the introduction of the 'environmental infraction' legislation of 1983. The case concerned the coal-fired thermal power station at Cercs, in Catalonia, which had been emitting illegal quantities of sulphur dioxide and poisoning vegetation for miles around. The prosecution won the case and the Supreme Court stiffened both the prison sentence meted out to the plant's director and the fine. A vital precedent had been set.

If industrial pollution is one of Spain's great challenges, so too is sewage disposal. Spain lags far behind the other industrialized countries in this respect. According to a detailed report published in February 1991 by the Organization for Economic Co-operation and Development, it was treating only 45 per cent of its sewage. When the report appeared a Spanish official commented: 'In Spain we have very little water, we waste it and, moreover, we don't clean it.' Over the next decade, with EC assistance, a great improvement in this situation can be expected.

The Spanish Civil Guard is traditionally feared by the populace at large. An indication of how Spain's attitude to conservation is changing can be found in the fact that, since 1988, the force has had a special, 1,000-member 'green' arm, known as the Civil Guard's

Nature Protection Service. These men have proved particularly effective in the surveillance of the nesting cliffs of Spain's rarer birds of prey – eagles, vultures and falcons. Several spectacular arrests have been made, both of egg collectors and of those intent on stealing the chicks of the peregrine falcon, a species much prized by Arab falconers.

Things are improving on the conservation front. Lead-free petrol is available at more and more garages, demand for recycled paper and ecological detergents is slowly growing, the bottle-banks distributed in the towns and cities are catching on, arrangements are being made for the danger-free disposal of used batteries, there is talk of refuse separation... little by little Spaniards, so long cut off from Europe, are beginning to get the 'green message'.

One proof is the more than 700 local conservationist associations and ecological pressure groups up and down the country. On average they have only fifty or so members, but dedication makes up for lack of numbers. At the national level stand the Spanish branches of three powerful international organizations: ADENA (Association for the Defence of Nature), offspring of the World Wildlife Fund, Greenpeace and the Friends of the Earth. Each of these has made a vital contribution to the spread of environmental thinking in Spain. A special mention must go, too, to the Spanish Ornithological Society, which has close links with Britain's Royal Society for the Protection of Birds.

Perhaps Spain's greatest ecological success story, however, concerns the Madrid-based body CODA. The initials stand for Coordinadora de Organizaciones de Defensa Ambiental, that is, Federation of Environmental Defence Organizations. Founded in 1978, CODA is a grass-roots movement with 35,000 members belonging to more than ninety associations around the country. Although originally it was exclusively concerned with the protection of birds, the federation is now involved in all aspects of nature conservation. Since 1986 it has fought more than 500 ecological battles and, sometimes with Community backing, has won a high percentage of them; it is a member of the Bureau Européen de l'Environnement, the International Council for Nature Conservation and the International Council for Bird Preservation; its permanent representatives in Brussels keep the organization up to date on the latest developments in EC environmental discussion and legislation; it publishes frequent bulletins; its numerous commissions are competent to examine all aspects of the conservation issues now constantly arising in Spain; sixteen CODA offices are open to the public throughout the country; and whenever new ecological scandals hit the newspapers (as they constantly do) its spokesmen and women are invariably consulted.

One of CODA's most highly publicized campaigns has been against the Ministry of Economy's Plan for the Regions, submitted to the EC in 1989 in the hopes of obtaining 21 per cent of the necessary finance from the EC Regional Development Fund (which has participated in the infrastructure for the Madrid–Seville high-speed train, as we have seen). Environmentalists were convinced that the Plan, ostensibly designed to promote the development of Spain's poorer regions, would in fact impoverish these even further by destroying natural habitats and traditional agriculture. For example, it included four more high-speed-train lines, intensive tourist development along the northern coast (rather than the promotion of 'green' tourism), more motorways, ninety-two new dams, and massive reafforestation with eucalyptus in Andalusia and Galicia. Once again the stress was on economic growth at all costs, and regional cities took precedence over the countryside, which environmentalists felt sure would become increasingly depopulated as a result. With the debate in full swing it emerged that the Ministry of Economy had not consulted any of the leading conservationist organizations in Spain before finalizing the Plan.

CODA's energetic vice-president, Santiago Martín Barajas, co-ordinator of the document with which the federation launched its counter-attack, stated that to implement the Plan would mean 'the destruction of most of the natural wealth of our country'. In Spain, he explained, there are from 8 to 10 million hectares (some 25 million acres) of great natural wealth, where animals and plants that have disappeared from the rest of Europe still survive. These zones should be excluded from the Plan, and their traditional economies encouraged. The natural produce of such areas, if adequately promoted, could be successfully sold in an increasingly conservation-minded Europe; and future tourists would be looking more and more for unspoilt country. To destroy these regions, as much a part of the European as of the Spanish heritage, amounted to sacrilege.

CODA's criticisms of the Plan were taken into account in Europe. In March 1991 the media announced that 30,200 million pesetas

129

(about £151 million) had just been allotted to Spain by the EC Regional Development Fund specifically to help the country with its environmental problems, above all the treatment of sewage nation-wide and of industrial waste in three chosen areas: Huelva, Murcia and Alicante.

The contribution from the Regional Fund was further proof of the advantages of belonging to the European club. It is clear, indeed, that, if Spain had failed to enter the EEC when it did, the environmental situation in the country today would be very much more unsatis-factory than it is.

The fight to save what can be saved, and to restore what has almost been destroyed, is going to call for further huge efforts by conserva-tionists. Given the EC's encouragement and financial assistance, as well as the growing public awareness of the threats to the environ-ment, it is surely not too much to expect that Spanish politicians will now take the ecological message to heart, and act accordingly. If they can be persuaded to do so, much of Chapman and Buck's Wild Spain may be preserved for posterity. But the right decisions will have to be taken at once. *Mañana* will be too late.

– 8 –

The Basque Country

The Basques are a mystery race and their language an enigma. Nobody knows exactly where they came from, nor when. Some authorities maintain that they may well be the direct descendants of Cro-Magnon Man. Thousands of years before the rise of the Roman Empire they were already inhabiting a broad swathe of south-west Europe stretching from the northern coast of Spain to the Garonne.

Today their territory is much reduced. The French 'Pays Basque', with a population of some 230,000 people, is made up of the three frontier districts of Basse Navarre (Benavarra), Soule (Zuberoa) and Labourd (Lapurdi). The Spanish autonomous 'País Vasco' comprises the provinces of Vizcaya, Guipúzcoa and Alava. It is 2,836 square miles in area (almost twice the size of Kent) and has almost 3 million inhabitants, of which only a quarter, approximately, are ethnically of pure Basque origin (because of the potent industry of Vizcaya and Guipúzcoa, there has been massive immigration since the late nineteenth century). Approximately half the population of the Basque Country lives in and around the badly polluted city of Bilbao, capital of Vizcaya.

The neighbouring autonomous community of Navarre, to the east, with an area of 4,070 square miles and just over half a million inhabitants, is considered by Basques the 'mother' or 'cradle' of their stateless nation, and they will remind you that the Romans called the Basque language 'lingua navarrorum', 'the tongue of the Navarrese'. José Lizarrabengoa, the dashing lover of Carmen in Mérimée's short story, is a Basque-speaking *navarro* from the town of Elizondo. 'I am a Basque and an Old Christian,' he explains proudly. Although Navarre's Basque identity has been eroded over the centuries, mainly because its southern reaches in the fertile Ebro valley have good communications with the rest of Spain, the northern part of the region is still partially Basque-speaking. The radical separatists believe that the old kingdom should be 'reincorporated' into a future Basque State along with the 'lost' French provinces.

The Basques refer to their language as *euskera*, to the person who uses it habitually as *euskaldun*, and to their territory as either *Euskal Herria*, the traditional term, or, more frequently, *Euskadi* ('Gathering of Basques'), a word coined at the end of the nineteenth century.

Fundamentally an agricultural and fishing people, the Basques have produced excellent seamen and some famous explorers, among them Lope de Aguirre, who took part in the expedition that set off in 1559 in search of the mythical land of El Dorado, and Sebastián de Elcano, right-hand man of the great Portuguese navigator Magellan.

Fiercely independent, the Basques have always defended their largely mountainous territory (the coastal strip is narrow, as elsewhere in Spain) with relentless tenacity against all comers, beginning with the Romans, who never succeeded in subduing them completely. The Goths found them unmanageable, and the Muslims failed to conquer Vizcaya and Guipúzcoa. Right up to our own times the Basques have resisted every attempt at assimilation. Some etymologists hold that the root 'eusk' (that is, 'Basque') means 'self-sufficiency'. Certainly it would be fitting if it did.

The Basques were never subject to the feudal system, and have always been a people of individual smallholders with a strong democratic instinct. In the subconscious of every Basque, as a symbol of pristine felicity, is the image of the traditional homestead of the valleys, the *baserri* (in Spanish, *caserío*). These small farms are passed on from generation to generation on the principle of male primogeniture and, according to an unwritten law deeply embedded in the minds of the Basques, are inalienable. The *baserris* are the unit of social life, the very nub of the Basque way of being, and existed long before the arrival of villages and towns (the Basques were both the last Europeans to become Christians and the last to have towns). Habitually three or four *baserris* are grouped in close proximity and form a unit called the *auzoa*. The neighbours share certain common tasks, including the maintenance of the *baserris* themselves, in accordance with a time-hallowed code of co-operation known as *auzolan*. By this arrangement each homestead is bound to make available three people for communal work and, if it does not or cannot, must supply food in lieu. Any neighbour failing to comply with the obligations of the system is ostracized.

It seems fair to assume that anyone brought up in such a small and cohesive community will have a strong sense of personal responsibility, property, identity and team spirit. Perhaps it is not surprising that the Basque Country has produced the world's most exciting experiments in the field of industrial co-operatives.

Physically, the Basques have always been taller and burlier on average than other peninsular peoples (the difference is now being reduced as Spaniards grow in height). Alone of all peoples in the Iberian Peninsula, their blood group is predominantly Rhesus negative. They have long, thin, bony heads and high foreheads. The men are famous for their long, straight noses, and the women have a characteristically 'Red Indian' look, with a pointed nose (which tends to get hooked in old age), square shoulders and small buttocks and breasts. When a Basque woman wears her hair plaited and dons moccasin sandals she looks as if she has come straight off the set of a Western. Sometimes, through the industrial pall of a winter evening in Bilbao, you can see, standing at a bus-stop or crossing a street, a breath-taking female apparition from *Hiawatha*.

The Basques are deeply Catholic (both Ignacio Loyola, the founder of the Jesuit order, and San Francisco Xavier were from here) and sexually more timid than other Spaniards. Alone in Spain they are a non-swearing people, and, on the rare occasions when they feel the need to let fly a curse, they almost invariably do so in Spanish, not *euskera*. They love to go hiking in their mountains, and are much given to sports involving physical strength, such as weight-lifting, log-sawing and stone-breaking. Hearty eaters and deep drinkers, they have some of the best cooking in the land. There is no hake like Basque hake, and their vegetables, apples and cheeses are in a class of their own. As for the folklore and music of the region, they rank among the richest in Spain. The Basques vie with the Catalans as the most hard-working, industrious people in the country. Generous and, when the occasion calls for it, ebullient, they tend to maintain with outsiders what Rodney Gallop, in his *A Book of the Basques* (1930), called 'an impenetrable reserve'.

If in the rest of the country the mother exercises great domestic power, in Euskadi she reigns supreme. The anthropologists tell us that this society was originally matriarchal, and I can believe it: the Basque matron is an awesome figure. Women have always enjoyed more rights in the Basque Country than elsewhere in Spain, and a Basque friend assures me that, while brother-sister incest occurs with some frequency in the lonely inland valleys, no father would ever dare to go to bed with his daughter – he would be instantly castrated by the woman of the house!

The most noticeably distinctive aspect of the Basques, however, is their non-Indo-European language, which sets them apart from all the other peoples of the Iberian Peninsula (who speak derivatives of Latin). *Euskera* has been baffling the philologists since antiquity. Strabo, Pliny and Martial referred to it as barbarous in sound as well as incomprehensible. A saying recorded by Richard Ford in the nine-teenth century had it that the Devil spent seven years in the Basque Country trying to learn the language – and only managed three words. The most recent scholarship suggests that the language is linked to two tongues still spoken in the Caucasus, Circassian and Georgian, as well as to certain Berber dialects in North Africa.

There has also long been a debate about the extent to which Basque may be related to Iberian, which was spoken throughout the Peninsula when the Romans arrived and which is only now beginning to be understood, thanks to the recent deciphering of a lead tablet dis-covered in Serreta de Alcoy (Alicante) in 1921. Today's experts seem to agree that the connection between Basque and Iberian is beyond doubt.

A few basic characteristics of Basque can be briefly pointed out. It has no 'f', for example (other than in modern loan-words), and this peculiarity almost certainly influenced the development of Castilian, which in its early stages converted the initial Latin 'f' into an aspirat-ed 'h', unlike all other Romance dialects with the exception of those on the other side of the Pyrenees which had also come into contact with Basque. The language has no words beginning with 'r' (again, other than loan-words). In modern Basque the letter 'c' has been replaced by 'k', and Basque nationalists derive a grim satisfaction from blotting it out on signposts written in Spanish and in Spanish loan-words, substituting 'k's' and replacing the 'c' before 'e' or 'i' (the characteristic lisped 'th' of Spanish) with 'z's'. Where Spanish has 'qu' (a 'k' sound before 'e' and 'i'), Basque, again, has 'k'. Take any text in Basque and you will notice that the 'k's' proliferate. This is not only for the reasons just given but because the Basque plural is formed by adding a 'k', not an 's'. Spanish 'ch' (pronounced as in the English 'church') is 'tx', Spanish 'v' is 'b' and Spanish 'j' (similar to the 'ch' in the Scottish pronunciation of 'loch') 'x'. Some examples should make the pattern clear:

Spanish	*Basque*
Sondica (Bilbao airport)	Sondika
Eceiza (surname)	Ezeiza
Luchana (place-name)	Lutxana
Vizcaya	Bizkaia
chacolí (Basque wine)	txakolí
eusquera	euskera
Javier	Xabier

Here is a short passage of Basque taken genuinely at random from the separatist daily newspaper *Egin* (in which ETA, the terrorist organization, often publishes its communiqués). It is a political commentary:

> Buruzagi abertzaleak bere baieztapena ziurtatzeko, hauteskunde hauetan negoziazio gaia alderdi guztiak ikutu beharrekoa bihurtu dela esan zuen, 'diskurtso politikoaren erreferentzia gunea bilakatzen ari delako'.

Note particularly, apart from the panoply of 'k's' and 'z's', the number of Spanish loan-words in such a short passage: 'negoziazio' ('negociación'), 'diskurtso' ('discurso'), 'politikoaren' ('político') and 'erreferentizia' ('referencia'). Clearly modern Basque is heavily dependent on Spanish for its terminology. A Basque friend has translated the passage into Spanish for me. The sense in English is:

> The Basque patriot leader said, to support his assertion,
> that in these elections the question of negotiation [with
> Madrid about Basque independence] has become a topic
> that all the political parties should discuss, 'because it is
> becoming the focus of current political discourse'.

The Basques' problems with Castile began a long time ago, their
territory being annexed by Pedro the Cruel, King of Castile and León,
as early as the fourteenth century. They were allowed to retain their
traditional laws and economic privileges (*fueros*), however, and it
became customary for the Castilian kings to swear to uphold these at
their accession. The *fueros* were ancient rights, not concessions, and
the Castilian pledges were given under the sacred oak tree of Gernika,
near Bilbao, where since time immemorial the Basque elders had
gathered to deliberate. In 1476 (sixteen years before they gained possession of Granada) Ferdinand and Isabella travelled to Gernika to
take the oath; their grandson the Emperor Charles V did the same in
1526; and so the practice continued down the centuries. The Spanish
kings often tried to go back on their word, to find some way of reducing the Basques' rights. It was a constant tug-of-war between periphery and centre, with periodical suppressions and restorations of the
fueros, depending on the political situation.

Matters came to a head in the nineteenth century. On the death of
the tyrant Ferdinand VII in 1833 the Basques threw in their lot with
the pretender, Carlos María Isidro, brother of the dead king, against
Ferdinand's daughter Isabella, whom, in disregard of the Salic Law, he
had named his successor. The Basques' support of the pretender was
motivated principally by their determination to safeguard their freedoms, menaced by centralizing Madrid. When the Carlists lost the
war, in 1839, the Basques were deprived of their *fueros*. These were
restored later but then, after the second Carlist war, abolished for
good in 1876. In their place Madrid granted what was called a
'Concierto Económico' ('Economic Agreement') under which the
Basques were allowed to handle their own tax affairs and to pay a
fixed sum to the central Treasury.

Madrid's meddling with and final suppression of the Basques' traditional privileges had the effect of definitively alienating these independent-minded people, and made the rise of militant political nationalism inevitable. Throughout the Basque Country people will talk to you passionately about the Carlist Wars and the treachery of Madrid, a treachery which they see at work still today, despite the granting of regional autonomy. When we were filming the mother of the ETA terrorist Zabarte, then in prison in the Canary Islands, she spoke angrily about Madrid's treatment of the Basque Country over the centuries. The Spaniards long ago deprived her people of their *gozamen*, she exclaimed. I asked what this Basque word meant. 'It means our happiness, our liberty,' she replied.

Militant Basque nationalism, of which the terrorist organization ETA is the most violent contemporary expression (the letters stand for 'Euskadi ta Askatasuna', 'The Basque People and Liberty'), came into existence in the late nineteenth century. To a large extent it was the result of the efforts of one man, Sabino Arana y Goiri. Born in 1865, Arana inherited from his father, a supporter of the Carlist pretender, a hatred of Madrid and centralism. He early developed an interest in the origins and structure of the Basque language and sought to systematize its chaotic grammar, an almost impossible task given the huge variety of dialects, some of them incomprehensible outside their own valleys. He also invented the term by which the Basque Country is today most commonly known, Euskadi.

Until the advent of Arana, which led to the founding of the Basque Nationalist Party ('Partido Nacionalista Vasco', the PNV) – still the leading force in Basque politics – the Basques were a proud people, certainly, but far from being radical nationalists. Arana, whose battle-cry was 'God and our traditional laws!', preached that the foreign immigrants flocking into Euskadi as a result of the new industrialization were introducing evil habits, and maintained that 'mixed marriages' would have the effect of weakening the race. A true Basque would never marry an outsider! He himself rejected the love of a Castilian girl and married a Basque woman socially inferior to himself. The irony was that, when he died, in 1903, his widow married, of all people, a member of the Civil Guard, the Spanish rural police force traditionally loathed by the Basques.

The Basque industrial revolution at the end of the nineteenth century was based principally on the exploitation of Vizcaya's huge deposits of high-quality non-phosphoric iron ores. Other vital factors were an inexhaustible supply of local wood from the damp mountains facing the Atlantic, and the abundance of swift rivers plunging down through the valleys to the sea. But such natural advantages would have counted for little without this tenacious people's innate ability for hard work and their pride in their country. They took to business long after the Catalans and were soon their rivals; and, instead of copying the Asturians, further along the coast to the west, who seemed content merely to export their coal to England and leave it at that, the Basques began to invest the profits and to diversify. By the beginning of the twentieth century Bilbao's giant iron foundries, the 'Altos Hornos de Vizcaya', were as much a symbol of Spanish industry as the textile factories of Catalonia. Moreover the Basques had also become the nation's bankers.

The massive immigration from the rest of Spain occasioned by the Basques' industrial revolution had a devastating effect on the region's traditional way of life and, not least, the language. In the last third of the nineteenth century, 98 and 93 per cent respectively of the inhabitants of Guipúzcoa and Vizcaya spoke *euskera* (in Alava the proportion was much lower). With the influx of Spanish speakers the ratio soon changed for the worse (from the point of view of the Basque language) and by the time the Republic came to power in 1931 *euskera* had reached an all-time low.

The Republic quickly got down to drafting the Basques' Autonomy Statute. Originally it was intended that the Statute should apply not only to the three Basque provinces but to Navarre as well. In July 1932, however, the Navarrese delegation pulled out of the negotiations. Alava, Vizcaya and Guipúzcoa polled overwhelmingly in favour of the proposed law but the vote coincided with the accession to power of a right-wing government in Madrid. The new Parliament shelved Basque autonomy, and Basque nationalism grew increasingly virulent during the so-called 'Black Biennium' leading up to the victory of the Popular Front in February 1936. That October, a few months after the outbreak of the Civil War, Vizcaya and Guipúzcoa were granted a provisional autonomy statute for their loyalty to the Republican cause. Alava, like Navarre, had sided with Franco.

By allowing his Nazi allies to use the Condor Legion to bomb the 'sacred' town of Gernika on 26 April 1937, General Franco attacked the very heart of Basque nationalism, and the insult was deepened when, during the long years of the post-war regime, official propaganda maintained that the city had been burnt by the Basques themselves before retreating.

Franco never forgave Vizcaya and Guipúzcoa for supporting the Republic, and from the moment Bilbao fell, a few weeks after the bombing of Gernika, he repressed them brutally. No effort was spared to eradicate the language and to suppress Basque civilization in general. As a result, given the Basques' long history of fighting for their rights, the rise of an armed resistance organization was inevitable.

ETA was born in 1960. It drew its first members mainly from the farms, towns and villages of the valleys (localities such as Mondragón, Oñati and Vergara), not from the coastal cities. These were young people who had been reared at home in a traditional culture for which Spain, always the enemy, had become, under Franco, the devil incarnate. In school that native culture was spurned and the children were forced to learn Spanish, the language of the oppressor. The speaking of *euskera* on the premises was severely punished. A better breeding-ground for revolutionaries could hardly be imagined. Moreover, when the children from the valleys grew up and went to Bilbao and, to a lesser degree, San Sebastián in search of jobs, the poor labour conditions in the foundaries and factories increased their hostility to the regime even further.

Juan Miguel Goiburu, an intellectual ex-member of ETA who agreed to be interviewed for the 'Fire in the Blood' series, is a good example of the sort of Basque who was attracted to the movement in its early days. Born in rural Guipúzcoa and outraged by Franco's repression of Basque culture, Goiburu came to feel that it was his moral obligation to join the armed resistance to the dictatorship. This was a struggle against Fascism and oppression, and violence was not only legitimate but necessary. At the time there was massive support for ETA throughout the Basque Country and in Spain as a whole, and when, in 1973, the organization succeeded in blowing up Franco's prime minister, Admiral Carrero Blanco, the *etarras* became little short of national heroes. Even Spaniards who abhorred the gun could not fail to admire their courage and resourcefulness.

ETA received further support when the dying Franco committed the great barbarity, as well as political mistake, of executing two *etarras* and three members of a militant anti-Fascist group on 27 September 1975, despite worldwide pleas for clemency, including one from the Pope. The country was appalled by the declining dictator's gesture of ferocity, and ETA's stock soared.

When Franco died, the transition to democracy got under way and work began on the Constitution (which, as was pointed out in an earlier chapter, a majority of the Basque people failed to approve in the referendum), the big question was whether ETA would disband once Euskadi was granted its regional autonomy. It did not, although there were defections and splits too complicated to analyse here. Many of those who had fought against Franco felt that, when the Basque people gave their assent to the Autonomy Statute by referendum on 25 October 1979, it was time to put away their weapons. True, there had been a 40.23 per cent abstention on polling day, but of those who had voted, 90.29 per cent expressed themselves in favour of the Statute. Clearly, ETA could no longer claim to speak as sole mouthpiece of the Basque Nation.

Those who remained within the organization, seeing their vision of full Basque independence slip from them, then embarked on a campaign of wholesale violence which continues today. Their principal target, as before, has been the Civil Guard deployed in the Basque Country, but they have also killed army officers and members of the Civil Guard in other parts of Spain. Cynically, setting themselves up as fighters for human rights, they have also decided to liquidate selected drug peddlers.

If ETA constitutes the terrorist manifestation of radical Basque separatism, its political expression is Herri Batasuna (HB), perhaps best rendered in English as 'The People's Unity Coalition'. The *batasuneros*, as they are known popularly, seem from outside to be a wild, irrational bunch. They despise the State that has emerged from Franco's Spain, in which reform has been preferred to a clean, revolutionary break with the past, and appear to believe sincerely that, if Euskadi were an independent State, its problems would solve themselves automatically. Fanatical about the Basque language, the men, women and youth of HB will tell you that no one can be fully Basque if he or she does not speak *euskera*. Every time I hear this I am reminded of the compulsory Irish enforced when I was at school, and of the fanatics who used to proclaim that, if you did not 'have the language', you could not possibly consider yourself a true child of the Nation.

The polls have shown consistently that in all the elections held in Euskadi (local, autonomous and national) HB can count on some 200,000 supporters, that is to say on approximately 17 per cent of the vote.

Wherever the coalition has control of local councils it makes things as difficult as possible for the non-Basque-speaking immigrants in the community, known pejoratively as *maketos*. When we filmed in the HB-run town of Mondragón, for example, where approximately half of the population of 26,000 does not speak *euskera*, we found that not only were the *batasuneros* refusing to use Spanish at council meetings but the local TV station, funded by public money, was broadcasting solely in Basque. Bills for water, electricity and so on were issued exclusively in Basque, and those citizens wanting them in Spanish had to apply to have their names entered on a special register – a humiliating and highly discriminatory process deeply resented by the victims. Taking into account the true linguistic situation in Mondragón, HB's attitude could be seen as ruthlessly nationalistic.

You have to be very careful indeed how you use the word Spain in the Basque Country. While we were in Mondragón I made the mistake of repeating to a friendly barman what the writer José Bergamín, a dissident Catholic who had fiercely opposed Franco during the war, once told me, namely that Euskadi is 'the most genuinely Spanish part of Spain'. 'Rubbish!' snapped my new acquaintance scornfully. 'Rubbish! Euskadi has nothing to do with Spain!' 'Perhaps Bergamín meant it in the sense that the Basque Country is the most ancient community in the Iberian Peninsula?' I volunteered timidly. Luckily this suggestion met with approval.

If at that time I had read G.L. Steer's wonderful book *The Tree of Gernika* (1938), a contemporary account of the struggle and defeat of the Basques in the Civil War, I would have been more careful. 'There are few things the patient Basque will not tolerate,' writes Steer, 'and one is the suggestion that he is Spanish. For him, Iberian is the safer term: it nearly conveys the idea of that antiquity and Peninsular twilight in which the Basque finds his source.' After my encounter with the barman I asked Joseba, the mother of the imprisoned *etarra* Zabarte, what feeling the word 'Spain' evoked in her. She did not hesitate. 'Horror!' she exclaimed. 'Horror!' No less explicit was the dynamic mayor of Oñati, Eli Galdós, a Basque Nationalist Party man who had belonged to ETA under Franco but left at the advent of democracy. 'To tell you the truth, I can't stand being called Spanish,' he assured me.

The loathing felt for the Spanish flag by Basque nationalists of all degrees is only equalled by the veneration reserved for their own, the green and red *ikurriña*, which was ruthlessly suppressed by Franco. Zabarte's mother told me of the intense emotion that swept the whole Basque Country when, after the death of the dictator, the flag 'took to the streets' legally for the first time since the Civil War. What the separatists cannot stomach today is to see the *ikurriña* and the Spanish flag flying side by side. When we were filming the 'Day of the Basque Soldier' procession in Mondragón (a march held annually throughout the Basque Country in honour of the ETA members killed fighting for Basque independence) two hooded figures suddenly appeared before the crowd in the main square, right under the balcony of the Town Hall, and burnt a Spanish flag. An ecstatic round of applause greeted their exploit. A minor exploit, to be sure: this was a Herri Batasuna, pro-ETA preserve, and no police action would be forthcoming.

There can be no doubt that since the advent of the Autonomy Statute, popular support for ETA has been dropping steadily. A turning-point was the terrorists' assassination of their former colleague María Dolores González Katarain. 'Yoyes', as she was nicknamed, had joined ETA at the age of seventeen, and her impassioned dedication to the cause soon led to her being given important missions. After the death of Franco, however, and the implementation of the Autonomy Statute, she came to feel that it was futile, and wrong, to continue the armed struggle. She left the organization in 1979 and moved to Mexico. When she arrived back in Spain in 1986 to take advantage of an amnesty declared by the government, she was fully aware of the dangers. Friends had advised her against returning, pointing out that her ex-colleagues might take revenge. But 'Yoyes' was nothing if not courageous. On the morning of 10 September 1986 she was crossing a square in her native town of Ordizia with her three-year-old son when a masked man shot her three times at point-blank range and finished her off with a *coup de grâce*.

ETA stated that it had had no option but to 'execute' 'Yoyes' for what they deemed her 'betrayal' of the cause. Not only Spaniards at large but many previous supporters were disgusted. An organization capable of murdering its former members was a far cry from the one that had opposed Franco. Support for ETA waned further.

Juan Miguel Goiburu, who had left the organization in 1981, was nearby when the assassination occurred. He told me that for him it signified 'the death of a hope' – the hope that ETA would now allow the Basque people to decide for themselves, democratically, what they wanted. By this time, in Goiburu's opinion, the vast majority of Basques were sick of ETA's violence and all they desired was for the organization to opt out with some dignity while it still could, and for its gaoled members to be allowed home. The murder of 'Yoyes' was the most brutal proof imaginable that ETA had lost contact with decency and reality.

ETA did not see it like that, of course, and continued unperturbed with its policy of assassinations mixed with kidnappings and the extortion of protection money to finance its operations. Its most brutal achievement was to plant a formidable bomb in the subterranean car-park of a supermarket in Barcelona in July 1987. There were twenty-one dead and fifty wounded. Like the IRA, ETA has few scruples about killing or maiming people who get in the way.

The rejection of violence by the huge majority of ordinary Basques was reflected in the so-called 'Pacto de Ajuria Enea' in January 1988 (Ajuria Enea is the name of the Basque Parliament building in Vitoria), signed by all the Basque parties with the inevitable exception of Herri Batasuna. By the terms of the agreement the Basque democrats undertook to do everything in their power to eradicate terrorist violence in the community, which meant, in the first place, refusing to negotiate with ETA. The decision of the Basque Nationalist Party (PNV) to be a signatory to the agreement was particularly significant. Up to then the PNV had often proved ambiguous on the question of violence. Now it had made its position clear. Its decision has played a predominant role in the 'pacification' of Euskadi.

The *etarras*, of course, were not impressed by the Ajuria Enea pact, nor by the massive and deeply moving peace demonstration that took place in Bilbao in March 1989 and, ironically, perhaps contributed to the breakdown of the talks between ETA and the Spanish government that were then under way in Algeria (the terrrorists maintained that it had been organized by Madrid). Since then there have been partial truces, splits, defections and many arrests, but the assassinations continue. For the record, between 1968 and July 1991 ETA killed almost 750 people, as well as wounding many dozens more.

Recently ETA has taken sides with the environmentalists, of all people, in the polemic surrounding the location of the final ten-mile stretch of new motorway linking Pamplona (capital of Navarre) and San Sebastián (capital of Guipúzcoa on the Basque coast near the French frontier). The terrorist organization, with its record of bloodshed, wounding and bullying, now concerned about environmental issues? Certainly not, but any question touching a popular nerve in the Basque Country can be useful to ETA, and the fate of the beautiful valley of Leizarán falls into this category. During 1990 letter-bombs were sent to firms involved in the project, offices burnt down, grenades thrown, workers threatened, machinery destroyed. And, of course, the genuine conservationists who had initiated the protests were accused of having ETA sympathies. Popular rejection of the terrorists hardened and the motorway, partially funded by the EC, went ahead by almost common consent.

Herri Batasuna had not only voiced its opposition to the motorway but, it became known, intimidated some of those involved in its construction. As a result all the Basque democratic parties signed a pact, in January 1991, by which they undertook to co-operate in order to prevent HB from winning any town councils at the next municipal elections. This was a remarkable breakthrough, termed by one politician 'a giant step forward in the struggle against the men of violence'.

The motorway has provided further proof that more and more people are now prepared to speak out against ETA. Even in the ranks of Herri Batasuna, some voices are cautiously suggesting that perhaps it is time for the organization to bury the hatchet (one of its symbols). Recent research shows that maybe as many as half HB's voters reject ETA's violent methods, although very few are as yet prepared to say so in public, or to relinquish their dream of an independent Euskadi.

Meanwhile the Madrid government continues to state that it will not reopen the talks with ETA that fell through a few years ago (although contacts still undoubtedly exist) until the organization stops killing, while the terrorists carry on just as stubbornly demand-

ABOVE:

14 *Basque terrorism is the great thorn
in the flesh of the new Spanish
democracy. ETA continues to kill army
officers and policemen, despite the fact
that most Basques seem satisfied with
local autonomy within the Spanish
state.*

OVERLEAF:

15 *Madrid's seventeenth-century
Plaza Mayor is a favourite with
tourists and natives alike. It has seen
bullfights and auto-da-fés, and is now
at its most lively on Sunday mornings.*

ABOVE:

19 An anti-NATO march in 1985.
The Socialist Party had promised in
1982 that when elected they would hold
a referendum on NATO and advise
withdrawal. Once in power, however,
the Socialists recommended staying in
the organization, a U-turn which split
their own party and caused much
public protest.

ing political negotiation with no prior conditions. One thing seems certain. If no compromise is reached before 1992, ETA is bound to do everything in its power to draw attention to itself and its cause by attempting to sabotage the Seville World Fair and the Barcelona Olympic Games. The authorities, fully aware of the danger, are taking due precautions.

As more competences are transferred from Madrid to the Basque Parliament (in particular, the Basque nationalists want to have financial control of the Health Service), as the new Basque police force, the Ertzaintza, increasingly takes over the duties of the hated Civil Guard (by 1993 it will be deployed throughout the region), and as the consumer society makes further inroads into the traditional values on which the life of Euskadi has been based, it seems that ETA must eventually collapse under the weight of its own inconsistencies, anachronism and futility. Moreover, the fact that France is now collaborating much more effectively than before against the *etarras* operating on its side of the Basque frontier has dealt a tremendous blow to the organization. Its French 'sanctuary' is gone, and Paris has extradited several terrorists to Spain. The future, then, seems bleak for ETA.

Finally, what about the present situation of the language – after all, the Basques' most distinctive identity sign? Following the provisions of the 1978 Constitution, *euskera* is now taught in all the schools of the community, both State and private, on an officially 'co-existent' basis, just as Catalan and Galician are in their respective regions. On the surface, the health of the language would seem to have improved radically, a recent survey suggesting that about 25 per cent of the population now speaks Basque with varying degrees of fluency, while a considerably higher proportion understands it. But the future is far from happy. Those responsible for teaching the language are not at all optimistic. 'It's one thing for children to learn it at school,' the teacher of five-year-olds we filmed in Mondragón explained, 'it's another for them to speak it outside and to go on speaking it after they finish their education.'

It is impossible not to agree. The pressure of Spanish is overwhelming in the media. Take the case of Basque television. At its inception, in 1983, the plan was that the new station should play a leading role in the recovery of *euskera*. The programmes were to be completely in Basque, with Spanish subtitles. But the scheme proved impossibly

145

idealistic. Before the end of the year there were news bulletins in Spanish. In 1986 a second channel, entirely in Spanish, was introduced, and immediately captured the allegiance of non-Basque-speaking viewers in the community. In late 1990 it was officially reported that the second channel was watched by 28 per cent of viewers, the first, 'Basque', channel, by only 12 per cent. The majority were watching neither as a matter of course, preferring Spanish State TV or other options.

As for the printed media, the presence of *euskera* is negligible. Even the widely read nationalistic daily *Egin* has only a small proportion of entries in Basque. At the moment only one weekly entirely in Basque survives. For a language which can never be a medium of international communication, the chances of prevailing are slim indeed.

Which is not to say that, at the moment, there is not important literary work being done in the vernacular. Until the revival of the language that followed Sabino Arana's passionate defence of Basque nationalism at the end of the nineteenth century, little written literature had been produced in *euskera* (although the tradition of oral poetry and story-telling flourished, and still survives). Today the situation has improved further, and one talented young writer and poet, Bernardo Atxaga, won the National Prize for Literature in 1989 for a remarkable collection of short stories in Basque, *Obabakoak*, whose Spanish translation became a best-seller.

The Basques are conscientious, proud, hard-working and hard-headed. There seems to be no reason why their industries, particularly their iron and steel mills (which have gone through a painful process of restructuring under the Socialists), should not now compete successfully in Europe. For the Basque Country to flourish, all that is needed is an end to the violence. Since early 1991, the autonomous community has been governed by a moderate nationalist coalition with, this time, no Socialist participation — with, that is, no overt pressure from Felipe González's Cabinet in Madrid (between 1986 and 1990 the Basque Nationalist Party ruled in conjunction with the PSOE). Perhaps this government can bring ETA finally to heel, and set Euskadi firmly on the path to peace and prosperity.

– 9 –

Catalonia

The Principality of Catalonia, with the Basque Country and Galicia one of Spain's 'historical autonomies', comprises the provinces of Barcelona, Tarragona, Lleida (Lérida) and Girona, and shares some 150 miles of Pyrenean frontier with France. Catalonia's seaboard runs for 200 miles from the rocky Costa Brava, or 'Wild Coast' (until a few years ago the part of Spain best known to British tourists), to just below the delta of the peninsula's longest river, the Ebro, south of Tarragona. Westwards Catalonia flanks the old kingdom of Aragón. The Principality is a triangle, and has been likened to a half-open fan with its handle resting on the Valencian border.

With an area of almost 12,472 square miles, Catalonia is marginally larger than Belgium, although with far fewer inhabitants: six million to the latter's ten, 75 per cent of them living in Barcelona and its highly industrialized outskirts. Such a striking demographical imbalance between the capital and the rest of the region has given rise to some popular comparisons. According to one, Catalonia is a *cabezudo*, the dwarf with the outsize head and spindly legs whom you will see gyrating beside the giant in many traditional Spanish festivals. Another simile likens Catalonia to a tadpole: again, a large head with a tiny body.

It is worth stressing immediately that Barcelona, crowded into a

147

narrow strip of land between the hills and the sea, is not only the most densely populated city on the Mediterranean but the biggest in Europe not enjoying the status of national capital. In practice, however, Spain has two capitals, and Madrid and Barcelona, each with some 4,600,000 inhabitants (city and province) have always been great rivals, feelings coming to a head periodically in the football matches between their respective star teams, Real Madrid and Barça.

Although Spain's fastest train, the Talgo, still takes seven and a half hours to cover the 450 miles separating the two cities, an air shuttle links them every hour (someone has written that one of the characteristics of the 40,000 Catalans working in Madrid is their 'unashamed passion for the shuttle'), and the motorway between them has just been completed (previously it was agony to drive to Barcelona from Madrid). Catalans are indignant, however, that as yet work has not begun on the promised high-speed train line between the two cities and from Barcelona up to the French frontier, the central government having given priority to the line from Madrid to Seville (with Expo 92 in mind), as we have seen. 'The high-speed train between Madrid and Seville can't get you to Europe,' the Catalan prime minister, Jordi Pujol, commented wryly in March 1991.

The experts disagree about the origin of the term 'Catalans', first recorded in the thirteenth century. According to one theory it derives from the same Latin root as 'Castilians', 'castle-dwellers'. Another view has it that the word preserves the name of a lost Celtic tribe. A further possibility is that 'Catalonia' is but the modern spelling of an unattested 'Gothalunia', 'Gothland', a reminder that the Visigoths entered Spain around the eastern, not western, edge of the Pyrenees. The 'Castilian' theory is the one most widely accepted by etymologists.

The Catalans are sharply differentiated from the Basques in that theirs is a Romance language, with none of the mystery (and the mystique) that surrounds *euskera*. Today it is spoken, with regional variations, by some 9 million people living in Catalonia, the Co-Principality of Andorra, the French *département* of Pyrénées Orientales, a fringe of Aragón, Valencia, the Balearic Islands and the city of Alghieri, in Sardinia (a relic of the days when Catalonia was a Mediterranean power). It is not, therefore, a language to be taken lightly, and one can understand the Catalans' annoyance when, as too often happens, someone suggests that they speak a 'dialect of Spanish'. In fact, of all Europe's stateless nations, Catalonia is the one with the most widely spoken native tongue.

In contrast to the situation with *euskera* in the Basque Country, if an immigrant from some other part of Spain who does not know Catalan decides to learn it, the problem is relatively simple, given the language's similarity to Spanish. And the immigrants' children, who learn Catalan in school, do not lose the language as soon as they finish their education, simply because in the outside world it is an everyday reality. This is borne out by the fact that, in the debates in the Catalan Parliament, the MPs speak Catalan as a matter of course.

Catalan is in fact much closer to French than to Spanish in its morphology, phonetics and vocabulary. It has a strong tendency to reduce two-syllable Latin words to one syllable. For example, Latin *noctem* 'night', *jocus*, 'game', and *totus*, 'all', give 'noche', 'juego' and 'todo' respectively in Spanish but 'nit', 'joc' and 'tot' in Catalan (compare French 'nuit', 'jeu' and 'tout'). The suppression of the final 'e' is very noticeable in adverbs, making another striking contrast with Spanish. Thus, where the latter says 'agradablemente', Catalan has 'agradablement'. Similarly, nouns ending in '-miento' in Spanish terminate in '-ment' in Catalan (for instance, where Spanish has 'ayuntamiento', 'town hall', we find 'ajuntament' in Catalan). All of this means that the rhythm of the two languages is quite different.

As for its sounds, the characteristic lisped 'th' fricative of Spanish ('c' before 'e' and 'i') is missing in Catalan; so too is the harsh 'j' (pronounced, as I said in the chapter on the Basques, like the 'ch' in the Scots 'loch'). The 's' between vowels is voiced (that is, pronounced like an English 'z'), in tune with French and Italian, not Spanish, and the 'e' tends to be rendered as an 'a', the 'o' as a 'u'. But the sound that other Spaniards most notice (and joke about) is Catalan's markedly palatal 'l'. Try the experiment of pronouncing very slowly, with your tongue as hard up against the roof of your mouth as you can manage when you come to the 'l', the name of Catalonia's most famous painter: Dalí. After a few shots you should be able to articulate the Catalan 'l' as effectively as the Surrealist master himself.

The fact that the language is so close to France gives the Catalans an advantage when it comes to understanding and acquiring their neighbours' tongue, a further factor setting them apart from other

Spaniards. Barcelona, the most European city in Spain, has always looked much more to Paris than to Madrid for its cultural inspiration, and holidaying Catalans prefer to travel to France rather than to the rest of Spain. It comes as no surprise to find the popular Catalan song-writer and singer, Joan Manuel Serrat, rounding off one of his best-known recent numbers, 'Malson per entregues' ('Nightmare in Various Instalments'), with a tribute to Charles Boyer in French. That would be unthinkable in a song composed in Madrid.

But how has this north-eastern corner of the Iberian Peninsula developed into the modern Catalonia, Spain's most industrialized (and the Catalans would have it, not without justification, most civilized) region? Some background is necessary.

Between AD 717 and 725 the Moors overran the area. The inhabitants quickly recovered its northern reaches, however, and by the end of the century the frontier between the Christians and Muslims had been pushed back almost to Barcelona, which was retaken in 801 with the decisive intervention of Charlemagne and his Franks. The territory, baptized by the latter as the *Marca Hispanica*, or Spanish March, was now incorporated into the Carolingian Empire and divided into several *comtats*, counties. That of Barcelona, already a thriving city, soon asserted its primacy and began to absorb the others.

There then took place an event of which the Catalans are inordinately proud: in 988 the Count of Barcelona, Borrell II, vassal, like his predecessors, to the *Rex Francorum et Romanorum*, at that time Hugues Capet, decided to cast off his feudal shackles. Barcelona was liberated from its subservience to the Franks and became the dynamo of the new Catalonia. As the power of the city grew apace the Count of Barcelona acquired what was practically the status of king of Catalonia.

In the eleventh century Barcelona embarked on a process of vigorous commercial expansion in the Mediterranean and participated energetically in the conquest of the land to its south, still in Muslim hands. The ancient city of Tarragona (capital of the Roman province of Hispania Citerior, and later, of Tarraconensis) fell to the Catalans in 1129, and in 1137 the then Count of Barcelona, Ramón Berenguer IV, became king of neighbouring Aragón by marrying Petronila, heiress to the Crown. It was the beginning of a dynastic confederacy under which Aragón and Catalonia each retained their separate institutions although Barcelona, not Saragossa, was the official residence of the Court. Ramón Berenguer's descendants carried on the work of wresting possessions from the Muslims, incorporating Majorca (1228–9) and Valencia (1232–45) to the Crown and taking the Catalan language with them.

In the thirteenth century a parliament comprising representatives of the nobility, Church and cities of the combined Aragonese and Catalan territories was inaugurated. Its function, as well as making laws, was to moderate the working of the monarchy. This institution gave rise, the following century, to the governing body known as the Generalitat, which gradually took upon itself the running of Aragón and Catalonia in collaboration with the Council of the Hundred, a commission of burghers entrusted with the organization of Barcelona.

In 1474 the crowns of Castile and Aragón were united by the marriage of Ferdinand and Isabella, the 'Catholic Monarchs', and Catalonia's destiny changed dramatically. When their daughter, Joanna 'the Mad', married Philip 'the Handsome', son of the Holy Roman Emperor Maximilian I, Spain – including, willy-nilly, Catalonia – entered the Habsburg era. By and large the 'Austrians', as the Habsburg kings, beginning with the Emperor Charles I, are commonly known in Spain, were respectful of Catalonia's institutions, although they continued the policy, imposed by the 'Catholic Monarchs', of not allowing the Principality to trade with the New World. One of the effects of this ban was to encourage Barcelona's stubborn self-reliance, already considerable, and to stimulate the city further to develop its Mediterranean commerce.

When, in 1700, Charles II, Spain's last Habsburg king, died without direct issue and named as his successor Philip of Anjou, grandson of Louis XIV, the Catalans feared the worst. As a result of the Treaty of the Pyrenees, made in 1659, Roussillon, Vallespir, Conflent, Capcir and part of Cerdanya, traditionally belonging to Catalonia, had been annexed to France. The Catalans could not forget this, and had little reason now to trust Spain's recently installed Bourbon monarch. So, as Europe became embroiled in yet another bloody conflict, the War of the Spanish Succession, they opted to support the Habsburg Pretender, the Archduke Charles of Austria, hoping that, if he prevailed, their institutions and way of life would continue to be respected.

But the Archduke Charles did not prevail. Aragón fell to the enemy first, then Valencia. Catalonia was occupied by French and Spanish armies in the summer of 1713, and Barcelona, by then a city of some 34,000 inhabitants, put up a furious resistance, holding out for more than a year. The terms of the surrender were not complied with, and the victors razed a third of the city to the ground.

The 11th of September 1714, the day on which Barcelona surrendered to the Bourbon troops, marks a watershed in the history of Catalonia. The date is etched as sharply on the Catalan consciousness as 1066 on the English, and, after the death of Franco, 11 September was restored as Catalonia's National Day, the 'Diada'.

Under the new Bourbon order the Generalitat (Parliament) and Council of the Hundred were suppressed and the Catalan universities closed down and replaced by a new institution, the University of Cervera; Castilian was imposed as the language of the administration, and concerted attempts were made to undermine the use of the Catalan language in other areas, but the people at large never stopped speaking their native tongue.

The Catalans were now fully in thrall to distant Madrid, their subjection symbolically expressed in the inexpugnable citadel the hated Philip V ordered to be erected on the outskirts of Barcelona, and which would not be destroyed until 150 years later.

The year 1714 also spelt the disappearance from the Catalan scene of the nation's aristocracy, which moved to Madrid and henceforth was to play little part in the affairs of the Principality.

Is it any wonder that, since the disaster of 1714, the Catalans have consistently felt themselves alien to the Spanish State? While their resistance to it has not usually been violent (by and large they are an orderly, peace-loving people), this latent hostility, often disguised as indifference, has been a constant factor in the politics and culture of the nation, and remains so today.

Deprived of their political freedoms, the Catalan townsfolk, always remarkable for their tenacity, self-assurance and industriousness, threw their energies even more vigorously into commerce, an activity for which they had shown great flair since the Middle Ages. As members of a community with a strong sense of collective identity, they never relinquished the hope that one day they would recover their old institutions. Meanwhile they made the best of the situation. During the eighteenth century Barcelona's merchants flourished, and the population of the city tripled. The mainstay of Catalan industry was textiles, in particular printed calicos. The Principality supplied most of the clothing and arms for the Spanish army, produced many varieties of woollens and exported wine, brandies, salt and oil.

Then, in 1756, the ban on commerce with the New World, imposed by Ferdinand and Isabella, was partially lifted and Barcelona was allowed to trade with Santo Domingo and Puerto Rico; shortly afterwards the permission was extended to all of Spain's possessions in South America. The Catalan economy moved into top gear. But it was soon forced to slow down temporarily as a consequence of the French Revolution and, shortly afterwards, the Napoleonic invasion, which led to what in Britain is known as the Peninsular War and in Spain as the War of Independence.

The growing commercial power of Barcelona during the eighteenth century had not altered the fact that Catalonia as a whole was still a predominantly agricultural region. Tarragona, for example, was well known for its almonds and dried fruits, and fine wines were being produced in the Maresme district and the Penedés. The landscape of this rural Catalonia was made internationally famous over a century later by the paintings of Joan Miró, Salvador Dalí and, to a lesser extent, Picasso.

The introduction of the steam engine in the 1830s gave Catalan commerce, particularly the textile sector, a tremendous boost. It was the beginning of an industrial revolution that set the Principality apart from the rest of Spain and was all the more meritorious in so far as, unlike Britain, the country had to import most of its raw materials. The Catalan industrialists sought to protect themselves against competition from the British and French by persuading the State to impose solid tariff barriers, a circumstance that naturally irritated their European competitors.

British travellers to Spain in the eighteenth and nineteenth centuries were very much surprised by Catalonia, which did not correspond at all their image of a romantic land of dark-skinned ladies, bandits and bullfighters. Henry Swinburne (great-great-uncle of the poet) visited Spain for the first time in 1774, entering the country at the Franco-Catalan border. He was impressed by the industry and resilience of the people. 'The loss of all their immunities, the igno-

153

minious prohibition of every weapon, even a knife, and an enormous load of taxes,' he wrote, 'have not been able to stifle their independent spirit, which breaks out upon the least stretch of arbitrary power.' In Barcelona Swinburne found that the Catalan 'thirst after lucre makes them bear with any hardships', and that the local worthies talked about Spain as if it were a foreign country, as alien to them as neighbouring France.

Seventy years later, when the French Revolution and Peninsular War had run their course and the Catalan industrial revolution was getting under way, Richard Ford gave a much fuller picture of the region in his *Handbook*. His feelings about the place were mixed. 'Catalans,' he wrote, 'are not very courteous or hospitable to strangers, whom they fear and hate. They are neither French nor Spanish, but *sui generis* in language, costume, and habits; indeed the rudeness, activity, and manufacturing industry of the districts near Barcelona are enough to warn the traveller that he is no longer in high-bred, indolent Spain.' Ford discovered that the Catalans had not a good word to say for Madrid and that they were always waiting for the moment of liberation: 'No province of the unamalgamating bundle which forms the conventional monarchy of Spain hangs more loosely to the crown than Catalonia, this classical country of revolt, which is ever ready to fly off.'

The Catalonia Ford visited was a veritable hive of endeavour, a Spanish Lancashire with Barcelona as its Manchester. There was nothing like it in the rest of Spain (the Basque industrial revolution had not yet begun). Once he had got over his shock, Ford could not hide his sneaking regard for these people, who had suffered so much at the hands of both the Spanish and French. 'Intensely selfish' they might be, and excessively protectionist, but who could blame them for seeking to assert through commerce and industry their difference from the rest of the nation? 'Trade was never thought here to be a degradation until the province was annexed to the proud Castiles, when the first heavy blow was dealt to its prosperity,' he mused. The Barcelona merchant, unlike the pedigree-obsessed 'proud pauper Castilian', Ford found to be an eminently practical man, brimful of confidence in his business ability and determined to get on in the world.

The Catalans today are still proud of the qualities identified as their hallmarks by the early travellers from Europe. They are less hectic than other Spaniards: they don't shout nearly so much, they ride quieter motorbikes and they stop at the lights. They believe themselves possessed of a sound common sense, called *seny*, that sets them apart from the rest of Spain – or, as they like to say, Castile. The term *seny* also implies moderation, serenity, reliability, equanimity, even phlegm. The much-respected Catalan conservative politician Miquel Roca i Junyent has put it nicely. Asked by a Madrid journalist in September 1990 if he considered Catalonia 'different', he replied: 'It seems clear that Catalan society is not as frivolous as the Madrid we see reflected in the media. Although we too have our share of frivolity (more than I, personally, would wish) Catalonia has tended more in the direction of Benedictine austerity, of, that is, a rich, comfortable austerity. I always say that one of the most impressive things about the great Benedictine monasteries is the sensation they give of solidity and good quality.'

Solidity and good quality – emphatically not characteristics that have defined Spanish life over the last few centuries.

Other Spaniards have mixed feelings about the Catalans. They are considered the only stingy people in the country, for example, and it is true that there are more savings banks in Catalonia than in the rest of Spain put together. The Delegate of the Generalitat in Madrid, Francesc Sanúy, has assured me that it is a custom in Catalonia to open a savings bank account on behalf of new-born children, the god-father being liable for the first deposit. Catalans do not like buying rounds of drinks (in the rest of Spain people would rather die than allow a foreigner to pay for the *copas*). Many jokes circulate in Spain about this propensity to meanness. 'What do you do when it gets cold in winter?', goes one I heard recently. 'Move close to the stove,' answers the Catalan. 'And when it gets colder?' 'Move closer.' 'And when it gets really freezing?' 'Light it.'

The Catalans' constant complaints about victimization gets on other Spaniards' nerves. 'They never stop moaning, always blaming Madrid,' a Castilian acquaintance who has worked for many years in Barcelona assures me. Catalans admit to this failing, termed by one writer 'a massive tendency to indulge in negative dramatization'. According to the outspoken Catalan architect Oriol Bohigas, one of those most responsible for planning the new 'Olympic' Barcelona, the tendency is perhaps due 'to the fact that we have been clobbered more than we should have been, given our economic and cultural merits'.

The Catalans' insistence on speaking their language even when some of those present only know Spanish, or when they are addressed in Spanish, also irritates many people from the rest of the country. Likewise, other Spaniards often question the Catalans' much-vaunted reputation as the nation's most industrious people. A Córdoba friend is adamant on the subject. For him, such diligence and enterprise are as much a product of circumstance as is the alleged laziness of many Andalusians. If Andalusia had not been divided up among the nobles of the 'Reconquest' into huge, unproductive estates with absentee landlords and only a handful of day labourers working them, my friend insists, then southern Spain would also be reckoned 'industrious' today.

The Andalusians, who for generations have been migrating *en masse* to Catalonia, feel that their contribution to the economic buoyancy of the Principality is often conveniently overlooked by the Catalans. The point was made to me repeatedly during a visit to Seville in 1990 to see the preparations for Expo 92. 'It was Andalusian sweated labour that made the Catalans rich,' a TV producer assured me, 'but, now that we have our regional parliament and more control of our own affairs than ever before, we're going to show them that we can work hard at home, too, when given the chance. They'll see.'

Richard Ford only witnessed the early days of Catalonia's industrial revolution, which gathered pace throughout the nineteenth century and, as immigrants poured in from the rest of Spain to man the machinery, gave rise to the first militant trade union movement in the country. It would certainly be a great mistake to think of Catalonia as a country only of solid burghers and rich, European-minded businessmen. The middle class may be proud of its *seny*, but there is also a Catalan word for the opposite side of the coin, the ability to suddenly flare up in a burst of passion and violence. It is called *rauxa*. Spanish anarchism, which proliferated in the slums and mills of industrial Barcelona, the seedbed of ferocious class hatreds, was impregnated with *rauxa*. The latter asserted itself on a famous occasion in 1908 when, during what became known as The Tragic Week, the enraged masses rebelled against the sending of troops to Spanish Morocco. As anyone who has read George Orwell's *Homage to Catalonia* is aware, the anarchists played a major role in preventing Barcelona from falling into the hands of the Fascists in 1936, and were possessed of a revolutionary fury unlike anything else in Spain. That, undoubtedly, was *rauxa*.

Some commentators have it that the Catalans always oscillate between *seny* (a rather stodgy philosophy and life-style) and *rauxa* (an excessively irrational one), never quite finding an acceptable equilibrium. Perhaps Dalí was a perfect case in point, his obsession with money and security corresponding to *seny*, his Surrealist frenzies to *rauxa*.

The late nineteenth century was for Catalonia a period of intense industrial growth and optimism symbolized by Barcelona's Universal Exhibition in 1888 and the completion of the city's Eixample, or Extension, a new, symmetrical quarter of wide, parallel streets which looks, from the air, like a giant chess-board. Designed by the architect Ildefons Cerdà, the Eixample had been begun in 1859 when, along with the hated Citadel, the restricting walls of the old city were torn down. Between 1860 and 1900 no fewer than 4,728 substantial blocks of flats were erected in the new quarter.

The same period saw a potent renascence of Catalan literature and, towards the end of the century (by which time Barcelona had half a million inhabitants), a flourishing movement in the arts, known as 'Modernisme'. Today this is particularly famous internationally for its fantastic architecture, one of whose principal exponents was Antoni Gaudí; his great unfinished cathedral, the Sagrada Familia ('Holy Family'), is the city's most striking landmark.

The men and women involved in Modernisme, a 'total' movement embracing all the arts, felt themselves intensely European as well as Catalan, but hardly at all Spanish, and were very much aware of the work of the Pre-Raphaelites, of William Morris and of French Art Nouveau. They believed in making objects at once useful and beautiful (something at which the Catalans have always been good), and were as concerned about the design of small domestic things as of large-scale factories or workshops. Their buildings were planned down to the very last detail in the same characteristic style, with a profusion of mosaics, wrought iron and painted glass. They had a strong dislike of straight lines, and the façades of Barcelona's dazzlingly coloured

Modernist buildings are an exuberant symphony of flowing curves and ellipses, which give the impression of being in constant movement.

As it approached the turn of the century, riding on the crest of the 1888 Exhibition's success, Barcelona, proud of its long history yet equally determined to be up to date, became fully aware of itself as a great European city. The young Picasso, who spent several years here after leaving his native Málaga, beautifully captured the mood of this Spanish Paris on the Mediterranean in his paintings of the period.

Not surprisingly, given Barcelona's supreme self-confidence at this time, the old nagging annoyance at being subservient to Madrid was considerably in evidence. Attempts were made over the following years to achieve some measure of local devolution, but in 1923 the successful *coup d'état* by General Miguel Primo de Rivera put the lid once again on Catalan pretensions to autonomy, and kept it there for eight years, until the arrival of the Second Republic. The period of the dictatorship was marked by the celebration in Barcelona of the 1929 Exhibition, which ushered out Spain's version of the swinging twenties, an extremely lively decade culturally if not politically.

On 14 April 1931, at the proclamation of the Republic, the Catalans resuscitated their medieval parliament, the Generalitat, which embarked on drawing up the region's Autonomy Statute. This was passed by the National Parliament in Madrid in September 1932, when the process of transferring powers to the Generalitat got under way in an atmosphere of intense enthusiasm and warm co-operation with the central government. The November 1933 general election, won by the Right, proved fatal for the Catalans, however. Relations between the Generalitat and Madrid grew intensely strained, and led to an armed rising in Barcelona on 6 October 1934. This was put down instantly. The Autonomy Statute was suppressed and most of the Catalan leaders were imprisoned, including Lluís Companys, president of the Generalitat.

In the years 1932–4 the Generalitat had not been able to achieve a great deal, although progress had been made in education, as it had in the rest of Spain, and the arts flourished in an atmosphere of freedom and liberalism.

When, in February 1936, the Popular Front won the elections, the Generalitat was restored and the Catalan nationalist leaders left prison amidst scenes of immense jubilation. But the damage had been done. Spain had become a battleground, attitudes had hardened and every day there were violent encounters, both in Barcelona and Madrid, between the Fascists and the various factions of the Left. From February onwards the nation embarked on what, in retrospect, can be seen as a relentless slide into civil war, a war in which the Catalans were to fight the rebels tooth and nail.

When Franco's troops entered Barcelona in 1939 at the end of the conflagration a terrible price immediately began to be exacted by the victors for the city's resistance – and that of Catalonia in general. The Catalans were forcibly reminded of what had happened in 1714 when Barcelona surrendered to the troops of Philip V. But this time it was even worse. We will never know exactly how many 'Reds' were executed in Barcelona between 1939 and 1942, but certainly the figure ran into tens of thousands. One of the worst outrages was that committed on the person of Lluís Companys, who was arrested in France by the Nazis, returned to Franco and shot in Barcelona in 1942. A mild man, with no blood on his hands, his execution was presumably intended to cow the Catalans into a state of utter moral apathy and dejection.

As for Catalan culture, Franco was implacable: every effort was made to eradicate the language, which was removed totally from the schools, prohibited in public, banned in newspapers, magazines and books and discouraged elsewhere – a resurrection, in practice, of the policy inaugurated by Philip V in 1714. The effect on the minds of generations of children forced to learn and use in school a language that they did not speak at home or in the street, and obliged to study other subjects through it, can be imagined. 'Our language and culture lost a richness that no one can ever restore to us,' laments a well-known Catalan journalist and politician, Maria Aurelia Capmany, in her recent book *What the Devil Is Catalonia?* Another Catalan writer has said that, between them, Generals Primo de Rivera and Franco almost succeeded in inflicting 'cultural genocide' on the Principality.

To find a closer-to-home equivalent we could perhaps reflect on the British repression of Gaelic in Ireland, effected with extraordinary brutality, which led to the almost total loss of the language, or try to imagine the reaction of the Welsh if Westminster decreed that they stop using their traditional tongue.

One small detail provided by Maria Aurelia Capmany demonstrates the utter determination of the Franco regime, at every level, to humiliate Barcelona. When, in the fifties, the city began to recover industrially, attracting massive immigration from the poorer parts of Spain, the authorities placed a limit on the number of car number-plates to be issued with Barcelona registrations, obliging people to purchase vehicles in Madrid. The city could not be seen to be acquiring more new cars than the capital of the nation!

If the Catalans did not offer violent resistance to Franco during the long years of the dictatorship, their cultural opposition was sustained, subtle and finally successful. One of the most efficient modes of passive protest was music. Among the outstanding singer-composers who, in the 1960s, achieved a multitudinous following in Catalonia were Joan Manuel Serrat (from Barcelona), Lluís Llach (from the Costa Brava), Raimon (a Valencian) and the Majorcan Maria del Mar Bonet. These performers created what came to be known as the 'Nova Cançon', or 'New Song'. They did not need to risk their careers by spelling out their rebellious message explicitly: it was enough to sing in their native language. Songs in Catalan were by then grudgingly allowed by the authorities (it was thirty years since the Civil War), and by singing wistfully of the region's hills and sea, its sadness or the nostalgia of its exiles, the point was obvious.

Progressive Catalan Catholics were also able to voice their rejection of the regime by protesting against Franco's habitual appointment of non-Catalans to the Principality's sees. A case in point was the decisive treatment meted out to the Castilian Marcelo González Martín, named archbishop of Barcelona in 1956, whose throne was set on fire. It may be added that the Catalan Church has traditionally been the most tolerant and civilized in Spain, that it has more worker priests than elsewhere in the country, and that today there is increasing support for the view that it should be allowed its own Bishops' Conference.

The ignorance in the rest of Spain about the reality of Catalan history, about 1714 and the successive attempts to put down the region's language and culture, is one of the chief causes of the 'Catalan problem'. Despite the explicit provision of the 1978 Constitution ('The richness of the different linguistic modes in Spain is a cultural heritage that will be the object of special respect and protection'), little has been done to encourage Spaniards living in other parts of the State to feel in a concrete way that Catalan is one of the nation's valuable assets, and only a handful of universities outside the Principality run courses on Catalan philosophy and culture. The populace at large knows nothing about Catalan literature, which was rich in the Middle Ages and, since its resurrection in the nineteenth century, has produced some outstanding writers.

It may be added, in general, that the lack of contact between the different languages and cultures of Spain is one of the great weaknesses of the current situation, a weakness which, if the will existed, could be remedied by a fuller implementation of the Constitution. Some people feel, for example, that Spanish children in the solely Castilian-speaking areas should be given basic instruction in one of the other languages of the State. Television, too, could be used more imaginatively, not only by running really lively courses in Catalan, Basque and Galician, but by making the regional programmes available nationally. A Catalan friend recently complained to me that in the five-star hotel where he always stays in Madrid he is able to watch Mexican satellite TV but not the all-Catalan Third Channel. 'Thousands of Catalan businessmen stay at the hotel each year,' he assured me, 'and only a handful of Mexicans. Yet it never occurs to the management to point their bloody dish at Barcelona.' It seemed to me a fair point – and a further indication of the cultural abyss separating Madrid and Catalonia.

A new difficulty arose for Catalan culture as a result of the massive immigration in the 1950s from the poorer regions of Spain, particularly Andalusia. This continued in the 1960s but began to dwindle to a trickle in the 1970s. One of the main consequences of the influx was linguistic: by the time Franco died there were some 3 million people living in Catalonia (that is, half the Catalan population) for whom Spanish, not Catalan, was their native tongue. Many Catalans felt that, once again, they were being victimized, that it was a deliberate policy on the part of the dictatorship to swamp Catalan culture under an avalanche of Spanish-speaking *xarnegos* (the word corresponds in pejorative impact to *maketos* in the Basque Country). But no such policy had been envisaged. The immigration had a merely economic basis. The outcome was the same, however: a huge new population had to be assimilated.

When Franco died in 1975 it soon became clear that the recovery of Catalan autonomy was inevitable. On 11 September 1977 (their National Day) a million people from throughout the Principality gathered in Barcelona to voice their demand for the return of the regional parliament. Then, on 23 October, Josep Tarradellas, president since 1954 of the Generalitat in exile, arrived back in Barcelona, having sworn never to do so until Catalonia was guaranteed the recovery of her liberties. Tarradellas's reappearance in the Catalan capital at this time, made possible not only by his own wise statesmanship but by the political vision and realism of Prime Minister Adolfo Suárez, was an intensely symbolic occasion. The city was overjoyed, hundreds of thousands of Catalans taking to the streets to greet the president. Tarradellas came out on to the balcony of the Generalitat in the Plaça de San Jaume to address the crowd. 'Ja sóc aquí!' 'Here I am at last!' were his first words.

The exiled president's return to Barcelona did not bring the full restoration of the Generalitat, of course – that would only come once the Constitution had been promulgated and the Autonomy Statute enacted. But it meant that such a restoration was guaranteed. Two years later the Catalans massively approved their Statute by referendum. Shortly afterward it was ratified by both houses of the Madrid Parliament and received the royal approbation. The Statute came into force on 31 December 1979.

Tarradellas's place was taken by Jordi Pujol, leader of the conservative coalition, CiU (Convergència i Unió – Convergence and Union), which in March 1980 won the first autonomous elections held in Catalonia since 1932. Since then it has never been out of office, always with Pujol at the helm. The president of the Generalitat, who was born in 1930, is the very embodiment of *seny*, the common sense so prized by Catalans. He has all the right qualifications for the job: business acumen (he is a banker), diplomacy, pragmatism, an ironic sense of humour, cunning, apparently sincere Catholic faith, a genuine love of Catalonia, a sociable personality and a great determination to succeed. The latter quality has been identified by the distinguished Catalan historian Vicens Vives as typical of the Principality, where the self-made man is deeply admired. It comes as no surprise to find Pujol stating that Catalonia 'is a small country but with a great will to be' (*voluntad de ser*). To cap it all Pujol (whose Christian name coincides with that of Catalonia's patron, Saint George) has an impeccable prison record: the dictatorship locked him up for three years (1960–3) for organizing a cultural act in which, in the presence of Franco, a Catalan nationalist hymn was sung – in Catalan.

Unlike the younger Felipe González, whose contact with the ordinary people of Spain has been minimal since he acceded to power, Jordi Pujol takes every opportunity to mix with his fellow countrymen and women, who respond warmly to him at street level whatever their political persuasion. Most Catalans are impressed by the president, and it is hardly an exaggeration to say that, in practice if not technically, he is head of State. In Catalonia, given the long history of Madrid-imposed repression, you would not expect people to feel great warmth towards the King of Spain. They recognize Juan Carlos's good qualities, certainly; appreciate his splendid efforts on behalf of democracy; will tell you that in him, at last, the Bourbons have produced a king who is no *farceur*. But they still consider the monarchy as something alien, distant. This was expressed graphically when, during a ceremony inaugurating the Barcelona Olympic Stadium in 1989, a sector of the Youth Organization of Pujol's party booed Juan Carlos, thereby greatly embarrassing the Catalan prime minister. Luckily the radical separatists, a tiny minority, are not as violent as ETA. In Catalonia the separatist tendency is strong but civilized. There is nothing corresponding to the sizeable following that, in Euskadi, supports the terrorists; no party comparable to Herri Batasuna.

Jordi Pujol has succeeded in convincing a majority of Catalans that in him are resumed the fundamental 'essences' of the nation. When seeing him in action it is impossible not to recall De Gaulle's 'La France, c'est moi.' The only other 'autonomous' prime minister who can vie with Pujol in terms of charisma and status is Manuel Fraga, who, unlike the Catalan premier, first made his political reputation in Madrid. But Fraga has only been head of the Galician government for three years, not long enough to make a profound impact. Who is prime minister of La Rioja, Asturias, Cantabria, Extremadura? Hardly anyone could tell you outside these regions; probably a high percentage of Spaniards would even be unable to say who heads the governments of Andalusia, the Basque Country – or Madrid. In Catalonia, with the same conservative coalition in power for ten years (there has never been any question of searching for a new prime minister), Jordi Pujol is an institution.

In December 1988 the Catalan Parliament celebrated the 1000th anniversary of Borrell II's severance of the link with the Carolingians, equating the date, somewhat arbitrarily, with the foundation of Catalonia as a nation. Behind the decision to celebrate the 'Millennium' lay, it is said, Pujol's desire to remind Madrid that, five hundred years before the 'Catholic Monarchs' embarked on their policy of unifying Spain, Catalonia was aware of itself as a nation in its own right. Perhaps the most memorable moment of the commemoration festivities occurred in Rome, where 5,000 Catalan pilgrims performed *sardanas*, the national dance, in Saint Peter's Square, and waved Catalan flags. The Pope made the mistake of beginning his homily in Castilian, a gaffe that inspired the more hardline pilgrims present to whistle their disapproval. Then, in Catalan, Wojtyla commended the visitors warmly to Our Lady of Montserrat, Patroness of the Principality. Jordi Pujol was among the pilgrims. 'I am here to demonstrate my Christian faith and my faith in Catalonia,' he told reporters.

Pujol, like the King, delivers an annual Christmas message to his 'subjects' on TV. In 1990, with a decade in power to his credit, he was his usual poised, avuncular self. He asked his viewers to make a determined effort over the *next* ten years to 'situate Catalonia in the front row' by dint of civic responsibility and excellence in every field of activity. In the 1990s, he said, 'we want more autonomy, more European integration, more respect for the environment, a higher standard of living and more welfare', all of this in order to achieve 'a European-style nation, small but very alive.'

'More autonomy'. This is the bone of contention, as in the Basque Country. Pujol is very guarded, astute and deliberately ambiguous in his public references to the question of Catalan independence, preferring to harp constantly on Madrid's unhelpfulness in implementing the full potential of the Autonomy Statute rather than to suggest that what the Principality needs is separation from the rest of the State. Pujol may dream of an independent Catalonia, but, as a hard-headed pragmatist (as much a pragmatist as Felipe González), he knows that, for the moment at any rate, such an eventuality is out of the question. Meanwhile he plays his nationalist cards with supreme dexterity.

164

Perhaps the most striking characteristic of Catalan political life since the Statute came into effect has been the fact that, while power in the Generalitat has been concentrated in the hands of Jordi Pujol and his conservative government, the Barcelona City Council is controlled by the Socialists. The elegant buildings of the Generalitat and the City Hall face each other across the historic Plaça de San Jaume, at the very heart of Old Barcelona, which therefore condenses most of the political life of the Principality, a political life marked by constant friction between the two institutions.

Given Barcelona's key role in the making of modern Catalonia, and the importance of the City Council since medieval times, it can be appreciated that whoever controls the latter is a person to be reckoned with. The present mayor certainly is. Pasqual Maragall, a tall, wiry fifty-year-old with a thick shock of greying hair, likes to set a good ecological example by cycling around the car-choked city. He has all Pujol's dynamism, intelligence and ability to mix with people, but a very different style: more low-key, less paternalistic. Maragall is hugely popular, for it was he who, more than anyone else, spearheaded the operation that led, on 17 October 1986, to the nomination of Barcelona as the seat of the 1992 Olympics. Since then he has become a power in the land.

From the very moment of its Olympic nomination, Barcelona put in motion a process of radical transformation and modernization in keeping with its tradition as a city both ancient and intensely contemporary. After all, such an in-depth renewal had been the whole point and aim of the campaign for the nomination, which was rooted in the conviction that if Barcelona was to be put firmly on the map of the modern world as it approached the year 2000, it was now or never. No time was lost, therefore, either in beginning the transformation of Montjuïc (the Roman 'Mons Jovis', or Mount of Jove) into the 'Olympic Hill' of 1992 and refurbishing the stadium built there for the 1929 Exhibition, or in implementing the ambitious plans for the city's new infrastructure. Never had Barcelona been so buoyant, so euphoric, not even when preparations got under way for the 1888 Exhibition.

One of the first tasks tackled by the undisputed monarchs of the moment, the architects and town-planners, was to give Barcelona back its seafront, from which it had been cruelly severed since the end of the nineteenth century by an agglomeration of railway lines, factories, docklands and customs buildings. This aim has now been achieved and the maritime promenade, which includes the Moll de la Fusta wharf, is one of the marvels of the new city. So too is the dazzling Olympic Village of Poblenou, constructed on the edge of the shore beyond the harbour where previously the railway to Mataró (now put underground) ran between abandoned mills. When the Games end and the cohorts of athletes depart, thousands of affluent *barceloneses* will move into this privileged quarter.

Numerous other initiatives to transform Barcelona in time for the Olympics have been successfully implemented. Restoration work has been carried out on the façades of Gaudí's astonishing blocks of flats, for example, and many of the venerable medieval buildings of the Gothic quarter cleaned; the interior decoration of the city's boutiques, discos, offices and bars is now more innovative and daring than anything in the rest of Spain; a combination of public and private enterprise has spruced up the city's once-famous bohemian avenue, the Paralelo, with its saucy music hall El Molino (Barcelona's answer to the Moulin Rouge), one of the few theatres surviving from the street's Golden Age in the 1920s; new, tree-lined squares mitigate the concrete desolation of the poorer areas (Barcelona has far fewer green spaces than Madrid, London or New York); quality publications on every aspect of Catalonia's history and culture pour from the presses, the City Hall vying with the Generalitat in this labour of promotion, analysis and reassessment; the airport has been modernized and extended; a new ring road, the National Theatre of Catalonia and a Music Auditorium have been constructed; and many other exciting modern buildings have sprung up.

Those who said Barcelona would never make it on time for the Olympics have been confounded.

With Spain's eventual entry to the EC a foregone conclusion by the early eighties, the Catalans were poised for an economic boom several years before the Common Market negotiations were concluded in 1985. Foreign investors, particularly the Japanese, were quick to perceive the advantages offered to them by obtaining a foothold in Spain prior to full European membership, and Barcelona seemed a far better bet than distant and poorly-communicated Madrid (90 per cent of Japan's new Spanish plant is in Catalonia, due in part to two visits to Tokyo by the persuasive and shrewd financier, Jordi Pujol). When the announcement came in 1986 that Barcelona had won the Olympic nomination, the potential of Catalonia was further enhanced.

One of the principality's showpieces is the technological park sited in the Vallès Oriental district, not far from Barcelona ('Oriental', 'Eastern', is not an allusion to the presence of the Japanese but a geographical designation), which has earned the nickname of 'Silicon Vallès'. Dozens of 'high-tech' firms, both foreign and Spanish, have set up here, specializing in such areas as biotechnology, telecommunications, microelectronics and fine chemicals. Another, but considerably more grimy, earnest of Catalonia's industrial power is Tarragona, which has Spain's most important petro-chemical complex and two nuclear power stations (one of which almost caused a disaster in 1989 and has since been closed down).

The Catalans, along with the rest of the Spanish business community, now have their eyes firmly fixed on the immediate post-Games future, when, on 1 January 1993, the European Single Market will come into operation. Being competitive in Europe is the obsession, and Jordi Pujol, to give him his due, is the only Spanish politician who has had the honesty and courage to say in public that for Spain, despite the ties of language, race and culture that link it to South America, Europe must now be the first allegiance. 'Our priority is Europe,' he stated in Mexico early in 1991, 'and we must make this clear. All too often discussion on the subject of Spain's relations with the Latin-American countries has been full of empty rhetoric.' Probably only a Catalan could have said that.

Europe, then, is the goal, and, more specifically, what has come to be known as 'The Toulouse–Montpellier–Barcelona triangle'. 'The Pyrenees have gone,' Louis XIV is reported to have exclaimed with satisfaction at the coronation of his grandson as Philip V of Spain. In fact it is only now, three hundred years later, that the gigantic mountain barrier separating Spain and France is finally being vanquished. By the end of the century two new trans-Pyrenean tunnels will bring the two countries very much closer: in 1992 work is scheduled to begin on the five-mile-long Puerto de Somport tunnel under the central Pyrenees, which will enable a new motorway to be built between

Saragossa and Pau; while the tunnel currently being excavated under the Puerto de Puymorens, just to the east of Andorra, will link Toulouse and Barcelona. As for the ninety-mile stretch of TGV (Train de Grande Vitesse) line between Barcelona and the French border at La Jonquera, the Catalan government has recently agreed on its exact route. Paris has just decided to give the Mediterranean frontier priority for the extension of the French TGV network to Spain, and the Catalans are euphoric. But it will be ten years before the TGV links Barcelona and the French capital.

There is little doubt in anyone's mind, north or south of the border, that Catalonia, Midi-Pyrénées (capital Toulouse) and Languedoc-Roussillon (capital Montpellier), with a combined area of 40,920 square miles and over 10 million inhabitants, are in the process of becoming a booming 'Euro-region'. Contacts between the three capitals are multiplying, co-operation schemes in education, research and industry are afoot, and both Pasqual Maragall and Jordi Pujol have close political friends in Toulouse and Montpellier. The motorway between Catalonia and France already means that it takes less than two hours to cover the hundred miles separating Barcelona and Perpignan, where more and more Catalans do their weekend shopping. Similarly, many Roussillon people drive south to Dalí's home town of Figueres, only twenty miles from the border, to shop at its well-supplied market and eat in the famous restaurant at Durán's Hotel, once frequented by the Surrealist genius and his friends. Such contacts are bound to become increasingly common.

Maragall has said that, when the Single Market begins to operate in 1993, Barcelona will provide services to 15 million people on both sides of the border. The 'Golden Triangle' may well become a European version of the American 'sun belt' that comprises California, Texas, Arizona and Florida. Some Catalans are worried by this prospect, fearing that the community's identity will be diluted in the process, and continue to dream of the day when the 'Catalan Countries' (Catalonia 'proper', Valencia and the Balearic Islands) will be linked as a homogenous unit. But such a prospect now seems unlikely, to say the least.

Catalonia today gives the impression that, for the foreseeable future, it will continue playing its role as the most European and technologically advanced region of Spain. My eye was caught recently by an article entitled 'The Spanish March' in Barcelona's leading newspaper, *La Vanguardia*, written by a Catalan representative in the Council of Europe, Lluís M. de Puig. In it he argued that, in the new Europe, with the gradual relinquishment of sovereignty by the member nations, there could be no question of setting up an independent Catalan State. Much more realistic would be to envisage some form of federal compromise within the European Community, in tune with Catalonia's destiny as a frontier region. 'The conditions of our future development', wrote M. de Puig, 'will depend on our ability to continue being a place of transit, a corridor of interchange, a meeting-place for people proceeding from different points of departure.'

It was Charlemagne and the Franks who first gave the name of 'Marca Hispanica', the Spanish March, to the region now known as Catalonia. The Principality's danger is the introspection and sense of victimization vis-à-vis Madrid that periodically assail its inhabitants, but full involvement in Europe may well free it from these bugbears. If it does so, industrious Catalonia, which one political wit recently termed 'a small European country between Spain and France', is likely to go from strength to strength.

$-10-$

At Home with Spaniards

What are Spaniards like? That is a daunting question, for, if generalizations about any nation are dangerous, they are peculiarly so in the case of Spain with its range of different peoples, languages and regional idiosyncrasies. I feel obliged to point out, moreover, that, although it has been my destiny, privilege and delight to explore Spain on and off for over thirty years, I have only resided for long periods in two places: Granada and, especially, Madrid.

What follows cannot claim, therefore, to be a comprehensive picture. Nor does it profess to be an unbiased one. I have been earning my keep as a writer in Spain since 1978, and was granted Spanish nationality in 1984. I am not here as a tourist, nor as a retired hispanist with a pension. I live and work among Spaniards, and about them, as about the people of my native Ireland, my feelings are mixed, a passionate compound of love and rage, with love predominating. One final point: much of what I say will have only a limited application to the Catalans, to my way of thinking the least 'Spanish' of Spaniards (although many Basques would, I know, disagree energetically, claiming for themselves this questionable distinction).

What are the really positive things one can say about Spaniards and their way of life? What does one admire about these warm-hearted, generous, incurious people who consistently run down their country, assert, often with scorn, that Spanish products are rubbish (*chapuza*) and will tell you, quite seriously (quoting Miguel de Unamuno or Salvador de Madariaga in support), that the National Vice is envy?

I rate, above all, their zest for getting the most out of the present moment. If ever there was a people who put into practice Horace's injunction to 'enjoy the day and trust as little as possible to the future', it is surely the Spaniards, an intensely sociable human group who like nothing better than spontaneous happenings, the sudden improvising of a party or outing. Observe them in a restaurant. It would be hard to imagine people enjoying themselves more fully. For sheer rollicking human exuberance, nobody can beat the Spaniards. And when the time comes for singing, every man, woman and child of them knows the words.

Gerald Brenan was right to talk of 'the huge animal vitality of this race'. To anyone arriving in Spain from more northern climes, such energy can be overwhelming. Personally I find it exhilarating.

The vitality is transmitted at an early age. Spanish children are not repressed. Far from it. Spain is a wonderful country for the young, who are encouraged to join in adult social activities and to perform. They are also much kissed and hugged. As a result they grow up very confident, and you will find few self-conscious Spaniards. The amiable lawyer so engagingly played by John Cleese in *A Fish Called Wanda* makes the point that the English are terrified of being embarrassed. Not so the Spaniards. Christopher Ricks has written a fine book called *Keats and Embarrassment*. I do not believe it would be possible to devote more than a few pages to the presence of this painful emotion in any Spanish writer of the early nineteenth century – or indeed of any century. The very notion of embarrassment, as understood in Britain, is difficult to convey in Spanish. The language does not make a distinction between 'flushing' (with anger) and 'blushing' (with shame), for example, and the vocabulary of shame is extremely poor by comparison with English. Spaniards look you straight in the eye and, when challenged or 'caught out', will rarely flinch. Perhaps it is because they are encouraged to be conspicuous as children that they so rarely seem to 'lose countenance' in later life. Does this mean that in some respects they are a rather insensitive people? I think so.

In Spain it is easy and fun to follow the example of the natives and begin to loosen up, to be more relaxed. Spaniards help you to cope with your aggression too, providing many daily opportunities for practice. Here if you don't assert yourself strongly you go under. Among its other virtues, in short, Spain helps one to express one's emotions more freely. Certainly it has helped me to, and I am grateful to the country and its people for the therapy.

In *The Bible in Spain* (1843), George Borrow, a consummate linguist, comments on the inability of the English to use their hands when trying to communicate. 'When they attempt to speak Spanish, the most sonorous tongue in existence,' he writes, 'they scarcely open their lips, and putting their hands in their pockets fumble lazily, instead of applying them to the indispensable office of gesticulation.' His complaint still applies, 150 years later. Spaniards speak not only with their vocal chords but with the rest of their bodies, particularly in Andalusia. So must anyone who wants to feel fully at home among them.

Spaniards love talking. Here you can strike up a conversation with anybody and not feel that you are intruding. And there is nothing approaching the peculiarly nasty form of stand-offishness practised in England, based on where (and what school) you come from. I find the lack of snobbery, and of anything approaching a 'posh' voice, a great relief. People revel in their local accents and would never dream of trying to disguise or lose them. Prime Minister Felipe González, for example, has a markedly Andalusian one and even on State occasions brazenly drops the 'd' between vowels (for example, 'tomao' for 'tomado'), a practice not considered 'correct' in Castile.

Foreigners visiting Spain in the nineteenth century were struck by the innate dignity of the Spaniard. 'He is not a common being; he is an extraordinary man,' wrote Borrow, who singled out as Spaniards' great virtues 'a spirit of proud independence' and a marked lack of bigotry. These qualities still hold, and Spaniards have been proving since the death of Franco just how tolerant they can be when allowed to think for themselves.

Spanish society, with its preference for street life over home entertaining, encourages those superficial friendships that so enhance existence. In Spain people will never tell you, as is so common in England, that 'It may take you a long time to make close friends here, but once you do it's for ever.' The Spaniards are fully aware that, since you can only form a few such friendships in a lifetime, what really counts is being able to have shallow ones whenever you feel the urge. They are good about buying drinks (with the exception of the Catalans), and after ten minutes' conversation over a *copa* make you feel you've always known them. An illusion, to be sure, but none the less acceptable for that.

With Spanish vitality goes an immense zest for night life. Here you don't have to join a private club to get a drink in the early hours. True, most bars close much sooner than used to be the case under Franco, but you will always find one open, and people in it to talk to, particularly in Madrid. The capital's late-night pub and disco scene, the *movida* (from the verb *mover*, 'to move'), is unparalleled in Europe, and perhaps anywhere. The basic requirement of the *movida* is that, having had your drink and seen who's there, you hurry on to the next fashionable venue – and then the next and the next. If there are traffic jams in Madrid at four o'clock on a Friday and Saturday morning during the winter, the reader will have no difficulty in imagining what the *movida* is like in summer, every night of the week. From mid-June to September the *jornada intensiva* comes into operation: the 'intensive', white-collar working day from 8 a.m. to 3 p.m. with no lunch break. What the young and able often do during these months is to stay up all night, go straight to the office, put in their stint, eat, sleep from late afternoon to midnight, and then get ready to plunge back into the feverish dance.

As for the Spanish morning, I am a fervent admirer. Mainly because it's so *long*. In France the shops snap shut, like Monsieur Hulot's canoe, at twelve on the dot, and a few minutes later the citizens are 'à table'. Not in Spain. Here they put down the shutters (with a crash) at half-one or two. This means that if you ever get off to a slow start, which can happen after a spell of *movida*, there is still plenty of time to get things done. Since I am constitutionally incapable of writing after lunch, Spain's long mornings have made it possible for me to survive professionally. Could I ask for more?

With the shops and offices closed, Spaniards begin to think about lunch – and make straight to a bar serving *tapas*, which deserve a short paragraph to themselves. Spain would be unthinkable without *tapas*. Along with the potato omelette, they are among its greatest contributions to gastronomy and civilization. Spain is the only country in Europe, perhaps in the world, where it is normal to have a substantial nibble before going home to eat. (And, not surprisingly, Spanish males tend to be pot-bellied before thirty.) Among the *tapas* (the word means 'filler'), fresh anchovies, *boquerones*, are my favourites. They are eaten raw in an overnight marinade of oil, vinegar, parsley and garlic. As long as my bar can provide me a few times a week with a *ración* of these delicacies, and a glass of wine to wash them down with, life is still worth living.

Wine! It is perhaps not widely appreciated, either in or outside Spain, that the country can boast some 4,500 different labels. One of the decisions I took years ago in the gloom of England was eventually to earn enough money to be able to drink at least half a bottle of decent wine each evening. A modest aim! I achieved it by coming to live in Spain. The difficulty, of course, is to avoid finding oneself repeating the same operation at lunchtime.

Until not so long ago life among Spaniards used to be wearing, a constant battle to get things done. EC entry is changing this (Spain is much more efficient than it was) and has also gone a long way towards restoring Spaniards' confidence in themselves as a nation. They take their acceptance by the European club very seriously. Indeed, they revel in it. Language teaching has improved and more and more young people are travelling and studying outside Spain. The old inferiority complex, the old gripes, are far less in evidence, and as a result people are easier to deal with.

There is a moment in *Don Quixote* when the hero and Sancho Panza arrive at the edge of a town in La Mancha called Puerto Lápice on the road to Andalusia (today skirted by the motorway). 'Here, Brother Sancho, we can sink our arms up to the elbows in what are called adventures!' the would-be knight exclaims. I often think of this episode when I set out from Madrid on one of my own explorations. Spain is still a place for adventures, giving the impression that anything can happen at any moment; a place where even the most modest excursion guarantees surprises; where, if the *paisaje* (landscape) can be stunning, the *paisanaje* (the locals) are always entertaining, and where there is now the certainty of comfortable lodgings and good (sometimes excellent) fare.

I have no regrets about having come to live in Spain. On the contrary. But, to expand what I said at the beginning of this chapter, I feel for the country a passionate attachment mixed often with a sizeable quantity of rage (and disappointment). Many, perhaps most, of my Spanish friends feel the same way. I hope that it will be understood that what follows is not intended as criticism. Rather, it is a reflection on some of the problems, failings and infuriating conditioned reflexes of a people who for centuries were deprived of security, stability and dignity. In self-defence, allow me to quote Manuel Azaña, prime minister during the first two years of the Second Republic, and later its president. 'The Spanish people never learn from their mistakes,' Azaña wrote. 'Although the nation is old, and hardened by misfortune, the discontinuity of its culture, which always appears sporadically in isolated groups, makes it a people without experience.' That was written in 1923, when the dictatorship of General Primo de Rivera had just plunged Spain into another period of obscurantism. Today Spain is set on a stable democratic course, but to a considerable extent Azaña's observation still holds true.

An Andalusian frind of mine likes to make a wicked distinction between Spaniards and Germans, having had ample experience of both. 'Spaniards,' she assures me, 'have breeding [*educación*], but no sense of civic responsibility [*urbanidad*]; Germans have a sense of civic responsibility, but no breeding.' I can't say if my friend is right about the Germans, but as regards Spaniards the observation strikes me as accurate enough. Concern for the common good is a rare commodity in Spain, as a thousand daily signs reveal, from the papers dropped on the floors of bars and cafés, the empty cigarette packets tossed out of cars or the rubbish that strews the woods and ditches of the countryside (chairs, mattresses, plastic containers... you name it), to the refusal to donate blood or take part in neighbourhood associations until the bulldozer is actually knocking down the walls.

Spaniards tend to be utterly scornful of the idea of making any individual sacrifice for society at large. Indeed, the 'common good' as a concept is almost as lacking today as it was when Ford arrived in Spain in 1830. 'Few dream of making a combined effort for the public good,' he wrote in his famous *Handbook for Travellers in Spain*; 'the very idea of making a combined effort would be scouted with *carcajadas* of derisive laughter.'

That is still largely the case today, as Spaniards admit openly and even gleefully. 'Solidarity is not our strong point,' I have been told again and again. Under Franco's long regime the tendency intensified. All interest in politics was discouraged. Football, TV and censored American films became the opium of the people. In such a situation, as so often in Spain's previous history, it was every man for himself (there's a ubiquitous, and cruel, schoolboy saying here which goes 'Maricón [or marica] el último', 'Whoever comes last's a queer'). Protest of any kind was futile as well as dangerous in Franco's Spain, and the result is that Spaniards today are still not as energetic as they should be in standing up against petty officialdom. Almost twenty years after the dictator's demise the country has made enormous progress in learning new democratic ways. But the old habits linger on.

The Spaniards, in fact, are so anarchic that even anarchism strikes them as too organized. Angel Ganivet, a brilliant young diplomat and writer from Granada who committed suicide at thirty-eight in 1898 (the year in which Spain lost its last American colonies), was perceptive about this characteristic of his compatriots. He saw it as a result of the loosening of legal ties that took place during the early centuries of the struggle against the Muslims. At that time it was common practice for those engaged in fighting the Moors to claim special privileges or exemptions, known as *fueros*. In Ganivet's view this process led to an 'atomization' of the law, to a belief that each group, each family, was virtually entitled to its own *ad hoc* legal code. Hence, he assures us, the country came close to achieving the 'juridical dream' whereby every citizen would carry in his pocket a legal document that read: 'This Spaniard is authorized to do whatever he likes.'

Should it surprise us that the Spaniards can make a good case for having invented guerrilla warfare, the military expression of every man for himself? I think not.

One of Spain's great literary achievements is the seventeenth-century picaresque novel, which gave rise to an enormous vogue throughout Europe, Le Sage's *Gil Blas de Santillane* being the most famous non-Spanish representative of the genre. In these fast-moving narratives of low life, the 'pícaro' ('rogue' or 'scoundrel'), faced with an implacably harsh world, tries to beat the system by using his wits. It is 'maricón el último' again.

The modern 'pícaro' exists at every level of Spanish society, if we are to believe what Spaniards tell us about themselves, and scarcely a day passes but someone in high places is found to have succumbed to the national picaresque tendency. In 1989 Pilar Miró, Controller of Spanish TV, was accused of spending excessive sums of public money on her private wardrobe. Eventually she was forced to resign, though alleging her innocence. A high official in Spanish TV was quoted as saying that it seemed to him unfair that, 'in a country of "pícaros" like Spain', the former Controller should risk ending up in prison for the mere peccadillo of misappropriating a trivial quantity of public funds.

Another famous case has been that involving Juan Guerra, the brother of Alfonso Guerra, deputy prime minister until his resignation in February 1991. Juan Guerra, it transpired several months earlier, had been running some of his own private affairs from an official Andalusian government office allotted to him by the Socialists. There is no doubt that he was making a fortune out of his 'family connection'.

In the world of TV, radio and business, bribery is now so commonplace that hardly anyone thinks twice about it. 'You have a project that you would like us to accept? There's lots of competition, you know. It may be possible but not, you must understand, without paying a . . . commission.' I know of one TV producer who, because he refuses to play this game, is shunned by his colleagues.

The activity in which 'pícaros' engage, and their philosophy, are known as 'la picaresca', and you find this word everywhere in Spain, used in such combinations as 'la picaresca nacional', 'la picaresca política', 'la picaresca de los negocios' (the business variety) and so on. Pilar Miró's mistake was to get involved in 'la picaresca de la televisión'.

Spaniards have traditionally assumed that anyone in public office uses his or her position to engage in picaresque activities. This is because for centuries no sensible Spaniard could have had any faith either in the honesty or the efficiency of the administration. Ford's *Handbook* is eloquent in this respect, as in so many others. He found that there were dozens of pithy proverbs expressing the Spanish people's utter distrust of their rulers and civil servants. One of the most apt was 'Quien el aceite mesura, las manos unta', 'Measure olive oil, and your hands get greasy.'

Another well-known saying in the same line, still current today, is 'Quien hizo la ley hizo la trampa', 'Law-maker, law-breaker'. And another: 'Allá van leyes do quieren reyes', 'Laws go where kings wish.'

A notable example of 'la picaresca' that recently came my way concerns the Spanish equivalent of the MOT test. If your tyres are not in good order you don't pass this test which, in other respects, is not too exacting. The answer? To hire a sound set for the occasion, putting back the old ones later on. In Granada a firm offered this eminently picaresque service until it was uncovered and closed down.

It will come as no surprise to the reader to learn that smuggling has traditionally been a profession much admired in Spain, and that poaching is another national addiction. They are two further examples of the determination to beat the system. Not long ago the deputy president of one of the seventeen autonomous communities was forced to resign. In a country where hardly anyone ever resigns, he must have done something serious. He had. Despite being an ardent conservationist in theory, the police caught him shooting in a nature reserve. Another 'pícaro'.

'In Spain there are no businessmen, only speculators,' insists a neighbour of mine. This is of course an exaggeration, but it is true that when a Spaniard tells you that he is about to 'montar un negocio', or 'set up a business' (an expression one hears every day) what he really means is that he has devised a brilliant idea for making money quickly. To 'set up a business' and get out fast with the profits – this tends to be the Spanish view of what enterprise is all about. It is a picaresque view.

One way to make easy money in Spain has been tourism. The weather in most of the country is brilliantly sunny in summer, and there are thousands of miles of seaside. When the European sun-seekers began to arrive in the fifties, Spaniards suddenly realized that geography and climate were providing them with a fabulous new opportunity. Forty years later the results are there for all to see: the almost complete destruction of the Spanish coastline.

But the bonanza could not last forever, and rising prices, shoddy service and a changing world situation led to a rapid decline in the summer of 1990, when tourism, particularly from Great Britain, dropped so sharply that there was consternation on a national scale. 'Spain's Sun Loses Its Appeal for Europeans', 'Spain's Number One Industry in Crisis', 'The Tourist Crisis Is No Accident', 'Thunderclouds Over Spain's Tourist Industry', ran the newspaper headlines. The final figures showed that two million fewer tourists visited Spain in 1990 than in 1989.

After the panic came perplexity and then soul-searching. It was a sign of the growing maturity of Spanish society that the Tourist Board made no bones about what had gone wrong: quite simply, visitors were fed up with being ripped off.

In the New Spain the picaresque attitude to life may be waning. While people still believe that there is corruption in the administration, for example, it is no longer so common to hear blanket accusations of civil service improbity. Spaniards, like most people, hate having to pay taxes. Previously it was always assumed that they went to line the taxman's pocket. You don't hear that accusation so often now, although people still grumble that their taxes are not being used properly.

A stable administration has been one of Spain's most pressing needs for centuries, and is now becoming a reality within the framework of the EC. Such a revolution is leading to changes in the way Spaniards think about themselves and those who govern them, and will probably mean that the 'pícaro' becomes an increasingly rare species. In this, as in so many other respects, Spain is going to be somewhat less 'different' than formerly.

If what foreigners most appreciate about Spain is its sun (which luckily, as someone has pointed out, does not depend on national technology), what they most dislike, according to research by the Department of Tourism, is its noise.

Spaniards will accept, under duress, that theirs is the noisiest country in the world after Japan. Alan Bookbinder, BBC series producer of the 'Fire in the Blood' films, has experience of noise production in both countries. Over lunch in Seville, as the waiters crashed plates on the sideboard next to us and people roared at each other across the tables, he assured me that, while in Japan there is a constant industrial hum, nothing in that country can approach Spain for sheer, brutal, relentless, eardrum-shattering din. According to a report published by the United Nations Programme for the Environment, no less than 80 per cent of Spaniards are constantly subjected to noise levels in excess of 80 decibels, 15db louder than the safety limit set by the experts.

The noise has many sources. To start with the language itself, particularly when spoken by Castilians, can be harsh and rasping (in the mouths and throats of other Spaniards it tends to be softer), and these qualities are emphasized when people talk loudly, as they so often do. Numerous descriptions of the Spanish voice have been essayed by foreign hispanophiles. Laurie Lee, for example. In *As I Walked Out One Midsummer Morning*, he records that he heard men 'talking ceaselessly together with the dry throaty rattle of pebbles being rolled down a gulley'. That gets it well. So does Victor Pritchett's definition. 'It is a dry, harsh, stone-cracking tongue,' he observes in *The Spanish Temper*, 'a sort of desert Latin chipped off at the edges by its lisped consonants and dry-throated gutturals, its energetic "r's", but opened by its strong emphatic vowels.' Pritchett goes on to make another point, which may offend some but with which it is difficult not to agree. 'Castilian,' he says, 'is above all a language which suggests masculinity, or at any rate it is more suited to the male voice than to the feminine voice which, in Spain, shocks one by its lack of melody.'

Add to this the fact that most Spaniards are intensely gregarious, self-assertive and talkative. In order to make themselves heard (the main object) they must perforce raise their voices. They must also speak fast. Children born into this environment learn to shout very early on in order to get attention, and since such behaviour is not frowned upon by their noise-intensive elders they never lose the habit.

Spain's conversational hullabaloo is not a new phenomenon. Many nineteenth-century visitors commented on it. 'There is more row aboard a Spanish fishing-smack than an English line-of-battle ship,' Richard Ford found in the 1830s.

One odd by-product of the Spanish attitude to noise is that in this country you will only very rarely hear people whisper in the English sense of the term. When an attempt is made to do so (in cinemas or other public places) the vocal chords come into automatic operation and produce a resonant low growling to which the Spanish term 'cuchicheo' hardly does justice. From the public gallery during a parliamentary debate I was once almost able to follow a private conversation between two representatives sitting below me. No doubt they believed they were whispering. Sometimes I wonder if, just as the Great Auk's wings became atrophied through lack of use, Spaniards will one day find themselves literally unable to have recourse to this subtle form of verbal communication.

Domingo García Sabell, distinguished doctor, writer and member of the Spanish Royal Academy, has long been asking himself why Spaniards shout at each other instead of simply talking. Himself a quietly-spoken Galician, he has come to the conclusion that behind the vociferation (and its attendant gestures) lies the desire to reduce the opposition to silence. It is often difficult to retain Spaniards' attention during a conversation. Observe any group of people talking and you will notice how they switch off, or become intensely impatient, when anyone holds the conversational stage for too long. Spaniards are terrible listeners. My dentist assures me that all his countryfellows want is to hear the sound of their own voices.

The novelist Anthony Burgess is well acquainted with Spanish noise. He speaks the language, is popular here, and sometimes turns up to promote his work at the book launches which, in Spain, are multitudinous social occasions, mainly because of the drink and canapés liberally provided. Few of the guests attend to the official business, unless, that is, the event is held behind closed doors in a room with seats. At one of Burgess's launches (it was the no-seats, no-closed-doors variety) he and others tried to talk about his work. To no avail. The fatal error had been made of serving drinks before the speakers performed, and the guests were talking to each other at the tops of their voices. Pleas from the organizers produced each time a brief silence, but soon the hubbub rose again, a tidal surge, and the voices from the platform sank beneath the flood.

When Pope John Paul II visited this country a few years ago he was struck by the Spaniards' inability to keep quiet. 'El Papa también quiere hablar', 'The Pope too would like to talk', he told the large, chattering crowd which had turned up, supposedly to listen to him, at an open-air mass in Madrid.

The other noises? Well, motorbikes in general and two-strokes and mopeds in particular (the adolescents tamper with the silencers); car horns, used habitually in self-affirmation ('get out of my way!') and angrily by drivers blocked in by the double- and triple-parked vehicles that are a permanent feature of city life in Spain; pounding car radios; the manic whistles of the traffic police; ambulance, fire brigade and police sirens, far more strident than is necessary; faulty burglar alarms suddenly going off accidentally; ear-splitting pneumatic drills; madly barking dogs (every chalet has one); rattling air-conditioning systems; the open-air terraces with their throbbing music; revellers bellowing at each other in the early hours of the morning as they empty out of bars and discos; blaring TV sets placed by open windows, or in private gardens, on summer evenings; refuse collections in the early hours of the morning . . . the list is endless.

Spanish bars are the noisiest in the world. TV, a panoply of fruit machines (which, when nobody uses them, draw attention to themselves with maddening snatches from 'The Harry Lime Theme' and 'La Cucaracha'), talking cigarette-dispensers, videogames, radios or cassette-players emitting non-stop rhythmic backing, cacophonous expresso machines and coffee-grinders – frequently all this paraphernalia operates at the same time, forcing the clientele to raise their voices even more.

They now provide background music in what until recently was my favourite restaurant in downtown Madrid. A friendly house, old-style, comfortable. I liked the place among other reasons because the acoustics were good. So I gently upbraided my friend the owner. He turned the music off, slightly offended. The next time I went it was on again – the same tape, the same infuriating anthology of Russian pop classics. 'The other clients haven't complained,' he assured me, more offended than on the previous occasion. I said there was no accounting for tastes. I haven't been back.

According to a press report appearing in October 1988, 20 per cent of Spanish adolescents suffer from hearing loss caused by the excessive noise generated in discothèques and bars.

Forty-four per cent of Madrid's streets were found in 1990 to have continuous noise in excess of the limit considered tolerable by the World Health Organization. It is believed that the 70 million aspirins swallowed annually in the metropolitan area of the capital are not unconnected to this circumstance.

People thinking of spending a summer holiday in Spain should avoid at all costs renting a property with sleeping accommodation giving on to an inner patio. These deep pits are an inferno of noise pollution. Windows are kept open, the TVs throb relentlessly, the domestic activities of the families inhabiting the block are generously communicated (and Spaniards stay up very late at night, particularly in July and August). If the bedroom looks over the street the noise level may be minimally lower, depending where the house (I assume it to be a block of flats) is situated.

More and more Spaniards are aware of this problem. In Madrid the 'Green Patrol' was reintroduced, after a previous experiment, in 1989. This tiny police corps is responsible to the Environment Department of the town council. According to a report appearing in the press in May 1990, 30 per cent of the complaints received by the Department concerned noise. 'The people of this city are suffering from noise mania,' one officer told me, using a newly coined term that had not come my way before, *ruidomanía*. There are laws, regulations . . . but, in accordance with the maxim, 'Never do what you're told unless you absolutely have to' (Spaniards habitually do the *opposite* of what they're told), they tend to be disregarded. Madrid's Green Patrol is powerless to penalize more than an infinitesimal percentage of infractions.

One of the worst legacies of the Franco regime was a country with few public libraries and the lowest reading index in Europe (Portugal excepted). The State had no interest in encouraging reading among young or old, since book-lovers tend to be thinkers and can easily become opponents. Anyone who used the 'facilities' of the National Library in those days will remember the atmosphere of distrust that pervaded an institution where the volume consulted on Monday evening was often 'unavailable' on Tuesday morning.

The New Spain is trying to improve the situation, but it is an uphill battle made all the more difficult by the circumstance that the country is now television-mad, particularly since several private channels started transmitting in 1989 and 1990. After the British, in fact, Spaniards watch more TV than any other nation in western Europe, which seems unbelievable given the fact that, thanks to the good climate, they live so much of their lives out of doors. According to a recent survey, they are spending more and more time every day in front of the set, an average of 183.8 minutes in 1990 compared to 173 in 1989. If the standard were high, perhaps the situation would not be so serious. But it is woefully low, and even State TV interrupts its programmes with commercial advertising.

Where newspapers are concerned the figures for 1988 show that only 80 copies were reaching every 1,000 Spanish citizens. In Sweden and Japan the ratio was 500 per 1,000; in the other Nordic countries, and in Great Britain and Switzerland, 300–400. Even Italy and

Greece were doing slightly better than Spain. Since a ratio of 100 newspapers per 1,000 inhabitants is the dividing-line set by UNESCO to distinguish between developed and underdeveloped countries, Spain, by this token, is still a backward nation.

More than half the population never reads books, according to an opinion poll carried out by *El País* in 1985. When, on 1 January 1986, readers were hit by the imposition of 6 per cent VAT on books, despite massive opposition from the publishers and booksellers, the result was to push purchases down to an all-time low. The trade feels that in this respect Spain's EEC entry negotiators failed miserably in not securing the zero rating on books enjoyed by some other member countries.

According to a table published by the Madrid daily *El Independiente* in April 1990, the percentage of Europeans who habitually read was then as follows (the list of countries is incomplete):

1	German Federal Republic	74%
2	Low Countries	71%
3	France	57%
4	United Kingdom	55%
5	Italy	48%
6	Spain	36%

The Spanish performance was dismal indeed, much more dismal than the casual visitor to the Madrid Book Fair, held annually in the Retiro Park, might guess from the crowd milling among the hundreds of stalls.

As for public libraries, in 1983 there were 1,459 throughout Spain, and the number of library books per inhabitant was in the region of 0.30. Since UNESCO sets the acceptable national level at two or three public library books per inhabitant, Spain was, once again, floundering in a Third-World category. Sweden, by contrast, offered 4.71 volumes per person.

By 1986 the number of public libraries had grown to 2,500, a considerable achievement but still far from the target of 5,000 recommended by UNESCO. Much of the credit for the improvement was due to the autonomous regions. Valencia had proved particularly go-ahead, having decided that within a few years all towns with more than 3,000 inhabitants were to have their own public library.

In 1987 the Spanish publishers' guild stated that almost 8,000 municipalities throughout the country lacked even the most basic library facilities. This meant that some 10 million Spaniards were still being denied free access to books. The publishers added that, while in the USA and the majority of West European countries sales to libraries accounted for 20 per cent of the total, in Spain the figure was only 1.5 per cent – a disastrous situation not only for publishers but also for writers. Three years later figures issued by the Ministry of Culture showed that, of all the European countries, only Greece had fewer public library books per inhabitant. The Spanish ratio was then 0.35 books per citizen.

According to an official report published at the end of 1990 Spain has 10½ million 'functional illiterates' (people over fifteen lacking the basic reading and writing skills) and 1½ million complete illiterates, two thirds of them women. This out of a total population of 39 million. In a society dominated by TV, these people have little incentive either to learn to read or to improve their ability: far easier just to sit hour after hour watching the imported soap operas now provided every day after lunch, or the quiz games included daily on the channels' menus.

In order to change a nation's reading habits, you must reach the young. But the young, alas, are more interested in TV than books.

Almost forty years of negligence on the part of the Franco authorities and now increasing audiovisual competition make it impossible to feel optimistic about the future of reading in Spain. 'The best way to keep a secret in Spain is to publish it in a book,' said Manuel Azaña in the 1930s. Unfortunately this is still true today, sixty years later.

If, rather than reading, Spaniards prefer to watch torrents of TV, they also devote much time and vast quantities of money to gambling, an activity nowadays liberated from the strictures that fettered it under Franco. In 1990 Spaniards spent some £17½ billion on games of chance, which means, on average, approximately £450 per capita. According to Spanish sources the country comes top of the international gambling addiction league. Daily lotteries (the results of which are announced on TV), football pools, horse racing, fruit machines, bingo, casinos . . . gambling, in one or other of its expressions, gives full-time employment to over 250,000 people.

Hundreds of thousands of Spaniards are hooked on games of chance, almost half of them on the fruit-machines or one-armed bandits known popularly as 'tragaperras', 'small-change-swallowers', without which no Spanish bar would now be felt to be complete. A report appearing in 1988 revealed that these ubiquitous gadgets had earned £6 billion the previous year. By the end of 1989 Spain had 371,000 of them (compared with Britain's 170,000), with Madrid and its periphery accounting for 63,600. Indeed, according to the most recent figures, for every 100 pesetas spent on gambling, sixty go on fruit-machines. One of the most serious aspects of the phenomenon is that in the bars, so central to the Spanish way of life, children not only see their parents playing these machines, and absorb the excitement, but are themselves initiated into the coin-operated world thanks to the videogames also provided. The atmosphere conduces to dependence, and the moment the children come of age at eighteen, and it is legal to play the *tragaperras*, the pattern continues.

A name has been invented for the national gambling disease: *ludopatía*, 'ludopathy' (from the Latin *ludus*, 'game'). At a private clinic in Madrid set up for the treatment of ludopaths, several hundred victims are treated each year. 'The situation is bound to get worse in the future,' the establishment's psychiatrist, José Luis García, said in January 1991, after Spaniards had just spent £750,000,000 on the Christmas lotteries, 'because consumerism and the desire for easy money are growing apace.' According to the same authority, between 300,000 and 600,000 Spanish ludopaths are in urgent need of help.

The taxman loves a lottery, and the Treasury skims £3 billion a year from this particular Spanish passion. It's no wonder that the State does little to discourage 'ludopathy'.

Each December Spain's gambling mania works up to its annual fever pitch. The National Lottery's special Christmas draw, 'El Gordo' – 'The Big One' – is approaching. On 23 December the nation waits with bated breath while neatly dressed teenagers from a children's home chant the results on TV. Once the astronomical prizes have been announced Spaniards relax and get down to the business of celebrating the birth of the Saviour. Then, coinciding with the day when Spanish children traditionally receive their presents, Twelfth Night, the National Lottery has another special draw, known as 'El Niño',

'The Infant Christ'. The results, like 'El Gordo', make media headlines.

One of the most remarkable business organizations in the country is the ONCE, set up with Franco's approval in 1938. The letters stand for *Organización Nacional de Ciegos Españoles*, the National Organization for Blind Spaniards. Among its activities the ONCE runs a daily lottery from Monday to Friday whose proceeds fund salaries for the 13,000 blind and 8,000 handicapped men and women who sell the 100-peseta tickets (200 pesetas on Fridays) throughout Spain, and finance many other initiatives on behalf of the unsighted and disabled. The ONCE has been headed since 1986 by the dynamic lawyer Miguel Durán, himself blind, who for his financial acumen and ruthless dedication has earned himself the nickname of 'Al Cupone' ('cupón' is the Spanish for 'lottery ticket').

The ONCE, now one of the five largest companies in Spain, has among its wide-ranging investments a 25 per cent stake in Spain's most blatantly commercial private TV channel, Tele-5, of which Durán is chairman. Also with a 25 per cent holding in Tele-5 is Italian media magnate Silvio Berlusconi, whose presence tells in the channel's style. Each evening Tele-5 runs a fifteen-minute programme called 'Telecupón' in which the ONCE lucky number of the day is drawn by provocatively dressed girls carefully chosen for their voluptuous proportions. 'Telecupón' must surely rate as one of Spain's, and perhaps Europe's, most unashamedly materialistic TV spots.

Does this form of advertising encourage the spread of addictive 'ludopathy'? Ex-gambler Mariano Carnicero, one of the founder-members of an association set up in Madrid to help sufferers, is certain it does. 'The Government should ban all such advertising,' he insists, 'and every lottery ticket should have a government warning printed on it like on cigarettes packets, saying that it can be dangerous to health.' Carnicero knows that there is little chance that any Spanish government will ever heed such counsel. Quite simply, the State's income from gambling is so astronomical that it cannot afford to relinquish its cut.

Manna from heaven, never to have to work again in your life . . . it's a dream in which Spaniards are encouraged to indulge by the State itself.

*   *   *

If gambling is one way of living dangerously, reckless driving is another, and more lethal. As you are, so you drive, and seeing how Spaniards handle their cars, particularly young Spaniards, one is not surprised at the huge number of deaths on the roads. The tendency is to deny that the mentality of drivers is to blame for the situation. It's the poor condition of the roads: if only the Ministry of Public Works would improve them there would be far fewer accidents! But the Ministry *has* improved the roads and the deaths continue. The trouble lies with the drivers.

Having an impressive car, and driving it fast and ostentatiously, is clearly one of the compulsive needs of today's Spanish male. The car is Spain's new idol, the BMW the leading yuppie status symbol. The compulsion is fuelled by TV advertising, which puts great emphasis on the opportunity to acquire the car of your dreams, instantaneously, for 'minimal' monthly repayments. The connection between success and the possession of an alluring automobile is underscored by the media. The repayments will continue for years, but who cares? What counts is the appearance of affluence and success, here, now, immediately.

The obsessive keeping up of appearances goes back a long time in Spanish history. In his picaresque novel *The Swindler*, published in 1626, Francisco de Quevedo introduces us to an impoverished squire who explains how he and his like hire a carriage once a year and an elegant shirt-front to go with it. As they are driven slowly round and round the city's fashionable districts they present a resplendent façade to the public while keeping a sharp eye out for acquaintances, who receive profuse salutations. Thanks to this annual subterfuge they will be accounted men of substance! To the petty nobleman in question, the idea that someone like him should actually *work* to better his lot is abhorrent. Work! Old Christians do not work! Till the land with one's hands? Never! The point is to maintain the *appearance* of affluence.

Two centuries later things had not changed much, and foreign travellers noted that Spaniards, even when they didn't have a penny to their names, took pains to dress as nattily as possible. Visitors received the impression that there were no lengths to which Spaniards would not go in order to offer a well-turned-out exterior to the world.

Nowadays credit facilities make it possible for almost anyone to have a suitably impressive car, whereas, until not long ago, a Fiat 600 was the most the average citizen could ever hope to own. Spaniards, someone once said, love things foreign but are less keen on foreigners. There is truth in this. In a country that has had little in the way of indigenous technology, modern machinery and innovations have had to be imported ('Let the other countries invent!', Unamuno once exclaimed in an attack of pique). To possess them has been a hallmark of success, a gaudy feather in the cap. The foreign car is an obvious case in point and nowadays you can have one at the stroke of a pen. Forty per cent of Spanish car sales in 1990 were of imported models.

It is not only the owners of potent cars (and today almost all cars are potent) who put their foot down. So too, given a chance, do the drivers of lorries and even buses. Spaniards do have tremendous vitality, and this is bound to be expressed when they get behind the wheel. The King, by all accounts a first-rate driver, is no exception to the national obsession with speed. He has a collection of fabulous motorbikes and cars, including a Porsche 959 (which can accelerate from zero to 75 m.p.h. in four seconds), and every so often is reputed to escape from his modest palace outside Madrid to put them through their paces.

You will notice again and again the prevalence of broken glass at Spanish crossroads. This is the result of drivers' determination to get through the traffic-lights at all costs, certainly if they have changed to orange and often when they are red. Since the drivers waiting to draw away from the lights in the other direction feel exactly the same, the ensuing mid-street crashes are inevitable. At every junction in Madrid you will see cars hurtling through the red lights in the teeth of the oncoming traffic. Hence the strewn glass.

Because of the determination to beat the traffic-lights at all costs, the crossroads in the capital, even those marked out with a 'box', are frequently blocked. This produces turmoil – and a constant din of protesting horns. I once asked a taxi driver why Spaniards crash the lights. 'In Spain we all want to be number one,' he replied without hesitation. Other people have confirmed this interpretation. 'If you stop when the lights are orange you feel like a *gilipollas*,' one said. The word is difficult to render into polite English. A stupid twit, let's say. This very macho notion has been assimilated by many women drivers, too, whose gestures of annoyance I often catch in my rear mirror on

189

those occasions when I resist the infectious urge to crash the lights myself.

If a lot of drivers charge up to the traffic-lights and make only a last-second decision to stop, the majority of motorcyclists and moped riders consider that they are under no obligation to halt at a red light at all if they are turning right. They will slow down initially for reasons of self-protection, but, having ascertained that the way is clear enough to proceed, carry on blithely. I have never seen anyone pulled in by the police for doing this – and everyone does it.

The traffic situation in the cities is further exacerbated by drivers' parking habits, which include leaving their cars in the bus and taxi lanes – often rendered inoperative as a result. Wherever you go in Madrid you will see double-parked cars, frequently with their emergency lights winking. The latter gesture, very indicative of the Spanish temperament, means: 'This is my car, there is no emergency but, since I know that technically I shouldn't be here and am probably blocking you in, I'm letting you know that I'll be right back. Try to be understanding. You'd do the same thing. If you need me in a hurry, blow your horn.' The trapped victims *do* blow their horns, and the din produced is one of the characteristics of city life. A member of Madrid's 'Green Patrol' interviewed for the 'Fire in the Blood' series told me that, when he went to buy a car recently, the dealer informed him that the model he was interested in 'was equipped with emergency lights for double-parking'!

Fines are imposed by traffic wardens on the parking infractors, but only a very small proportion are collected. The average reaction is to tear up the ticket in the sure knowledge that the municipal authorities cannot cope with the magnitude of the problem and that the chances of having to fork out are minimal. If you are one of the unlucky ones whose car gets towed away, then that is a different, and costly, matter. But there aren't enough such trucks to go round.

I have been unable to find a term in Spanish to render the English 'to barge'. Perhaps this is because barging in one form or another is taken so much for granted in Spain that no word is necessary. Spaniards hate queues, and the tendency to jump them, to sidle in, is widespread. People barge their way into buses and the underground, or run ahead of the foreigners lining up for taxis at the airport. It's very difficult to get served in a crowded Spanish bar if one doesn't learn to assert oneself forcefully. As for the drivers, well, they too barge a lot, cutting in, weaving, pushing. They consider zebra crossings as much a nuisance as traffic lights and as you make your way across will often flash past within a hair's breadth. Don't step on unless the way is absolutely clear. Most drivers will only halt if your determination to cross is made very obvious indeed.

Even though the use of seat-belts is now compulsory except in towns, Spanish males are reluctant to employ them. I imagine that they see their use as another intolerable attack on their personal freedom and virility. Motorcyclists cannot so easily avoid their legal obligation to wear helmets, however, and these are now almost universal on Spanish roads (although not in the towns). The Civil Guard, responsible for policing the highways and the only force of law and order commanding healthy respect in Spain, has seen to that.

In April 1990 a highly advertised new Road Safety Act was introduced, with sweeping powers to make Spanish drivers behave better, including the introduction of breath tests and stiff fines for serious infractions. There was a great deal of fuss the first few days, with thousands of police interventions, and it seemed that drivers were responding to the call for a greater sense of responsibility. But then the old habits began to assert themselves again. Despite the decrease in accidents since April, August registered an all-time record for deaths.

Commenting on this relapse, a reader wrote to the Madrid daily *El Sol* (19/8/90): 'The basic problem is the lack of culture on the part of drivers, a failing which can be resumed in a nutshell as a lack of respect for others. The same phenomenon occurs in Spanish society at every level and the roads could hardly be an exception.'

The figures for road deaths over the Christmas period showed that the Act was indeed making little impact. Between 21 December 1990 and 1 January 1991 almost two hundred people died. The figures for 1990 as a whole were 5,935 dead. Shortly afterwards it was announced that fines were to be further increased, driving licences confiscated for a wider variety of offences and breath tests made more stringent. Spaniards themselves say that they will only behave when the authorities are tough, so perhaps such measures will gradually bring about a change in the nation's performance behind the wheel. For the moment, as Barcelona's head of traffic said in April 1991, 'In

Spain to get a fine for driving too fast is considered an achievement. Here no one will boast of jumping a red light, but any self-respecting driver will tell you that he can do 125 miles in an hour and a quarter.'

But what about the proverbial Spanish insistence on not doing today what can be put off until tomorrow or preferably the day after? Foreigners have always been irritated, and sometimes maddened, by this particular Spanish 'difference'. The Duke of Wellington, for instance, despaired during the Peninsular War at the constant stalling of his Spanish allies (while greatly admiring the fighting qualities of the ordinary Spanish soldier), and those of us who live here today know that you really must start worrying when a Spaniard says: 'No problem, it's as good as done' (*Esto está hecho*).

The best satirical comment ever produced on the national tendency to procrastinate (a proclivity to which, once again, Catalonia is the exception) was penned by the journalist Mariano José de Larra, who committed suicide in 1837 at the age of twenty-eight. Just before blowing his brains out Larra published a newspaper article entitled 'Vuelva usted mañana' ('Come Back Tomorrow'), in which he chronicled the sad case of an enterprising Frenchman who arrives in Madrid with the laudable purpose of setting up a business. The answer in every ministerial department is 'Come back tomorrow'. Finally, in despair, the would-be entrepreneur goes home. Things have improved dramatically since then, particularly now that the EC pressure is on. But the inclination to postpone action is still there, and one must beware of taking anything for granted until the contract has actually been signed.

One of the consequences of procrastination is that sensible precautions against things going wrong are habitually not taken in Spain until it is too late. The nineteenth-century English travellers, ever on the lookout for 'Moorish influence', noted that Spaniards had what they interpreted as an Oriental fatalism about accidents, seeing them as inevitable rather than the result of a lack of foresight. A century later things have improved – but not that much. Thus a leader in *El País* complained in August 1990, as Madrid's temperatures topped 100° Fahrenheit, that adequate provision had not been made to prevent the telephones, always affected by excessive heat, from collapsing and causing chaos at Barajas, the city's international airport. It was discovered that a few days earlier the airport's control system had been out of action for over six hours due to an easily predictable breakdown at the local telephone station, with the result that the airport was cut off from almost half the country. During these hours no aircraft had taken off from Barajas, but many had flown in through the blackout area, receiving instructions from Barcelona. *El País* expressed horror at the lack of co-ordination between the telephone company and the Department of Civil Aviation.

At the bottom of my road there is a pedestrian island in the middle of which the remains of a lamp-post base with four protruding bolts lie in wait for the unwary. It has been there for ten years. I admit that I haven't rung up the local authorities to suggest that they remove it before somebody trips in the dark and is hurt. Nor have I suggested that they cut down the several dead trees outside our block of flats which, sooner or later, are likely to fall and kill somebody. After almost fifteen years in Spain you catch yourself shrugging your shoulders more often than you used to. You put things off. You leave them until *mañana*.

I said at the beginning of this chapter that my feelings about Spaniards are mixed and passionate. I hope that it's now reasonably clear why this should be so. I have come to see, moreover, that in Spain there is no option but to take the good with the bad, since both are inseparably related – the inhabitants' extremely attractive ebullience, for instance, being the cause of the fact that it may be difficult to get to sleep at night in the summer. If, as a result of EC membership, Spain were to change too profoundly (to become, let's say, a Mediterranean Germany) I'd be tempted to pack my bags. But I don't envisage any such contingency. 'We in this country all have a depth of "Spanishness" that not even torture could wring out of us,' wrote the Andalusian novelist Juan Valera in 1888. Those words, happily, are still true.

-11-

A Nation at Work

By the time Franco died the Spanish people were desperate for change. Luckily the politicians, themselves an expression of the popular will, rose to the occasion. Luckily, too, King Juan Carlos proved himself to be just the right man at the right moment.

One cannot over-stress how well the King has done his job. It is tempting to say that his role has been providential. Charming, an excellent mixer, genuinely modest, firm when necessary, imposingly tall (this has been important, too, in a country where people are still small), he has had exactly the touch that was needed. Santiago Carrillo, the veteran Communist leader, reflecting on the King's contribution in the early stages of the transition to democracy, once put it nicely. 'I am now a convinced Juan Carlos Republican,' he joked. That about sums up, I think, how most Spaniards feel about the King and the country's current condition: the monarchy is working, there is peace, we are in Europe, and if, in the future, we decide to change the Constitution and bring in the Third Republic, we can do so. Meanwhile, what's the hurry? It is very rarely indeed that one hears Republican arguments put forward in Spain today. The few old Republicans who continue to express their disillusionment are hardly listened to. They are fossils. As for the Anarchists, they have almost disappeared off the map.

Perhaps there is a tendency to forget, after ten years of Socialist government with all too little opposition and a considerable degree of complacency, if not arrogance (they have won three successive general elections), that not only the PSOE but all the political parties contributed to the making of the consensus Constitution of 1978. That Constitution, which enshrines the principles of compromise and tolerance that have been so lacking in Spanish life over the last five centuries, was a major achievement by Spaniards as a whole.

It is true, however, that the story of The New Spain is to a large extent that of the Socialists' decade in office, a decade marked by their gradual conversion to centre-of-the-road liberalism.

Over the years Felipe González has taken on increasingly the role of Mr President, ably supported by his deputy prime minister (until January 1991) and fellow Sevillian Alfonso Guerra, a brilliant organizer as charismatic as González but in a different style. Whereas the imperturbable 'Felipe', as he is universally known in Spain, almost always expresses himself with consummate diplomacy, Guerra has a vitriolic wit and a tongue that at any moment can (and often does) run away with him – to the delight of his innumerable admirers. González is not only prime minister but secretary general of the Socialist Party, of which Guerra is deputy leader. As a result the Tweedledum-Tweedledee 'duumvirate' wielded immense power for almost ten years. Guerra's resignation as deputy prime minister marked the end of an epoch (his place was taken by a rather dour Catalan, Narcís Serra, previously minister of Defence), but he retains his position as deputy leader of a PSOE more and more divided between González-inspired pragmatists and those who, like Guerra himself, retain some flicker of allegiance to the old revolutionary ideals.

At various points in this book I have nailed my colours to the mast and expressed my disappointment with some aspects of the PSOE's performance in power while, at the same time, indicating what I think can fairly be considered its successes, not least a considerable advance in human rights. Perhaps above all one must be grateful to the Socialists for providing a political stability quite new in Spanish life. I believe that this has had a deeply calming effect on society.

The balance is positive, although not quite so positive as, perhaps naïvely, one had hoped.

Felipe González and his colleagues won the biggest overall majority in Spanish history in 1982 after promising a new, ethically-orientated politics and, in particular, a referendum on NATO in which the government would recommend that the country withdraw from the Alliance ('OTAN, de entrada, no' ran the electoral slogan). Unfortunately the ethical revolution was never effected and, where NATO was concerned (very much an ethical issue, this), the PSOE did an about-turn. The referendum, as mentioned earlier, was put off for four years and only held, in March 1986, once Spain was safely in the EEC.

The referendum campaign had a devastating effect on hundreds of thousands, perhaps millions, of PSOE supporters who were against Spain's membership of NATO. At the time I had the opportunity to talk to many Socialist mayors and town councillors around the country. 'Personally I'm for leaving NATO,' one mayor told me, 'but the party has decided we should stay put. My job and family are my first priorities, so publicly I'm in favour of remaining in.'

Similar confessions could be heard everywhere in those days. Within the Socialist family the campaign set father against son, brother against sister, cousin against cousin. It spread corruption and confusion and it poisoned friendships.

The main argument used to justify staying in NATO was economic. If Spain withdrew, the Socialists maintained, not only would the country be weakened internationally but foreign investors, vital to galvanize the economy, would go elsewhere. All the ethical arguments against Spain's membership used by the Socialists in 1982 were conveniently forgotten. They had been sacrificed on the altar of 'pragmatism', a pragmatism that meant, first and foremost, keeping in with the USA.

Felipe González is nothing if not pragmatic. It was pragmatic for the party formally to abandon Marxism (which he forced it to do shortly before the PSOE won the 1982 general election), pragmatic to change its policy on nationalization of the banks, and now pragmatic to stay in NATO.

The prime minister's last speech before referendum day, seen on TV, had a decisive influence on the outcome of the poll. Speaking from a podium of Mussolinian dimensions he insisted that withdrawal would spell economic disaster, and proclaimed that messages supporting the PSOE's pro-NATO stand were pouring in from Europe and (of all places) South America. NATO, the prime minister assured his audience, was 'the only path open' to Spain. Neutrality led 'nowhere'. Ethics professor José Luis López Aranguren – one of Spain's most respected thinkers, *sui generis* liberal Catholic and lifelong adversary of the politicially powerful, beginning with Franco – figured prominently among those who wanted the country out of NATO. Aranguren, today in his eighties, has repeatedly lamented the failure of the Socialists' promised ethical revolution and denounced a society where far too many posts are occupied by people appointed simply because they are card-carrying members of the PSOE. In particular, Aranguren regrets the way in which many self-styled intellectuals have put themselves at the service of the party in return for favours of one sort or another. 'The NATO referendum showed on which side of the fence such intellectuals stood,' he said recently, 'and the Gulf War made it even clearer. Such individuals feel at home in the present situation, naturally. They've been domesticated by those in power.'

The Socialists' general failure to give an ethical lead to the country, their abandonment of any semblance of radicalism, gave rise at the time of the referendum to a memorable witticism. According to this the PSOE had now settled for 'changes' of a more materialistic nature. These were 'the three "c's"': *coche* (a new car), *compañera* (a new girl-friend) and *casa* (a new house).

Following the NATO referendum a noticeable disillusionment (*desengaño*) began to affect the progressive sector of the populace. It found voluble expression two and a half years later when, on 14 December 1988, Spain was brought to a standstill by a general strike called by the Socialist trade union, the UGT (General Union of Workers), and supported by the Communists. 'Spain Was Paralysed Yesterday Non-Violently by the Biggest General Strike in its History', ran the front-page headline of *Diario-16*. 'Yesterday's General Strike Paralysed Spain', *El País* proclaimed. A Socialist trade union, the largest in Spain, organizing a strike against a Socialist government? Something very odd indeed must surely have happened for such a move to have been thinkable – and for 8 million citizens to come out. It had: the unions were convinced that the government was now more interested in pleasing Spain's businessmen and bankers (who had never had it so good) than in attending to the legitimate demands of the working class, the old age pensioners and the unemployed.

The UGT wanted what their leader, Nicolás Redondo, termed a *giro social* ('social change of direction'). Felipe González, seriously alarmed by the huge success of the strike, parleyed with Redondo and other union leaders, and some shifts of policy were agreed. But this was only wallpapering. The change of direction was not forthcoming. It was too late.

It is worth remembering that the initials PSOE stand for Spanish Socialist *Workers'* Party. The majority of the party's voters are no longer 'workers', however, and sooner or later, perhaps sooner, the reference to them in the party's name is bound to go. Indeed, it is already proving something of an embarrassment. Recently, as more and more divergences have emerged within the PSOE, Felipe González has intimated that he might be prepared to govern in coalition if the party does not win another outright majority at the next general election (which must take place by October 1993 at the latest).

That election, whenever held, is not likely to be won by the Right, that is, by the Partido Popular, led at the moment by José María Aznar. Much of the conservatives' ground has been occupied by the PSOE, and the government's relations with the business and banking worlds are generally cordial (despite occasional friction). In such a situation it is difficult for the PP to manoeuvre, and Aznar's lack of charisma does not help. For the foreseeable future, therefore, it seems likely that the PSOE is going to control the government.

The party has drawn up a document setting out its aspirations for Spain's immediate future. Entitled *The 'Programme 2,000' Manifesto*, it has a preface by Willy Brandt and is sandwiched between a prologue by Alfonso Guerra and an 'epilogue' by Felipe González. The document breathes the assurance that in the year 2000 the PSOE will still be in power.

Felipe González himself seems to be in no doubt about it, and in May 1991 said that he was prepared to govern for a further ten years if the party so wished in order to finish the job of 'modernizing' the country. There is a recent book on González called *La ambición del César* ('The Ambition of the Caesar'). It is by the Madrid journalist José Luis Gutiérrez and the sociologist Amando de Miguel. The authors suggest that the prime minister genuinely believes he has been allotted by destiny the heroic task of bringing Spain truly up to date. González admires François Mitterrand, and it is not surprising that the two get on well. As the years pass and his hair modulates from black to elegant grey, González is acquiring an undoubted air of 'grandeur'. Already prime minister longer than any man in Spanish history, it may well be that he remains in the saddle for many years to come. It is not a prospect that either the Right or the Left relish.

But whatever the next election results, the country has got to pay its way. After decades of protectionism, the Spanish economy has undergone major diversification in the last twenty-five years, especially since the death of Franco. Spain is no longer a mainly agricultural country (exporting particularly olive oil, wine, fruits and vegetables) but an industrial power, classified as the world's tenth. The four years following EC accession registered the fastest economic growth in the Community, and it may come as a surprise to some readers to learn, for example, that Spain is now the EC's third biggest car maker and the world's largest producer of short-fibre pulp (as well as of mussels and sparkling wine). Since EC incorporation in 1986 foreign investment has rocketed, not only in Catalonia, and there is no indication that it is about to slow down. On the contrary.

According to the report *Human Development 1991*, published by the United Nations, Spain today can boast the twentieth highest standard of living in the world (Britain comes eleventh). Not bad going for a country 45 per cent of whose adult population, in 1936, worked on the land (today agriculture accounts for only 14 per cent of the labour force) and which, three years later, was left in ruins by a terrible civil war.

The picture is not entirely rosy, though, and the experts seem to agree that the country is going to face some serious problems when the European Single Market begins to operate on 1 January 1993. Modernization and competitiveness are to the forefront of everyone's mind in Spain's industrial and business worlds today, but there is a lot of leeway to be made up before the country reaches the level of, say, France or Germany. In particular, there still needs to be a great deal more investment in research and development, although significant strides forward have been taken in this area since the Socialists came to power in 1982.

According to the Ministry of Economy, 92 per cent of Spain's businesses are small- or medium-sized. In such a situation you would not expect to find much investment in other countries, and it comes as no surprise to learn that, of Europe's 15,000 largest enterprises, only 2.8 per cent are Spanish. A recent report by the Economist Intelligence Unit revealed that, while from September 1988 to September 1989 foreign concerns injected $2,000 million into the Spanish economy, Spanish businessman only invested $250 million abroad. That is a huge, and worrying gap: little wonder that there is now a strong tendency among Spanish businesses to merge or seek to become part of multinationals. By the end of 1989, thirty-two of Spain's leading companies were foreign-controlled. Today the multinationals are present in almost every area of the economy. One has the impression, indeed, that before long most of Spain's big business will be in the hands of outsiders (the car industry already is), not least those of the Japanese. Nor is there likely to be any government opposition to such a trend, for the prime minister and his advisers are determined that Spain must be fully exposed to market forces before the European barriers come down in January 1993. 'Market forces', apparently, are the panacea for Spain's economic ills.

No discussion of the Spanish economy can fail to leave out tourism. More than 50 million people visit Spain each year, and since the 1960s tourism has been the country's biggest foreign exchange earner, accounting for some 10 per cent of Gross Domestic Product. But in 1990, as mentioned in the last chapter, the number of visitors plummeted.

This trend was partially reversed in 1991, thanks to the Gulf War, which dissuaded millions of potential tourists from visiting the beaches of North Africa and made Spain an obvious substitute. But the quality of the offer will have to be improved greatly if the decline can be corrected definitively – it is now clear that guaranteed sunlight is no longer enough. The relevant authorities are keenly aware of the need for change. It has been announced that Spanish hotels are to undergo a shake-up, and plans are afoot, also, to open up the country's exciting hinterland ('Unknown Spain', 'Hidden Spain') to a more up-market sort of tourist. Meanwhile the Andalusian coast is seeing a massive boom in the construction of retirement villas, flats and building estates for rich northern Europeans and Japanese. Spain looks set fair to become Europe's leading retirement destination.

'Productivity', 'competitive capacity', 'modernization', 'development' – these are the primordial concerns of Spain's government today. Nowhere is this more evident than in the series of official advertising supplements that, under the title *Spain. Western Europe's Last Frontier*, appeared in *Time* magazine in the run-up to 1992. In a recent number the key term is 'pan-European', used obsessively in reference to Spain's EC involvement. 'The Spanish are enthusiastically embracing this pan-European influence which is obvious throughout the country,' the report assures us; Spain 'promotes a pan-European security policy and has adopted many EC directives as national regulations'; 'Pan-European headquarters have been set up in Spain' – and so on.

There is a phrase in Spanish which often crops up when the subject of 'modernization' is aired, as it so often is nowadays. This is 'quemar etapas', which means, literally, 'to burn up stages' in the sense of making up as quickly as possible for lost time and opportunities. The lost time in this case is the four decades of Franco. Felipe González and his men have set themselves the task of propelling Spain to the top of the European ladder as fast as possible, whatever ideals may have to be sacrificed on the way. For as George Foyo, managing director and chief executive officer of AT&T Microelectrics, says in the special advertising section just mentioned, 'The Spanish consider it a matter of national pride to catch up with Europe.'

One area in which the obsession to 'burn up stages' has led to astonishing progress has been in road building. At Franco's death in 1975 the country lagged far behind Europe in motorway construction (not even Barcelona and Madrid were linked) and it took several years before this situation began to be improved. Spain, as the reader is aware, is the second most mountainous country in Europe, with difficult overland communications. Motorways are a necessary evil if it is to get its goods, and particularly its fresh produce, quickly to EC markets. In 1984 a national road-building plan was launched by the Socialist government. At that time Spain had only 1,125 miles of motorway. Now it has approximately 2,400. The Madrid–Barcelona and Madrid–Seville connections have been completed and work is pushing ahead on that between Madrid and the Basque frontier with France. Down south in Andalusia the situation has improved beyond recognition, thanks largely to the powerful stimulus provided by Expo 92. By the end of 1992 Spain's motorway miles will total 3,750 and, if work goes ahead as planned, a further 2,500 will have been added by the year 2000 – a spectacular exploit by any standards. There is a problem, however: the motorways are almost all two-lane, not three, and a sharp increase in road transport could soon lead to saturation and the need for widening.

'Spain is a new Penelope and spends her entire time weaving and unweaving the same tapestry.' This was the conclusion of the nineteenth-century journalist Mariano José de Larra, to whom I referred in the previous chapter. He had in mind the ploy devised by Ulysses' wife for keeping her unwanted suitors at bay while she waited for the great man's return: she said she would choose a lover when she finished her tapestry, which of course she took care to unpick every night. Many of the foreign visitors to Spain in the 1800s, and certainly Richard Ford, would have agreed with Larra's despairing definition of his country, for they were forcibly struck by the abject fatalism they found among Spaniards, by their rooted conviction that Spain would never change. It was the state of mind diagnosed in our own century by the great historian Américo Castro as 'vivir desviviéndose', literally 'to live unliving oneself', that is, without faith or hope.

The mood of Spain today is much more positive, and the opinion polls carried out periodically for *El País* to measure what the newspaper terms 'the vital tone of the nation' suggest that a majority of Spaniards look to the future with considerable confidence, whatever their grouses about the politicians. This despite the fact that at the moment there is between 15 and 16 per cent unemployment (the highest in the EC) and that, according to Spain's leading charity organization, Caritas, no fewer than a million Spaniards live on or below the poverty line. What most strikes one about Spain, indeed, is its new-found optimism, the growing conviction that at last, after centuries of instability, isolation, *coups d'état* and civil wars, there is now a good chance that sustained progress may be possible within the stable framework of the EC. That a great deal remains to be done, particularly to reduce social injustice, few would deny; but the will to do it is there and I believe that the division of the country into seventeen autonomous communities, each knowing what is best for it, will make the task easier.

202

On the eve of Expo 92 and the Barcelona Olympics the conditions exist for Spain to become one of Europe's, and the world's, most desirable countries: only continued hard work is needed to make the dream a reality.

Index

205